THE LIMITS OF COMMON HUMANITY

The Limits of Common Humanity

Motivating the Responsibility to Protect in a Changing Global Order

SAMUEL JARVIS

McGill-Queen's University Press
Montreal & Kingston • London • Chicago

ISBN 978-0-2280-1077-7 (cloth)
ISBN 978-0-2280-1078-4 (paper)
ISBN 978-0-2280-1296-2 (ePDF)
ISBN 978-0-2280-1297-9 (ePUB)

Legal deposit second quarter 2022
Bibliothèque nationale du Québec

Library and Archives Canada Cataloguing in Publication

Title: The limits of common humanity : motivating the responsibility to protect in a changing global order / Samuel Jarvis.
Names: Jarvis, Samuel, author.
Description: Includes bibliographical references and index.
Identifiers: Canadiana (print) 20220135207 | Canadiana (ebook) 2022013524X | ISBN 9780228010777 (cloth) | ISBN 9780228010784 (paper) | ISBN 9780228012962 (ePDF) | ISBN 9780228012979 (ePUB)
Subjects: LCSH: Responsibility to protect (International law) | LCSH: Humanity.
Classification: LCC KZ4082 .J37 2022 | DDC 341.4/8—dc23

This book was typeset by True to Type in 10.5/13 Sabon

Contents

For
Louise

Preface

At the heart of the long-term challenge faced by the Responsibility to Protect (R2P) principle is an overlooked moral question: why do states act to protect populations outside their borders that are threatened by mass atrocity crimes? This question is critical to debates about human protection and atrocity prevention policy, yet it has not been sufficiently explored by scholars. Typically, academics and policy actors appeal to a common humanity that demands that states respond to crimes that shock the conscience: the mere existence of our shared humanity corresponds to an equally powerful motivation to act in its name. But why are some crimes viewed as conscience-shocking in the first place? And how do such acts relate to the metaphysical idea of a motivating common humanity?

This book provides the first in-depth evaluation of the theoretical concept of common humanity and its influence on the creation and moral purpose of the R2P principle. It examines the origins of the R2P's moral underpinnings and assesses the extent to which the principle's moral framing has influenced how states now weigh their responsibilities to others in situations involving mass atrocities. Critical to this analysis is understanding why moral arguments in the name of humanity have not translated into greater concrete action in support of the R2P principle, despite the international legal and political structures currently in place. While our common humanity is now key to our identification of distinct global harms, moral arguments for us to act to defend or protect common humanity have proven far less effective. In other words, appeals to the concept of humanity may be helpful in determining what we *ought* to do or how we *could* organize international political and legal structures, but they are not enough to motivate states to bypass competing national interests. Consequently, it is argued that the future application of the R2P principle will require a stronger emphasis on the interaction between the national and international politics of states when it comes to human protection, so as to recognize the contrasting and often contradictory ways that states approach the protection of human beings in a variety of contexts, both internally and outside their borders. This book, then, lays out a path for rethinking how state-based self-interest can be better harnessed for the wider recognition of common human conditions, without explicit moral appeals solely to our humanity.

This book also provides an important counterpoint to recent R2P scholarship, which has focused mainly on the role of global institutional reform at the expense of better understanding and theorizing about how national actors weigh competing domestic and international pressures to act in response to mass atrocities. In a rapidly changing global order, one in which rising powers are increasingly pushing a more pluralist agenda, it is vital to reappraise the core moral idea of humanity that underpins the R2P. This book therefore offers a much-needed new appraisal of the R2P and outlines how it can continue to function in a world that has begun to shift away from the liberal and cosmopolitan values that informed its creation.

Acknowledgments

My first debt of gratitude goes to Garrett Brown and Adrian Gallagher. I first met Adrian when I was a third-year undergraduate student at the University of Leeds, and it is thanks to his encouragement and expert guidance that this book has been written. I vividly remember my first meeting with Adrian to discuss my undergraduate dissertation on Barack Obama and his approach to the Libyan intervention. Our ensuing discussions over the next few months helped spark my interest in an academic career. Adrian has been an invaluable intellectual guide to the world of academia, and his resolute support and astute criticism have been essential to the writing of this book. Through Adrian, I met Garrett and decided to pursue a PhD at the University of Sheffield. Garrett's consistent enthusiasm and support for this project has been incredibly motivating, and his thoughtful critical engagement with my work has allowed me to develop as a scholar. His wise words of encouragement and all-round positivity have been a great inspiration. I am extremely grateful to Adrian and Garrett for all their support and encouragement in the writing of this book.

I would next like to thank a number of other academics who have had a significant influence on my academic journey. Jason Ralph, along with Adrian, encouraged me to pursue a PhD and supported my efforts to do so. He invited me to present my early research during an ISA panel in New Orleans, which proved to be an incredibly formative experience, for there I was able to test my ideas and learn more about the ins and outs of academic conferences. I am grateful for all his support and advice over the years. I also want to thank a number of supportive academics I have met through the R2P network in particular, including Jess Gifkins, Aidan Hehir, James Pattison,

Cristina Stefan, and James Souter, who have provided helpful advice and encouragement.

I also wish to acknowledge the ESRC and White Rose for funding my PhD project, without which I could not have written this book. My White Rose funding allowed me to share in the experience of writing a PhD with my follow R2P colleagues Daniel Wand and Chloë Gilgan. I thank them both for sharing in many interesting discussions and debates.

I must also thank Richard Baggaley for his excellent guidance and support as editor throughout the writing of this book, and the two anonymous reviewers for their helpful feedback and engagement with the manuscript. Their comments have helped me strengthen several key sections of the book as well as its overall contribution.

My next debt of gratitude goes to a number of academic colleagues who were supportive of my work while I was writing this book. They include Anastasia Shesterinina, Jonathan Joseph, John Hobson, Alasdair Cochrane, Clara Sandelind, and Simon Rushton at the University of Sheffield; Pia Riggirozzi, Russell Bentley, Jack Corbett, Christian Enemark, Will Jennings, Jonathan Havercroft, Matthew Ryan, Ingi Iusmen, Ben Saunders, and Eloise Harding at the University of Southampton; and Matthew Denton, Christopher Kirkland, Alexander Beaumont, and Esther McIntosh at York St John University.

On a more personal note, this book would not have been possible without the loyal friends I made along the way, particularly during my time as a PhD student at the University of Sheffield. A special thanks first of all to James Chamberlain, my "Christmas Party" planner in crime, whose generosity and all-round friendship was so important to me at Sheffield. Other heartfelt thanks go to Scott Lavery, Davide Schmid, Sam Morecroft, Lynzi Duncan, Rasmus Hansen, Robbie Pye, Vanessa Bilancetti, Johnny Webb, and Katherine Smith for their friendship and shared enjoyment of many nights of escapism at The Wash. Finally, thanks to Xavier Mathieu, Barbara Buraczynska, Lucy Parry, Gemma Bird, and Alex Dietzel.

I would also like to mention my friends beyond academia, in particular my fellow bandmates in Talons. The band itself has long provided me with an essential outlet away from academia, along with the social camaraderie that can only come from touring and recording music together. A special mention also to friends from Leeds, Manchester, London, and Hereford. While our paths may cross less frequently these days, I still look forward to sharing stories and making new ones together.

A large debt of gratitude is owed to my family, in particular my Mum and Dad, whose endless support, guidance, and love has been integral to my journey through life so far. Also, a special thanks to my sister Meggan for her patience, even during my "soapbox moments"!

Lastly, my endless gratitude to Louise. I was able to complete this book only because of her relentless support and uncompromising belief in me. I can never thank her enough for all she has sacrificed over the years and for being my favourite person to talk to, no matter the time or place. I will always be forever grateful for all her love and support. This book is dedicated to her.

PERMISSIONS

The following permissions are gratefully acknowledged. An adapted version of chapter 6, "Assessing the R2P's Motivational Capacity: The Role of Humanity," appears in the *Journal of International Political Theory* 14(1) (January 2018), 107–24. Material from chapters 1 and 2 features in a book chapter titled "A Critical Examination of Humanity," published in *Protecting Human Rights in the 21st Century*, edited by Aidan Hehir and Robert Murray (London: Routledge, 2017).

THE LIMITS OF COMMON HUMANITY

INTRODUCTION

The Missing Role of Humanity

The institutionalization of the Responsibility to Protect (R2P) principle in the 2005 World Summit Outcome Document greatly reframed long-standing debates about humanitarian intervention. Over the preceding decades, the UN had failed on multiple occasions to sufficiently address outbreaks of mass atrocity crimes, because agreement was lacking regarding the legality and legitimacy of military intervention for humanitarian goals. The R2P was intended to shift debate away from a supposed right to intervene and toward a shared responsibility to protect. Since 2005, the principle has enjoyed a meteoric rise within the UN system; as of October 2021, it has been referenced in eighty-three UN Security Council resolutions,[1] and a majority of UN member-states have offered it vociferous support (Gifkins 2016). Yet despite mounting rhetorical support for and scholarly interest in R2P, its implementation has often been blocked, and this has led to concerns over a widening motivational gap – that is, states have too often failed to build consensus on appropriate action. Furthermore, in the context of a growing nationalist backlash against multilateralism and human rights, coupled with the rise of emerging powers strongly protective of their sovereign integrity, many critics have begun to question the long-term viability of the principle. In light of all this, it is vital to examine the moral claims that drove the creation of the R2P and to ask why, precisely, states should act to protect populations threatened by mass atrocity crimes beyond their borders.

That question is central to debates over the implementation of humanitarian protection and prevention policy, yet it is usually overlooked in the current R2P literature. Many scholars continue to suggest that the obligations generated by R2P, in relation to stopping the most "conscience-shocking" crimes, are so obvious as to be incontestable – quite simply, our common humanity demands that we act (Evans 2008a; Thakur 2015). Similarly, other prominent R2P scholars such as Alex Bellamy (2015a), have questioned whether we need to return to the foundational debates that inform the R2P principle and argued that the focus should now be solely on practical questions of *how* to implement the principle. But such assumptions raise a further question: if the R2P principle has already clarified why states should be preventing mass atrocities and/or protecting the targeted populations, then how are we to explain the continued contestation surrounding the R2P, particularly when it comes to motivating states to respond to such crimes? In this book, I will argue that we cannot answer this question solely by engaging with the practical politics of implementation policy; we must also develop a more theoretically informed response to two further important questions: first, what role has the concept of humanity played in the development of the R2P?; and second, why have moral arguments in the name of humanity not generated stronger support for concrete action to uphold the R2P principle?

In addressing these two core questions, I will be focusing on the nebulous relationship between the R2P principle and the concept of humanity. A systematic examination of that relationship will shed light on the tensions at the heart of state decision-making and, ultimately, on how the moral aspirations underpinning the R2P principle interact with competing national and international pressures. Consequently, it will be possible to provide new insight into how political, legal, and moral arguments interact during processes of collective and national decision-making. This book will articulate the centrality of humanity to an understanding of global harm as well as the normative limitations of humanity as a motivational force. To begin this process, it is vital to first of all set out the way the concept of humanity has so far been utilized by both scholars and diplomats and to demonstrate the need for a more systematic examination of humanity and its influence on current R2P debates.

THE MISSING ROLE OF HUMANITY

As Gallagher and Brown (2016, 8) have noted, "despite the vast amount of literature written on the R2P over the past ten years, relatively little research has explored the relationship between the R2P and humanity."

This seems strikingly at odds with the significant weight that both scholars and diplomats place on the concept and with the metaphysical heavy lifting they assume the word "humanity" can provide to any moral argument. This is illustrated by a number of statements made by prominent R2P advocates and early initiators of the principle, such as Ramesh Thakur (2015, 23), who argues that the R2P is underpinned by "our common humanity" and hence demands "acceptance of a duty of care by all of us who live in zones of safety towards all those who are trapped in zones of danger." This is echoed by Gareth Evans (2008a, 229), who suggests that the case for R2P "rests simply on our common humanity." Furthermore, humanity plays an ongoing role in the diplomatic framing of the R2P principle, reflected in the 2017 report of the UN Secretary-General on the R2P, in which it was reaffirmed that the moral responsibility of the international community to contribute to protecting populations from harm "stems from our common humanity and solidarity" (Guterres 2017, 6). Yet as Maja Zehfuss (2012, 862) has rightly argued, "most often 'humanity' is not considered a category in need of explanation," leading to the assumption that "it self-evidently deserves protection." In these examples, the concept of humanity provides the central philosophical principle underpinning the moral weight of the arguments being made, yet the concept is presented without further comment and is simply taken as an uncontested truth. Consequently, while humanity as a concept is tied to the very moral foundations of the R2P, research that would explain the significance of this relationship has been notable by its absence.

One can further highlight this oversight in relation to ongoing debates surrounding the ethics of armed humanitarian intervention, exemplified most notably in a 2014 volume edited by Don E. Scheid. That book focuses on the moral rationale for intervening in specific regard to the R2P principle, yet it makes only fleeting reference to the concept of humanity and does not interrogate it. Most surprisingly, its introductory chapter takes as a given that "morality must encompass all of humanity" and ignores the role humanity plays in answering this central question: "What responsibilities are owed to distant strangers?" (Scheid 2014, 6). This lack of engagement with the concept in ethical debates around the R2P and humanitarian intervention more generally is surprising and further highlights a clear oversight in the R2P literature.

While more recent scholarship has attempted to fill this void – an example being an *International Politics* special issue on "The Responsibility to Protect 10 years on from the World Summit" (2016) – and has focused more specifically on the relationship between humanity and the R2P, there remains a tendency to overlook the complexities of humanity's moral foundations and its subsequent impact on the framing and construction of the R2P. One can highlight this oversight within the special issue, in which the concept of common humanity is most often utilized as a theoretical benchmark for measuring the current progress of the R2P. In this sense, the focus often concerns "whether the Responsibility to Protect promotes a common humanity" (Waldorf 2016, 50), or the extent to which the R2P can represent an "expression of common humanity" (Newman 2016, 32). Subsequently, those who appeal to humanity in R2P situations have most often failed to provide a persuasive account of why the existence of humanity serves as a powerful motivation to act on behalf of a common humanity in the first place. Thus, rather than analyze the R2P as simply an attempt to live up to or put into practice the universal value of humanity, one must further interrogate the points of contestation within this relationship, in particular the extent to which states acknowledge the link between humanity's role in identifying collective harm and its ability to then inspire action through the framework of the R2P. This book will investigate this lacuna, systematically examining humanity's interaction with legal and political pressures when it comes to a shared global responsibility to prevent and/or respond to mass atrocity crimes.

Furthermore, the lack of engagement with the concept of humanity has led scholars to overlook the central connection between humanity and the very crimes the R2P is attempting to protect human beings from. Beginning to address this oversight will require closer assessment of the significance of labelling certain crimes as "against humanity." As Hubert and Blätter (2012, 35) have noted, there has so far been surprisingly little research by R2P scholars into the "specific crimes that the doctrine exists to prevent and to halt." Implicit in our understanding of the crimes of R2P is therefore an assumption that they can be sufficiently separated from other acts of extreme violence that do not require a "global" response. In this sense, we can assume that a certain hierarchy exists that allows one to dictate which crimes are of shared concern for all states. However, this assumption has yet to be fully interrogated by R2P scholars. There is a vital need, then, to develop a more interdisciplinary approach to our understanding of humanity and the R2P principle that will help us address this significant lacuna. Doing so will allow for a more theoretically informed and expanded explanation of what differentiates the harm caused by R2P crimes from that caused by other violent acts, thus highlighting the importance of humanity to our understanding of the R2P.

It is also essential to briefly reflect on some of the reasons for the lack of engagement with moral principles, such as humanity, in R2P scholarship. One possible reason for this oversight may be connected to the speed with which the R2P concept has moved from a loose abstract framework to an idea recognized by all states in the 2005 World Summit Outcome Document (WSOD). The fanfare generated by the referencing of the R2P concept in the build-up to the 2011 Libyan intervention, and its growing presence in UN Security Council (UNSC) resolutions since then, has resulted in many supporters signalling that "the normative arguments about R2P [have been] largely won" (Bellamy 2015a). Consequently, academic interest in re-examining the normative foundations of the concept has been sparse, as those who support the concept continue to question the relevance of returning to such discussions. The debate has now turned to the challenge of implementation, with the focus being shifted to practical questions surrounding *how* the R2P principle can be realized. Thus, the lack of critical engagement with the concept of humanity has to some extent clouded normative judgments concerning the influence of humanity on the shaping of the principle and how this influences decision-making around motivating action in the name of R2P.

To What Extent Can the R2P Speak for a Common Humanity?

Another pressing debate concerning the motivation for protecting those threatened by mass atrocity crimes, one that has often been overlooked in certain parts of the R2P literature, relates to whether universal concepts such as the R2P can avoid becoming tools wielded solely by powerful Western actors. Traditional accounts of the evolution of international law have been strongly tied to the European experience, with colonialism and non-European societies viewed as peripheral to the discipline (Anghie 2006, 739). For example, in nineteenth-century international law, humanity itself was seen as divided between the non-European barbaric Other and the "civilized" Europeans. Sovereignty was thus for a long time viewed as a privilege enjoyed only by Europeans and by those seen as "civilized" enough to conduct their own affairs (Glanville 2020). This gave rise to "civilizing missions" that justified the "continuous intervention by the West in the affairs of Third World societies" (Anghie and Chimni 2003, 85). It can be argued that elements of these missions have endured, albeit in a different form, and that debates over human rights, democracy, and good governance are still being utilized to justify exploitative and interventionary practices (86). Thus the rights of sovereignty, gained by many in the Global South through decolonization, are being strongly defended, with states using international law and sovereignty claims to guard themselves against intervention and interference. Yet at the same time, non-Western scholars have emphasized the potential of critical Third World approaches to international law to promote the global common good and the safeguarding of "our common humanity" (Chimni 2018, 46). International law, in this view, can be utilized to protect peoples from their own state and various international actors. In this sense, claims to the protection of humanity are not simply rhetorical tools wielded by the powerful to shield their own interests. As this book will show, theorizing the concept of humanity and locating the global harms caused by atrocity crimes is critical to our ability to call out the passivity and inconsistency of state responses and to better understand why such crimes concern us all as human beings. As Anghie (2006, 752) has since argued, this critical question remains: how can international political and legal structures work to further the interests of the peoples of the Global South, protecting them from mass atrocity crimes, while also "advancing their interests in the international sphere?" The idea of universal humanity continues to play a central role in such debates, especially regarding how these competing demands can be more effectively reconciled as we reimagine a fairer and more just world. As the current Special Adviser on R2P, Karen Smith (2020), has argued, the ethical premise that underpins the R2P – that of a responsibility to others – is shared across "many different cultural and religious traditions," as is the claim that those in authority have a responsibility to their own citizens. Thus, a critical challenge moving forward is how to motivate these responsibilities effectively in ways that do not simply benefit powerful Western states but protect all of humanity from mass atrocity crimes. As chapter 1 will examine, the efforts made by non-Western states to curtail the West's use of coercive practices under the R2P principle have tended to focus on calling out the ulterior motives of Western powers, particularly as they relate to regime change. As a consequence, non-Western powers are playing an increasingly important role in shaping how the R2P is understood and applied (Stefan 2017). Moreover, non-Western states often simultaneously utilize and appeal to the concept of humanity when they try to hold intervening states to account for their actions. This suggests that at the heart of such debates are two questions: How do moral motivations translate into actions? And how can the power imbalances between states be better managed? Furthermore, as chapter 4 will scrutinize in detail, the UN has been forced to grapple with what are often competing responsibilities: to defend the international order and the sovereign integrity of states, and to protect human beings from mass atrocities. The inconsistency and hypocrisy of current state practices therefore require a stronger emphasis on initiatives that can help strengthen motivational support for the shared goal of R2P (see chapter 6).

Conceptual Literature

Before discussing the theoretical framing of humanity that underpins this book, I must briefly acknowledge that while the R2P literature has engaged relatively little with the concept of humanity, a wide range of philosophical literature has examined more explicitly the role of humanity and its relationship to mass violence and global harms (Gaita 2000; Teitel 2011). Much of that literature has developed around issues of human progress, detailing how rising human interconnectedness has steadily influenced significant shifts in state behaviour as well as the expectations placed on states' actions towards humanity. In this vein, recent work by Andrew Linklater (2011, 76) has questioned how much progress today's states have made in acknowledging "the obligations they owe all other people by virtue of shared humanity." Ruti Teitel (2011) has drawn attention to how humanity-based claims are at the forefront of contemporary foreign policy and diplomacy with the result that a humanity-based morality is becoming increasingly prevalent. This literature provides a useful starting point for analyzing the interaction between claims made in the name of protecting humanity and states' motivations for preventing mass atrocities and protecting people who are threatened by them.

Moreover, in the literature on international law, there has been considerable debate over the concept of humanity – most specifically, over the normative foundations of crimes against humanity. For international legal scholars such as May (2005) and Luban (2004), much of the focus has been on examining what sets international crimes apart from domestic crimes – specifically, how the concept of humanity can help differentiate between these two categories. In addressing this issue, scholars have been exploring the influence of humanity, understood as either humanness or humankind, in order to develop a greater understanding of the specific harms caused by such crimes. These arguments have then been used to theorize claims regarding why the prosecution of those who commit such acts must be of concern for the whole of the international community. These discussions thus feed into conceptual questions of how we understand crimes against humanity and also into normative questions concerning the international community's role in prosecuting these crimes (Renzo 2012). The concept of humanity is thus explicitly tied to key understandings in international law, which is where that concept has arguably undergone the greatest amount of philosophical inquiry to date as to its meaning and application. Furthermore, debates around the legal right to prosecute crimes against humanity can provide a useful foundation on which to formulate and theorize humanity-based arguments in support of state obligations to protect. This book will build on the current debates in international law around the prosecution of mass atrocity crimes and apply them more comprehensively to debates surrounding prevention and intervention initiatives.

The failure (so far) of these distinct fields of research to fully communicate with each other has brought about a significant lacuna in the literature, one that could be filled by a more interdisciplinary approach to our understanding of R2P and its relationship to the concept of humanity. A more informed conceptualization of this relationship would have significant theoretical and policy implications, which this book will explore, in terms of how to address the R2P's implementation gap and the possible limitations of current UN reform proposals.

THEORETICAL FRAMEWORK

To incorporate and analyze this wide-ranging literature will require a theoretical approach that is able to prioritize normative theory, particularly regarding state decision-making. Consequently, this book puts forward a specific understanding of the key relationship between the practices of politics and normative ideas themselves, by first asking how moral ideas about international order have influenced political behaviour (Hurrell 2007, 19). One can then begin to move the debate toward a broader discussion of the nature of ethical conduct and "what ought we to do?" (Hurrell 2007, 19). The starting point in all this is the recognition of a distinct dual understanding of humanity, one that is socially constructed and thus given shape through language and performative action. This book is therefore built on a cosmopolitan perspective that prioritizes the value of humanity as central to our understanding of the harms caused by the four crimes of R2P and thus makes it possible to re-examine R2P's role in guiding moral and political decision-making.

Cosmopolitanism is built on the idea that all humans deserve equal moral standing. Accordingly, both individuals and states have responsibilities that extend beyond their borders. These duties are arguably based on the existence of a shared humanity, which also underpins practical calls for responding to those who are threatened by mass atrocity crimes or are suffering as a result of them. Yet the extent to which appeals to humanity generate change in state behaviour remains deeply contested. In an increasingly divided world, the challenge is how to balance between "responsibilities to fellow nationals and larger responsibilities to humanity" (Beardsworth et al. 2019, 4). This balance has arguably come under increasing threat in recent years, since the rise of powers such as China, Russia, and Brazil, which have championed a more pluralist and statist approach to the management of the international order. As Yongjin Zhang (2016) has argued, China in particular has become increasingly active in contesting liberal cosmopolitan values in its attempt to reshape the today's normative order. Alongside this evolving dynamic is the growing Western backlash against cosmopolitan claims and responsibilities, exemplified by the election of Donald Trump and the spread of right-wing nationalism across Europe. The United States under the Trump administration abandoned its global responsibilities, including its key support of multilateral institutions, and thus added significant support to anti-cosmopolitan sentiments. It is in response to these shifts that this book seeks to examine what traction moral claims in the name of humanity can have when it comes to activating global responsibilities.

When locating the shared responsibilities connected to preventing mass atrocity crimes, one must begin by recognizing these crimes as representing a shared notion of "the bad life," by which conceptions of the wrong are seen to provide a better way to traverse cultural differences concerning cruel or inhuman behaviour (Linklater 2011, 106). It is argued that the best way to protect our cultural diversity is by locating a universal conception of harm, that is, by underscoring the existential threat that mass atrocity crimes pose to diversity as well as to humanity itself. Thus, our ability to relate to common humanity can be best located in our shared capacities as human beings. That means acknowledging universal solidarity so that we are able to recognize "common vulnerabilities to mental and physical suffering." This in turn will provide us with a greater opportunity to forge agreement on universal harms (111). Hence, the cosmopolitan argument put forward is one very much founded on the primacy of negative duties aimed at the avoidance and limitation of specific extreme harms (Shapcott 2008, 196). This book will reinforce a "thin conception of universality" in order to defend the ideal that every human being belongs to a single community of humankind and that everyone therefore shares the same natural capacities (Bartelson 2009, 171). What follows from this claim is that the key moral precept must be the "requirement of mutual respect in the face of human diversity" (Bartelson 2009, 178). Through this thin universalism, we can make subsequent claims that torture is abhorrent and that the right to life must be respected. Consequently, an acknowledgment of a thin universalism is essential to providing a basis for making normative judgments, reinforcing claims regarding what acts can be seen as representing universally accepted human wrongs.

Theorizing the Dual Function of Humanity

Building on this thin conception of universality, this book focuses mainly on providing a more comprehensive understanding of the concept of humanity and its complex relationship with the R2P principle. Without a clear theoretical and philosophical grounding of the concept of humanity, it will be increasingly difficult to express why the international community should take up the responsibility to protect populations when a state fails to do so. Key to the premise, then, is the argument that one needs to better understand the existence of humanity in order to explain why we must "act to save strangers" (Bain 2007, 561).[2] Unless we locate universal harm through a conception of our common humanity, we will be unable to fully conceptualize the extent of the crime and its possible ramifications.

Building on the idea of a distinct human wrong, humanity must first of all be understood as creating a moral demand as a form of reflection, whereby humanity can be seen as providing a foundational moral concept for categorizing mass atrocity crimes as universal wrongs. In this sense, rhetorical agreement on the four crimes of the R2P (genocide, war crimes, ethnic cleansing, and crimes against humanity) demonstrates that states are willing to acknowledge or recognize some form of universal harm connected to such crimes, located in an understanding of common humanity's emotional pull factor. It follows that the idea of humanity is central to our ability to imagine a global condition and for constructing ideas of universal jurisdiction, concerning attempts to both prohibit and respond to the most heinous crimes against human beings. While most of the literature concerned with humanitarian intervention and the R2P has so far been thought of as separate from debates over the philosophical underpinnings of the very crimes that interventions attempt to protect individuals from, this book presents an argument in support of transferring the prosecution-based focus of previous arguments to the question of why states should have a responsibility to both prevent mass atrocity crimes beyond their borders and protect those who are threatened by them. In doing so, this book puts forward a new theoretical approach for conceptualizing the distinct global harms created by crimes against humanity, thus providing a comprehensive answer to the question of why humanity matters and ultimately why states have a responsibility to respond to mass atrocity crimes beyond their borders.

The second role of humanity in relation to the R2P is to provide a motivational push, for this affects how states weigh the need to effectively respond to mass atrocity crimes. In this sense, humanity is seen as providing a moral cause that should motivate actors to respond to crimes that are deemed to threaten the concept of a shared humanity. The argument is that humanity creates obligations beyond simply recognizing conscience-shocking crimes as universal. The shock of such crimes is thus seen to generate a push factor, one that calls for states to take action that will potentially clash with other interests, as any decision to intervene in such cases will almost always require states to put their own troops or material wealth in harm's way in order to save and protect others. The motivational push factor must therefore be powerful enough to compete with or compliment a variety of other state preferences when it comes to protecting those threatened by mass atrocity crimes. Consequently, while the strength and motivational purpose of the R2P is inherently tied to the power of humanity as a moral force for change, the ability to assess this potential for change requires a much deeper understanding of the complex dual function underpinning humanity's use. It is through such analysis that one can begin to demonstrate and explain the motivational challenges currently facing the R2P in a changing global order.

CONTRIBUTIONS

The book makes two central contributions. First, as outlined earlier, by developing a unique analysis of humanity's dual function, it makes it possible to better explain both the role humanity plays in conceptualizing distinct global harms and its role in shaping motivational debates concerning state action and response. Through recognizing and exploring this critical dual function, this book highlights how moral arguments in the name of humanity have failed to translate into more effective state support of prevention and protection practices. Despite the collective legal and political structures that the R2P reinforces at the international level, states have continued to argue over when mass atrocity crimes should be identified as posing a threat to international peace and security, as well as the extent to which global harms caused by such crimes should require states to reconfigure their international and national priorities. Second, this book develops this argument further by contesting the liberal and teleological assumptions often made related to the R2P's influence on debates over human protection responses. In this regard, humanity must be understood as a motivating principle that ultimately diminishes in influence as the R2P principle is launched into action. This is important, for the assumptions made about the motivational qualities of humanity do not just impact on abstract theoretical debates; they also frame and support practical claims in response to mass atrocity crimes. In this sense, if the concept of humanity is to remain an essential part of the language used by both diplomats and academics to support and justify specific decisions, then the salience of these claims must be sufficiently interrogated.

Consequently, this book argues that there are significant limits to the moral imperative of humanity: national concerns, whether it be sacrificing troops or resources, ultimately shape state decision-making in mass atrocity crime situations. This has significant implications for the current R2P reform agenda and thus requires a renewed emphasis on how state-based self-interest can be harnessed for the wider recognition of common human conditions, without explicit moral appeals to our humanity alone. Critical to addressing the current R2P implementation gap is therefore the need to move beyond the focus on the binary playoff between humanitarian objectives and the role of state sovereignty, to begin to develop a more expansive approach to the challenge of mobilization, one that will reflect the ways that humanity, law, and politics interact at the global level. This book therefore provides the foundations for constructing a more intuitive framework for understanding the complex mobilization factors involved in generating collective responses to the threat of mass atrocity crimes.

PLAN OF THE BOOK

This book begins by outlining the motivations for the development of the R2P principle, highlighting how it was designed to address previous constraints on more consistent international responses to the threat of mass atrocity crimes. Chapter 1 therefore emphasizes how specific interpretations of past intervention failures continue to strongly guide the R2P, shaping its connection to moral claims in support of protecting humanity. Despite these influences, the R2P continues to be contested by states, whose competing visions of how best to motivate its application place cosmopolitan and statist claims in competition with each other. This division highlights the need to better conceptualize the complex interaction between moral claims to humanity's protection and narrow political interests.

Chapter 2 begins to unpack the complex relationship between the R2P and the concept of common humanity. It outlines an understanding of humanity, articulated by two interdependent definitions of the concept, namely humankind and humanness. It will argue that a dual conception of these two understandings of humanity is essential to our ability to theorize mass atrocity crimes as universal harms. Following on from this discussion, the chapter analyzes approaches that seek to deny the existence of a common humanity, focusing on communitarian and anti-foundational challenges. This is critical to demonstrating how these contrasting approaches continue to fail to move beyond the idea of shared human capacities, which are ultimately rooted in a universal conception of common humanity. The chapter concludes by underscoring the need to apply this theoretical framework to our understanding of the four major crimes of R2P, to better locate the distinct global harms created by such acts.

Chapter 3 addresses directly the question of why it is possible to insist that other nations not commit mass atrocity crimes against their own populations. It focuses on the need to move beyond claims that such crimes are simply "conscience-shocking," presenting a theoretically informed argument that addresses how we can conceptualize the impact such crimes have on the values and ideas that are argued to be essential to our existence as human beings. By building on the theoretical conception of humanity outlined in the previous chapter, we will be able to examine how mass atrocity crimes can be viewed as a challenge to dual conceptions of humanity, generating not only harms against the diversity of humankind but also challenging our distinct humanness, understood through our ability to coexist as political animals, as well as our capacity to reason and develop moral rules. The chapter provides a comprehensive reply to the questions of why humanity matters and why states have a responsibility to respond to crimes against humanity beyond their borders.

The book then turns to assess the extent to which the concept of humanity has influenced state behaviour at the UN level, by examining the historical trajectory of threat expansion that led up to the creation of the R2P and the actions and debates that surrounded the 2011 Libyan intervention and the ongoing Syrian Civil War. Rather than understanding threat expansion in the UN Security Council as a fixed linear progression, the historical analysis in the chapter demonstrates the lack of a consistent pattern in the way both the UNSC and individual states have chosen to categorize the scope and impact of mass atrocity crimes, despite consistent rhetorical claims as to the distinct threat they pose to our common humanity. In this regard, the chapter examines why state conceptions of international peace and security remain so fundamentally contested and how this has affected the capacity of the current R2P concept to fundamentally shift political will in the UNSC. It is then argued that despite an increased focus on the motivational force of humanity, states have so far been unwilling to acknowledge potential restrictions on how they interpret threats to international peace and security. This analysis is critical to further understanding how normative arguments concerning the motivational qualities of humanity feed into current debates about the R2P's implementation gap and how it can be addressed.

Building on the arguments so far presented, chapter 5 focuses on the severe shortfall in analysis of humanity's function in helping locate moral harm and provide a motivational cause that can drive human protection practices in support of the R2P principle. In response to this lacuna, the chapter puts forward three ways to hypothesize humanity's motivational role in this process: (a) humanity functioning as a rhetorical tool with no motivational qualities, (b) humanity as a concept that works to redefine sovereignty in support of the R2P, and (c) humanity as a motivating principle that ultimately diminishes in influence as the R2P principle is diffused into action. Through this analysis, the chapter offers a more rigorous and systematic evaluation of humanity's limitations as a moral motivator for generating a collective response to mass atrocity crimes, highlighting the need to further develop understanding of the complex interactions among morality, politics, and law in international decision-making. In this sense, the chapter challenges assumptions often made about the motivational capacity of humanity, thus raising significant questions about the processes through which debates take place over motivating state actors confronted by mass atrocities. It is argued that there must be space for a more critical approach to conceptualizing the constraining realities of international decision-making as well as a greater recognition of humanity as an increasingly contested and diminishing source of moral responsibility once the R2P is put into action.

If the R2P is limited in its ability to function as a motivating principle that can galvanize action in response to mass atrocity crimes, then what role or *added value* can the R2P provide to the overall challenge of preventing mass atrocity crimes and protecting people from them? And what might this claim mean for how we understand ongoing debates over R2P reform initiatives moving forward? Chapter 6 rejects the highly institutionalist focus of R2P literature and argues for a better understanding of how moral imperatives interact with political and legal pressures to influence the overall motivational consensus around responding to atrocity crimes. Central to this chapter's core argument is thus the claim that appropriate mechanisms through which to address mass atrocity crimes are available to UN member-states, yet as will be examined, their application has been inconsistent as well as at times contradictory. This suggests that the international community's ability to respond effectively to mass atrocity crimes is most often connected to a lack of consensus around generating sufficient moral sacrifice in light of competing demands, rather than to direct procedural concerns; this in turn creates a divide between how states wish to respond and the realities of upholding the UN's institutional framework. Consequently, the chapter emphasizes the role that state-based self-interest can play in the wider recognition of common human conditions and highlights the need to better understand how national actors weigh up competing domestic and international pressures to act in response to mass atrocities.

In its conclusion, this book reinforces the critical importance of political will and its relationship to state mobilization and argues that we must be more aware of how a variety of humanitarian protection norms interact and compete with one another and the impact this has not just on the R2P concept, understood in narrow terms, but also on the goal of protection and prevention of atrocity crimes more expansively. Moving forward, there is a need to move beyond the binary nature of previous R2P research, which has most often placed key normative values and beliefs in direct competition with one another rather than fully conceptualizing the complex intersubjectivity of these apparent dualisms. Consequently, when talking about motivation and political will in regard to the R2P, one cannot separate it from broader discussions concerning how states approach the protection of human beings in a variety of contexts. The current political climate of human rights pushback must therefore be seen as a significant obstacle to greater consensus on R2P mobilization, and thus as a direct challenge for us to start reconceptualizing a future strategy for new R2P initiatives beyond institutional rule changes and toward more national-facing and politically motivated initiatives. This book thus concludes by outlining practical drivers for state motivation that must be seen as the starting point for developing a more effective response to mass atrocity crimes in a changing global order.

1

The Development and Contestation of the Responsibility to Protect

The purpose of this chapter is threefold. First, it is to outline the genesis of the R2P, in specific relation to the role played by the moral language of "never again" and the concept of common humanity, in order to demonstrate the crucial link between previous mass atrocity prevention failures and the new moral authority seen to be generated by the R2P principle. This will help greatly to highlight how the R2P is ultimately a product of a long history of international attempts to bring an end to mass atrocity crimes, all of which are deeply connected to the important motivating role played by the concept of humanity. The second is to critically examine the contestation that currently surrounds the R2P principle, with a particular focus on the issue of motivation. The R2P principle was developed and refined specifically to address earlier motivational barriers surrounding the prevention of mass atrocities as well as responses to them. This included reimagining state sovereignty, the scale and scope of acts justifying action, and the institutional framework required for authorizing humanitarian responses. It was argued that each of these required refinement and clarification in light of the perceived limitations and ambiguities surrounding past humanitarian intervention norms. However, competing interpretations of the R2P's form and focus have continued to divide UNSC members, among whom the dominance of the sovereignty-versus-humanity dichotomy in R2P discussions has made generating consensus for action increasingly fraught. This suggests that views regarding how best to motivate and implement the R2P are becoming increasingly opposed as cosmopolitan claims compete with statist ones. Third and finally, in response to the contestation over the current R2P implementation gap, this chapter reflects on the ongoing challenge of generating political will in response to mass atrocity crimes and the problem of inconsistent state practice. To conclude, this chapter will argue that if we are to move beyond the current dichotomy, we will require a better conceptualization of the complex interactions among competing moral, political, and legal pressures surrounding state decision-making in R2P situations. And the starting point for that must be a clearer understanding of the role humanity has played as a central moral foundation in the creation of the R2P principle and its limits so far in driving motivational change.

THE GENESIS OF THE R2P

The R2P principle was initially driven by a commitment born out of the international community's past failures to respond to genocides and mass atrocities around the globe. The original language of "never again" can be traced back to the Holocaust; in its aftermath, states agreed that lessons must be learned and past mistakes never repeated and that the crime of genocide must be outlawed once and for all. As Adrian Gallagher (2013) argues, it was the "moral abhorrence felt toward the Holocaust" that dramatically altered "international society's moral, constitutional and legal expectations" (94). In response, the UN General Assembly unanimously adopted the Convention on Prevention and Punishment of the Crime of Genocide in December 1948. It explicitly recognized the "great losses on humanity" that genocide had caused; most notably, it stated under Article VIII that any party would be able to call upon the United Nations to "take such action under the Charter of the United Nations as they consider appropriate for the prevention and suppression of acts of genocide" (UN 1948). For the first time, then, genocide was understood to be of international concern, which meant that states now recognized a legal obligation to override the rights of sovereignty wherever genocide was being committed (Gallagher 2013, 115). Yet despite the initial moral outrage created by the Holocaust, events in the coming decades would provide little support for realizing the ambition of "never again." The international community's response to the genocides in Cambodia, Rwanda, and Bosnia demonstrated a lack of support for the principles laid out in the Genocide Convention, highlighting in particular the weakness of its legal enforcement in international relations.

This consistent failure to make the most conscience-shocking crimes of greater concern to states led many to call for the UN to change its approach to preventing and responding to mass atrocity crimes. Driving the debate over such changes in the post–Cold War era was UN Secretary-General Kofi Annan, who realized that the international order would suffer if the UN kept failing to uphold its responsibility. He suggested that "if the collective conscience of humanity ... cannot find in the United Nations its greatest tribune, there is grave danger that it will look elsewhere for peace and justice" (Annan 1999a). Annan (1999a) challenged the UN's member-states to "find common ground in upholding the principles of the Charter, and acting in defence of our common humanity." This statement reflected his belief that the UN must better represent humanity in order to maintain its legitimacy as a force for peace and justice; states needed to be prepared to act in the name of humanity's collective conscience. Arguably, the symbolic appeal to humanity continues to provide the R2P with much of its moral authority in international affairs and to underpin a key motivational element of the concept. Indeed, the language of "never again" is inherently tied to an understanding of common humanity, according to which mass atrocity crimes are so shocking that we must all collectively pledge to never let them occur again. The articulation of never again is founded on a respect for humanity that is understood as both universal and an end in itself. The concept of humanity provides the essential emotional pull and motivational push of R2P, through which many argue humankind can move toward eliminating mass atrocity crimes once and for all. The R2P is supported by an assumption that normative pressure rooted in the ideas of "never again" and common humanity can compel states (powerful states in particular) to adjust their foreign policy calculus. In this sense, the R2P can be understood as "essentially a narrative of guilt on the part of dissident former UN diplomats" that is utilized to help "operationalize moral determinism more effectively" (Lucas 2014, 37). The political failures of the past are very much embedded in the moral fabric of the concept as well as the institution of the UN, such that the failure to respond to situations that "shock the conscience of mankind" is viewed as representing an abandonment of the UN's key mission (Orford 2016, 19). While some R2P advocates may reject this particular reading, the statement does highlight how significant political failures of the past are woven deeply into the very moral fabric of the concept. As Stephen Hopgood (2014, 182) argues, "the politics of the R2P are intimately interwoven with the politics of stopping genocide": "it was the ghosts of Rwanda and Srebrenica that haunted advocates." This suggests that appeals to humanity and its protection are at the same time tightly linked to memory and the need not to repeat past failures.

Yet it is important to reflect on the argument that a collective responsibility to protect need not be grounded in the potential harm to humanity generated by mass atrocity crimes. Indeed, one could locate the starting point for collective responsibility in the existence of inter-state agreements, such as the Genocide Convention, that recognize international crimes and make them *de facto* matters of international concern. States have made political commitments to bring an end to mass atrocity crimes; given this, it can be argued that the normative idea of consent provides the guiding motivation to address those crimes. As Reus-Smit (1999) has argued, "for almost 150 years the fundamental institutions of contractual international law and multilateralism have provided the basic institutional framework for interstate cooperation and have become the favoured institutional solutions to the myriad of coordination and collaboration problems facing states in an increasingly complex world" (3). Thus, a state that wishes to depict its actions as legitimate will most often be compelled to justify such acts in relation to the primary norms that govern the system as a whole (35). So, do we need the normative idea of humanity in order to explain why states should care about mass atrocity crimes, when we already know that states have recognized such acts as wrong, thus shaping the contours of legitimate action? And if we do, what values and beliefs are able to influence and shape the foundations of international legal principles and the governing norms of the international system in the first place? What is it about the acts themselves that have compelled states to outlaw them and deem them to be outside the acceptable norms of international society? The concept of humanity is thus critical to making sense of the development and formal recognition of these acts as international crimes that concern us all. Even if humanity does not provide the central motivation for compliance today, it is impossible to make sense of the historical shift in state recognition of international crimes without reflecting on the idea of humanity as a guiding principle. As chapter 3 will explore in detail, engagement with the theoretical idea of humanity makes it possible to locate what global harm is generated by mass atrocity crimes and thus why states have come to formally recognize a shared responsibility for preventing them.

CONTESTING THE BARRIERS TO IMPLEMENTATION

As outlined so far, the creation of the R2P as an international principle has been a response to a long lineage of collective failures when it comes to averting mass atrocity crimes. The R2P provides a new focus for debates surrounding the challenge of protection, whereby states are now arguably tied to a stronger moral and political obligation, one that demands they work harder to both prevent and react to mass atrocity crimes around the globe. Yet despite this new focus, the R2P remains a deeply contested principle in international relations. To explain this pushback, I will begin by describing how the R2P was designed to overcome past barriers to the mass atrocity protection practices. This will allow me to examine recent contestations surrounding the R2P and explain why states have continued to want to privilege other principles and objectives in mass atrocity crime situations.

Sovereignty as Responsibility

Perhaps the most significant theoretical innovation put forward by the R2P is the concept of conditional sovereignty. For centuries, sovereign equality and non-intervention were guiding principles in the management of international relations, and the absolutist quality of these principles only became further embedded in the international community during the twentieth century (Glanville 2013). The importance of Westphalian sovereignty as an "institutional arrangement for organising political life" was reaffirmed in the 1945 UN Charter, underpinned by two key principles: "territoriality and the exclusion of external actors from domestic authority structures" (Krasner 1999, 20). Article 2(1) of the Charter thus states that "the organisation is based on the principle of the sovereign equality of States"; furthermore, the principle of non-intervention in the internal affairs of states is recognized under Article 2(7). The conception of sovereignty outlined in the Charter works to support the right of states to govern themselves without outside interference and helps build respect for territorial integrity in international relations. As a result, a state's internal actions against its own people have largely been viewed as outside the remit of the international community, and instead, the management of international order *between* states has been seen as the central objective. Sovereignty in this sense provides a way to manage differences between states.

Westphalian sovereignty is often referred to as absolute, yet it has long been the case that these principles have been violated depending on the motivational interests of state leaders (Krassner 1999, 24). However, in the post–Cold War era, with the rise of universal human rights norms, the individual has taken on increasing importance in international law and the principles of Westphalian sovereignty have come under increasing challenge. Hilpold (2012) writes that "'sovereignty' is no longer interpreted in the traditional Westphalian sense as the 'supreme authority within a territory' but as a concept based on human security and implying, as a consequence, also responsibilities" (68). However, outside the West many states have long been skeptical of attempts to challenge their sovereignty and territorial integrity, having fought for so long to gain legal recognition of both. Yet a fundamental challenge to this traditional understanding of sovereignty came from the former Sudanese diplomat Francis Deng and his colleagues, who in *Sovereignty as Responsibility: Conflict Management in Africa* (1996) wrote that "sovereignty can no longer be seen as a protection against interference but as a charge of responsibility where the state must be accountable to both domestic and external constituencies" (33). Moreover, Deng's early involvement in shaping the R2P speaks to the need to challenge the idea that the R2P is simply a Western construct and to highlight the variety of global voices that have been involved in its creation. This idea of sovereignty as *responsibility* has been highly influential and informs the arguments put forward by scholars such as Sampford and Thakur (2015), who have suggested that the traditional Westphalian concept of sovereignty was ultimately a "tyrant's charter," by which "the prior successful use of internal force justified the continuing use of internal force for any purpose that the sovereign saw fit" (52). In that regard, the upholding of sovereign non-intervention as a core international principle has provided cover for those wishing to commit atrocities against their own people, while at the same time giving other states a justification for their inaction.

So, it could be argued that the desire to do something to alleviate grave human suffering in mass atrocity situations was at odds with "the existing tenets of international law and specifically the rights of non-intervention afforded to sovereign states" (Hehir 2012, 182). However, the end of the Cold War brought with it a renewed sense of optimism regarding the possible good the UN could do as a more humanitarian-focused organization. Even so, debates during the 1990s over humanitarian intervention were still very much framed in terms of sovereignty versus human rights, and alternative conceptions of sovereignty received little explicit consideration (Glanville 2013, 181). Consequently, the confrontation between these two competing values became a major barrier to decision-making within the UN, most significantly in terms of responding to outbreaks of mass atrocity crimes in Bosnia, Rwanda, and Kosovo (Evans 2006). The UNSC's failure to sufficiently address those atrocities reignited debates concerning the strict absolutist view of sovereignty, which was increasingly seen as undermining the UN's legitimacy in terms of dealing with global threats.

In direct response to the UNSC's inaction in Rwanda, and its division in the case of Kosovo, UN Secretary-General Kofi Annan (2000) addressed the UN General Assembly to directly question the moral consistency of traditional Westphalian sovereignty, suggesting that "surely no legal principle — not even sovereignty — can ever shield crimes against humanity." He argued that "both the defence of humanity and the defence of sovereignty are principles that must be supported," calling for a reimagining of the relationship between the citizen, the state and the international community (Annan 2000, 48). This potentially contradictory statement highlighted the need to create a form of conditional sovereignty, one that would allow a strong defence of common humanity alongside efforts to maintain peace and security. Central to this proposal was the idea of the state as an instrument at the service of its peoples, and not vice versa; thus, the state must protect the fundamental freedoms of each individual first and foremost.

The task of putting this theoretical proposal into policy practice was taken up by the International Commission on Intervention and State Sovereignty (ICISS), which sought to build consensus within the international community around the proposition that major systematic violations of human rights must be stopped wherever they take place. Central to efforts to build this consensus was the idea of a "right to intervene," the argument being that a state had a responsibility to protect its own people; when it failed to do so, its non-intervention rights were void (Sampford and Thakur 2015, 45). Put another way, "only those states that protect the fundamental rights of their citizens and thereby fulfil their sovereign responsibilities, are entitled to the full panoply of sovereign rights" (Bellamy 2009, 19). This was an important reinterpretation of sovereignty, for it placed a new level of accountability on heads of state even while continuing to support the central principle of sovereign non-intervention. This meant moving away from the negative connotations associated with the "humanitarian intervention" norm, which had caused significant rifts within the UNSC after it was applied in Kosovo. The rules of intervention therefore began with "the need of human beings for help" rather than "the exceptional right of states to intervene in extreme cases" (Peters 2009a, 535). The R2P provided a bridge between the principles of humanitarian intervention and those of state sovereignty, thereby negating the idea that the two principles inevitably bred ongoing confrontation (Glanville 2013, 191). Thereafter, the international community's responsibility to respond to mass atrocity crimes would be triggered only where a state had manifestly failed in its own responsibility to protect its citizens.

However, despite efforts to frame the R2P as a new balancing force in the perceived battle between these competing demands, the relationships among sovereignty, humanity, and the R2P remain deeply contested. Scholars remain divided regarding the extent to which the R2P's creation has relegated sovereignty to a second-order norm and thereby reinforced the role of humanity as the ultimate normative source of international law (Peters 2009b, 155), and also regarding whether the R2P's implementation is still being undermined by the powerful role that sovereignty continues to play in international debates over the prevention of mass atrocity crime (Crossley 2016, 219). When examining recent actions by UNSC members, one can point most notably to the assertive approach taken by states such as China, which are explicitly challenging more "cosmopolitan notions of conditional sovereignty" and working to reassert the importance of the state as the central actor in protection (Welsh 2019, 61). Even when discussing the use of mediation activities in mass atrocity situations, China has argued that this must still be "based on respect for national sovereignty and non-interference in the internal affairs of others"; in other words, the consent must be secured beforehand and be fully respected (UN 2018a). This shift toward reinforcing the importance of sovereignty has been echoed in recent Secretary-General's reports, which place national governments front and centre in the analysis, emphasizing their particular role in prevention and stressing the need to view R2P as not just an international issue but a domestic one as well. States are now being encouraged to adopt mechanisms to protect their own populations (Guterres 2019). This has led to further pressure to shift the R2P away from debates on intervention and instead reframe its importance as a tool for strengthening state capacity through international assistance, again reinforcing a more state-centric conceptualization of the principle (Rhoads and Welsh 2019, 612). Yet it is also the case that the R2P can work to strengthen appeals to sovereignty in some circumstances and undermine it in others. This has significant implications for how motivation for action works in this changing global order (see chapter 5).

Refining the Focus of Humanity: The Four Crimes of the R2P

For supporters of the R2P, the 2005 WSOD was a watershed moment during which the tragedies of the past finally forced a "historic shift in international relations," reinforcing the idea of a "moral obligation to prevent and halt the most horrific crimes known to humankind" (Schmidt and Wolf 2012). Some even went so far as to claim that this R2P agreement in some way represented "the policy realization of the statement never again" (Stark 2011, 4). The language of never again would continue to be a feature of the diplomatic framing of this R2P document, with Slovakian delegate Michal Mlynar claiming during a General Assembly meeting on the R2P that "the 2005 World Summit, sought to ensure that the international community would never again fail to protect human rights and protect human beings from the worst crimes" (UN 2009). The initial optimism surrounding the realization of the R2P in the WSOD further strengthened the link between the language of "never again" and the moral principles underpinning the concept. R2P promised to make "never again" a reality, a goal that in many ways the WSOD had not set out directly to achieve. The intertwining of the "never again" narrative with the WSOD helped reinforce a key contradiction between the project's aim and its value as a moral tool for fundamentally changing state policy. In this sense, the construction of the R2P within the 2005 document acknowledged a specific pragmatic understanding of when states should have the responsibility to act – it would always be on a case-by-case basis. This refined version of the R2P was intended quite specifically to balance various imperatives and procedural considerations, and thus in many ways it contradicted the form in which the R2P was originally presented in the ICISS document.

The WSOD did have a notable achievement in particular, though: it had forged an agreement regarding the four mass atrocity crimes that would be covered under the R2P principle, namely genocide, war crimes, crimes against humanity, and ethnic cleansing. This marked an advance over the ambiguous wording of the ICISS report (2001, xi), which had located the threshold for intervention as incidents "where a population is suffering serious harm." The four categories proved vital in addressing many of the pressing questions left unanswered by the ICISS report, such as whether the R2P would apply to large-scale human rights violations or natural disasters, as well as major international crimes. States had long challenged the abstract wording and moral language used as triggers for humanitarian action, so it was seen as vital that such ambiguity be addressed in order to limit further contestation over thresholds in the future. As Michael Doyle (2014) acknowledged, there had been concerns as to the UNSC "acting far beyond the parameters of international peace and security" (191). By limiting the R2P to four major crimes, while recognizing each as a threat to "values considered vital to the international community," the R2P sought to build "a stronger imperative to respond," one that could fully recognize the need for a universal interest in repressing such crimes and one that acknowledged more stringent parameters for action (Welsh 2014a, 213). In this sense, the narrowing of the R2P amounted to a move toward creating a more precise legal underpinning, in that member-states now recognized obligations to prevent and punish genocide, war crimes, and crimes against humanity (Bellamy 2015b, 41).

These new standards also helped "preclude the trap of a genocide threshold for protection," which had previously been viewed as a major barrier to possible intervention practice and was often seen as setting the bar too high in terms of when states had a responsibility to protect those threatened by mass atrocity crimes (Doyle 2014, 203). This agreement strengthened the idea of a distinct moral threshold being broken when specific international crimes were committed, reinforcing a critical link between the R2P's normative ambition to redefine state behaviour in mass atrocity crime situations and the central moral imperative of humanity. Following on from the WSOD, the R2P concept was further refined through the introduction of a three-pillar system, introduced in the UN Secretary-General's 2009 R2P report. Pillar I outlined the responsibility every state has to protect its populations from the four mass atrocity crimes. Pillar II stipulated that the wider community has a responsibility to assist another state in meeting this responsibility. Pillar III specified that if a state is manifestly failing in its responsibility, then the international community must be prepared to take appropriate collective action in accordance with the UN Charter. Each of the three pillars was presented as equally important, and one need not follow them sequentially – it depended on the circumstances of the case.

The idea of "narrowing and deepening" the R2P's focus (Evans 2015, 27) was thus argued to be essential both for persuading states to endorse the principle and for helping strengthen the concept in terms of its application as a "mobilizer" or "rallying cry" for action (Evans 2008a, 64; Bellamy 2015b, 42). The concept of a shocked international conscience following the outbreak of mass atrocity crimes had found expression through the four crimes of R2P, and this helped apply moral indignation to concrete legal terms and reduce earlier ambiguities concerning the humanitarian scope of certain acts. Nonetheless, it is crucial to recognize that the 2005 WSOD did not itself create any new legal obligations, but instead "authoritatively interprets state's existing obligations to prevent and respond to atrocity crimes" (Welsh 2014b, 125). Thus, it provided a significant reminder to states of the "obligations they already owe to citizens as part of international law" (Welsh, 2014b, 130). By simply reinforcing existing international law, the document has left states to decide when and where they will choose to act upon the responsibilities outlined in the WSOD.

Despite the significance of the 2005 WSOD in refining the R2P's focus down to four major crimes, it has not ended debates as to when these four international crimes are to be considered threats to international peace and security and thus require an effective response from the UNSC. Contestation continues to be shaped by the extent to which states can define an appropriate threshold for when the outbreak of mass atrocity crimes demands forceful or coercive collective action (Jacob 2018, 396). States have continued to be selective as to when to expand (or shrink) their responsibilities for threat identification, instead of pursuing a gradual progression toward consistent expansion. This has dampened the human security–focused idea of R2P as well as strengthened a more state-centric conception of protection and prevention. The concept of human security in its original conception sought to challenge the state-centric nature of the international system; the R2P maintains the systemic status quo and treats states – and the state-based nature of the UN – as unalterable constants (Hehir 2017). As chapter 4 will explore in greater detail, the extent to which the UNSC has been willing to accept the increasing expansion of threats to international peace and security, even in regard to evidence of mass atrocity crimes, remains vehemently contested. The R2P is thus caught between competing ideological visions over when to recognize threats to humanity as also being threats to international peace and security that require a collective response. Moving forward, there is a need to reconcile the role of the state in promoting the cosmopolitan responsibilities that drove the R2P's original development, vis-à-vis an increasingly narrow conception of state interest when it comes to threat identification.

CLARIFYING THE UN'S INSTITUTIONAL FRAMEWORK

Finally, the R2P sought to address contestation surrounding the decision-making framework for protection practices. As the most powerful organ in the UN system, the UNSC is tasked with maintaining international peace and security. However, the Security Council was designed from the start to acknowledge the unequal capacities of states and to allow the great powers to dominate; specifically, those great powers enjoy permanent membership and the right to veto. Article 27(3) of the Charter states: "Decisions of the Security Council on all other matters shall be made by an affirmative vote of nine members including the concurring votes of the permanent members." Thus, each permanent member has the power to disallow a resolution by voting no to it (colloquially referred to as the veto) (Gifkins 2021, 4). The idea behind the veto is twofold: to ensure that the great powers remain committed to the UN, and to avoid great power conflict. It has therefore helped balance the competing interests of the great powers throughout the UN's history, and so far it has made direct conflict between them less likely. Even so, the great powers' veto privilege has long been a point of contention, with other member-states often viewing it as counter to the principle of the sovereign equality of states. The use of the veto has evolved significantly over the decades: in the 1950s nearly half of all draft resolutions were vetoed; by the 1990s, it was less than 2 percent (Schindlmayr 2001, 226). The extensive use of the veto during the Cold War era limited the effectiveness of the Security Council in matters of international peace and security; in the 1990s, the opportunity arose for a more activist council, and the council felt itself pressured to involve itself in human security issues. In the twenty-first century, however, the council's record has been mixed. In the 1990s, the veto was used only nine times; since 2010, twenty-five times. Alongside this, the increased resort to closed-door meetings has led to more informal vetoes, with states threatening to block resolutions before they are publicly tabled. The recent high-profile use of the veto in mass atrocity crime situations, such as in Syria, has generated calls for restrictions to be placed on the veto power.

Before the R2P, many of the disagreements around authorization concerned which body could legally authorize humanitarian intervention and when the Security Council might be bypassed. Such debates were intensified by NATO's decision to act outside of the UNSC, after the international community failed to reach consensus over the Kosovo crisis and Russia threatened to use its veto power. This kick-started discussions regarding the need to develop further constraints on the expansive humanitarian intervention norm. Absent a clearer idea of who could authorize such actions and when, that norm would remain deeply controversial, particularly in the eyes of states that in the past had suffered significantly at the hands of imperial states. The result was considerable distrust of any attempt to forge a "right of intervention." So it was vital that the R2P be crafted in such a way as to recognize and attempt to address these concerns and that it make clear which body could authorize intervention in mass atrocity cases. In light of these concerns, the report of the ICISS (2001, xii) went on to argue that there was "no better or more appropriate body than the UNSC to authorize military intervention for human protection purposes." Yet at the same time, the ICISS (xiii) report did hint that "states may not rule out other means to meet the gravity and urgency of that situation." The 2005 WSOD made a strong effort to address the concerns of all member-states on this issue and to clarify the UNSC's role in sanctioning collective action against mass atrocity crimes.

The UN member-states, especially those on the UNSC, remained deeply reluctant to engage in discussions about adapting the UN Charter, which ultimately meant that the 2005 WSOD was framed in such a way as to reinforce the UNSC's discretion on issues of protection, which would be taken exclusively on a "case-by-case basis" (Welsh 2008, 548). The R2P as formulated in the 2005 agreement thus worked with the current principles of the UN Charter and the rules concerning the authorization of force, so as to make it clear that R2P-related crises would be dealt with through the UN's normal peace and security mechanisms and would not require exceptional measures (Bellamy 2010, 160). As Doyle (2014, 206–7) highlights, the decision to keep authorization powers under the UNSC's umbrella allowed the R2P to function as a "leash" on past intervention practices, which had taken place "without restraint or credible attention to 'international'"; at the same time, the R2P provided a "licence" for action – that is, it offered greater legitimacy for action in R2P cases. Yet this decision did not resolve the critical question of what to do when the Security Council was deadlocked as a result of competing geostrategic interests. Since then, R2P supporters have kept trying to push the R2P beyond the initial 2005 agreement, arguing for stronger imperatives to dictate when the Security Council must act. Peters (2011), for example, has called for a strong legal interpretation of the R2P and for the Security Council members to be placed "under a legal obligation to authorize or to take sufficiently robust action in R2P situations." This can be linked to a continued emphasis on the need to put in place a "Responsibility Not to Veto (RN2V)" principle, as first proposed by France and Mexico in August 2015[1] and reinforced by the ACT group's "Code of conduct regarding Security Council action against genocide, crimes against humanity or war crimes" (ACT is a group of small and medium-sized states) (UN 2015). Both initiatives have been discussed and supported by a range of states during General Assembly debates on the R2P, and 103 states have now signed on to the Mexico–France initiative. In the 2019 General assembly debate, Mexico argued that "the veto is not a privilege, but an international responsibility" and that "in the face of atrocities, political agendas are simply not justifiable" (UN 2019). However, permanent members such as Russia have long pushed back against any form of veto restriction, arguing that keeping the veto power is vital to ensuring international peace and security and suggesting that "the use of the veto more than once has spared the United Nations from getting involved in dubious enterprises" (UN 2018b). The current contestation between permanent and non-permanent members over the need to introduce such a proposal reminds us again how states continue to dispute the responsibilities outlined by the R2P, as well as the extent to which those responsibilities should constrain state decision-making further than the original 2005 WSOD. In other words, many UN states view the case-by-case approach for addressing mass atrocity crimes as still allowing permanent members too much discretion in their use of the veto. This suggests that the

R2P's refinement in the WSOD has failed so far to end a range of debates concerning the process for authorizing coercive responses to mass atrocity crimes. As Ademola Abass (2012) has argued, the Security Council's costly inaction in African conflicts has left many African states doubtful whether decision-making should be left to the whims of the Security Council, and this in turn has energized calls for greater regional autonomy in terms of responding to mass atrocities. Chapter 4 will explore the significance of all this and the potential for greater consensus as to the UNSC's role.

Summary

The R2P can be viewed as an attempt to weaken the apparent obstacles to mass atrocity protection. As a principle, the R2P must also be understood in relation to past moral failures to act. Given the significant hostility to the previous idea of humanitarian intervention, distancing the R2P from this norm was crucial to the eventual unanimous agreement among member-states to the 2005 WSOD (Bellamy 2009, 194). Arguably, the successful adoption of the R2P in 2005 was achieved through efforts to address some of the most pressing questions surrounding intervention debates at that time: When can sovereignty be overridden? What body can authorize such action? Which acts constitute legitimate grounds for action? In helping forge greater consensus on these issues, the R2P has been recognized by its many advocates as a "game-changer" (Thakur 2011a) and an idea that "has begun to change the world" (Bellamy 2014, 111). However, the extent to which the R2P has been able to exert greater pressure on state actors to reassess their core responsibilities and motivations is much more contested. Despite the growing consensus and perceived clarity on many of the issues (see above), contentious debates have continued, especially regarding the UNSC's role in authorizing intervention and the challenge of specifying a trigger point for action. The ability to address these concerns therefore will require greater engagement with the R2P as it exists today, which is, as a moral and political principle that is seeking to change how states react to mass atrocity crimes by embedding a more collective understanding of responsibility rooted in the imperative of our common humanity. While much of the remaining contestation can be viewed as existing in regard to unresolved tensions over sovereignty and territorial claims, there are more fundamental disagreements besides — in particular, those concerning what protection and prevention should look like and under what circumstances the motivation of humanity can override or connect directly to a state's strategic and national interests.

TRANSFERRING MORAL SENTIMENT INTO POLITICAL WILL: REFLECTING ON THE R2P IMPLEMENTATION PUZZLE

It has been argued in recent years that the increased presence of human-centric security practice within the UNSC has created the impetus for states to become more accountable to the so-called wishes of humanity. Matthew Weinert (2015, 84) contends that in recent years human beings have increasingly, if inconsistently, been situated at the forefront of the UN's work. The assumed value of common humanity now features consistently in the normative appeals made by R2P scholars, to the point that it is often framed as *the* central issue in challenges to alter states' positions on intervention against mass atrocities. As highlighted by this chapter so far, at the heart of the original motivation for creating the R2P was a moral sentiment, one built on the idea that states can more strongly recognize obligations to common humanity and that this can be achieved by reiterating the scope of their responsibilities in an international doctrine. However, placing value on strangers' lives may well require states to risk their own citizens to protect them, besides risking political fallout from domestic audiences. As Bellamy (2009, 58) previously acknowledged, preventing future Rwandas boils down to overcoming one key obstacle – the need to persuade states "to accept risk in order to save people in distant lands, when there are few strategic interests at stake." Regarding the R2P, it remains unclear how the principle can better work to shift the political will of states. We must therefore examine the broader context in which the political will of states is influenced.

First and foremost, we must acknowledge that every humanitarian intervention is influenced by a range of factors and motives, which include self-interest and power management. This is not to suggest that an intervention cannot also be influenced by humanitarian motives. Roland Paris (2014, 573) writes that "patterns point to an interplay of material self-interests and humanitarian norms in intervention decisions." Whatever the claims by realist scholars that humanitarian intervention is only ever a cover for self-interest and power hunger, some recent studies demonstrate that interventions reflect a combination of values and material interests (Binder 2009;

Murray 2013; Kreig 2013). As Simon Caney (2005, 242) acknowledges, it is unrealistic to assume that states can never be motivated by other concerns, which must be seen to include ideological commitments. Furthermore, it is also clear that a state's pursuit of the national interest can include a commitment to humanitarian ideals, so it is artificial to "separate interests from their values" (Caney 2005, 242). This was expressed rhetorically by President Barack Obama with regard to the 2011 Libyan intervention, when he declared that "there will be times, though, when our safety is not directly threatened, but our interests and our values are. Sometimes, the course of history poses challenges that threaten our common humanity and our common security. These may not be America's problems alone, but they are important to us" (Obama 2011). Obama in this statement was recognizing that protecting those facing the threat of mass atrocity can be in a state's key interest, even when that population cannot directly threaten state security. In this sense, it is important to conceptualize state interest as involving much more than security. Values and norms can significantly influence state policy. So creating political will must be understood as a multi-front battle.

Challenging Western Motivation and Inconsistency

Much of the recent academic criticism of the R2P has focused on its failures to launch military intervention under Pillar III of the norm – in particular, its failure to bring about peace in Libya (Dunford and Neu 2019). Non-Western states have continued to emphasize the issue of what motivates R2P responses in the first place. Most controversially, these states claim that the R2P is simply a smokescreen for other political projects, such as regime change. With regard to Libya, the insistence of the P3 (the UK, the US, and France) that "Gaddafi must go" lent support to claims that regime change was the primary reason for the intervention (Akbarzadeh and Saba 2018, 540). South Africa later accused NATO of "abusing the authorization granted by the Council to advance a political regime-change agenda" and called out the problem of selectivity as one that "gravely limits the credibility of the Council in advancing protection of civilians mandates" (UN 2011a). So it can be argued that the inconsistency of the R2P's application has more to do with Western powers only legitimizing the use of force when they can further their own geostrategic interests. Indeed, it can seem as if only narrow strategic interests have ever dictated how states respond to mass atrocities. Yet as Welsh (2014b, 137) has previously noted, it is far too simplistic to claim that "only pragmatism and self-interest, and not normative considerations, affect behaviour." In this sense, it is vital to acknowledge that both normative and non-normative considerations remain in play, leading to inconsistent outcomes. As the Libya case made clear, many voices within the P3 states saw regime change as the best way to protect civilians. Thus the line between which actions are viewed as legitimate when protecting civilians and which are not quite clearly raises normative questions alongside those of strategic interests.

Yet it is important to reiterate that the R2P is built upon a pragmatic interpretation of when states should intervene. Thus it is unable to manufacture a universally consistent response to mass atrocity situations. This creates a dilemma: "inaction in the face of mass atrocities stands to weaken R2P by making it seem hollow, but conversely, employing coercive force in the name of R2P highlights the unavoidable inconsistency of the international response, which is just as likely to cast doubt on the doctrine" (Paris 2014, 579). This contradiction lies at the heart of the R2P and confounds those who try to measure the success or failure of the doctrine in any concrete manner. Critics have responded to the current inconsistent reality by suggesting that the R2P is not yet "sufficiently consolidated to compel states to principled action to prevent and respond to genocide or mass atrocities" (Crossley 2012). This same key criticism has been put forward by Aidan Hehir (2011), who has questioned the strength of the moral principle seen to underpin the concept. He suggests that "action taken on the basis of a commitment to a principle derived from altruistic individual impulses cannot be reasonably cited as constituting a precedent or new norm" (19). He argues that while an increase in more altruistic state behaviour is most welcome, the behavioural change required can only be "impelled by a unique constellation of necessarily temporal factors," creating major inconsistencies in its use (19). In this sense, the R2P has not addressed what Hehir views as a fundamental problem, which is, its inability to change political will when it comes to humanitarian intervention or to address its perennial inconsistency in relation to humanitarian response. For Hehir, then, the R2P has been rendered toothless because it has not changed international law, nor does it hold states to greater account. As former UN Secretary-General Ban Ki-moon argued in his 2015 R2P report, "the Council's inconsistent response to situations featuring genocide, war crimes, ethnic cleansing and crimes against humanity continues to affect the standing of the responsibility to protect" (13). He called for the protection of populations to be "elevated above more particular political and strategic interests" and thus for states to recognise the R2P as an "enduring obligation," whereby the responsibilities it creates cannot be turned on and off by states (Ki-moon 2015, 16-18). These comments reflect the importance of moral arguments and the weight that continues to be placed on the potential for shared responsibilities to take precedence over political decision-making.

Despite the creation of the R2P, normative battles over state responsibility continue, as states struggle to weigh their obligations to humanity against other obligations. Yet one cannot instantly conclude from this that the concept of humanity has failed to have any impact on state decision-making in such situations. As earlier highlighted, the concept of humanity has been central to affirming much of the motivational thrust behind state agreement on the four specific crimes of R2P, outlined in the 2005 WSOD. However, in terms of creating a stronger motivational push factor that can be utilized to shape states' self-interest, the concept of humanity has been much more limited. As a consequence, the cosmopolitan motivating principle of humanity is increasingly seen as at odds with competing interpretations of the R2P's focus and aims. As outlined earlier, a more statist approach to addressing mass atrocity crimes has further limited the appeal of such motivational claims. Thus the continued inconsistency of state responses to mass atrocities can be seen as significantly challenging the original promise of never again, which raises the need to redefine how best to motivate the R2P in a changing global order.

CONCLUSION

In light of the critiques highlighted in this chapter, it is important to reflect on a number of pertinent questions concerning the future salience of the R2P principle. First, what is behind the UNSC's inconsistent response? As highlighted earlier, inconsistent state action in protecting those threatened by mass atrocity crimes has been a consistent feature of international relations since before the Cold War and throughout the post–Cold War era, including since the subsequent rise of the R2P concept. So it can be argued that the decision to structure the WSOD within a pragmatic "case by case" framework has done little to address the inconsistency that has long been a feature of UNSC decision-making. Rhoads and Welsh (2019, 616) contend that the R2P in many ways continues to be shaped by failure – by failure to respond in decisive fashion and by failure to fully implement its overall mandate for action. Yet it is also the case that these failures are not simply outcomes of "deficiencies in capacity and political will"; they are also products of the behavioural contestation that continues to surround the norm, with states seeking to block or redefine the accepted parameters for attempts to protect populations at risk (616). What this suggests moving forward is the need to further explore the drivers of state contestation and the extent to which the R2P has been reshaped by competing interests that run counter to its cosmopolitan origins.

Second, what role can humanity be seen to play in shifting the current behaviour of states toward greater consensus on R2P implementation? Ultimately, this comes down to a question of why states should want to live up to this so-called global responsibility in the first place. So it is important to continue tracing the moral underpinning of such responsibilities in order to assess the claim that political will can be changed to achieve the goals set out by the wider R2P project. Key to this process will be more carefully locating how the dual function of humanity interacts with competing political and legal pressures on overall state decision-making. As Brunnee and Toope (2006) argue, "the need for real commitment to the responsibility to protect is both ethical and pragmatic" (133); debates concerning political will relate to more than the dominance of security interests over ethics and moral principles. For the R2P to begin to address this tension will require a greater understanding of the complex interactions among moral, political, and legal pressures on state decision-making at the international and national levels. And the starting point for this must be to better locate what is being referred to when we appeal to humanity, by analyzing the philosophical roots of the concept and how they relate to the very crimes on which the R2P focuses.

2

What Is Humanity?

The discourses that surround the idea of humanity have rich and complex philosophical, theological, and historical origins, yet humanity has often been presented as a self-evident truth, so that the existence and importance of humanity is rarely questioned, and neither is the implied requirement to protect it. It is vital then to recognize that the concept of humanity is certainly not as clear as "its wide-spread appearance in political and ethical discourse might suggest" (Feldman and Ticktin 2010, 1). This has a number of significant implications, but most importantly for this book, it presents several pressing questions concerning how we can theorize what responsibilities we may owe to those beyond our borders and to what extent we can locate universal human harms. This chapter thus begins to interrogate the tendency to overlook the key philosophical connection between atrocity crimes and the concept of humanity itself. It will argue that only through greater recognition of the concept of humanity can we fully conceptualize what harm is generated by mass atrocity crimes and begin to assess the strength of moral imperatives in support of preventing such crimes and protecting those who are threatened by them, wherever they occur. Without greater philosophical scrutiny of our understanding of mass atrocity crimes and their connection to humanity, we cannot fully draw the link between the legal and the moral right of intervention.

The challenge we face when theorizing a conception of humanity is to reconcile a set of universal values with the plurality of values that are embedded in particular communities (Bartelson 2009, 7). We need to recognize that "particularism and difference are not incompatible with the existence of universal principles" (Boucher 2011, 283) and that the existence of many different "humans" who coexist in difference is part of the very definition of humanity (Mazlish 2009, 95). As Catherine Lu (2006) highlights, the idea of a common humanity is ultimately "an account of what is common and distinctive about being a human agent" (92), recognizing that we as human beings all share natural vulnerabilities. A "thin conception of universality" must be reinforced, for this is essential to defending the ideal that every human being belongs to a single community of humankind and that everyone therefore shares a set of natural capacities (Bartelson 2009, 171). Building on this thin universalism, this chapter puts forward a distinct dual conception of humanity, understood through the critical interaction between ideas of humankind and humanness and grounded in the moral status of human beings as creators of moral law. In this way, we understand humanity through the relations we must have with other humans, which in turn involves a clear political component linked to a basic moral right to recognition (Honneth 1995; Forst 2011).

This conceptualization of humanity is central to reassessing how we think about the harms generated by mass atrocity crimes and how we should attempt to formulate a response to them. Accordingly, I argue that any attempt to locate universal harms created by certain acts of violence must conceptualize the threat they pose to the collective ability to coexist within a social order underpinned by moral rules. Only then, having assessed this relationship between collective responsibility and universal harm, can one begin to talk of a specific moral obligation in relation to state actors. To locate the theoretical grounding for these obligations, this chapter begins by providing a clearer theoretical understanding of what we can refer to as our common humanity.

HISTORICAL CONTEXT

From a purely empirical point of view, it is perhaps obvious to suggest that our most basic understanding of humanity comes from its definition as a pre-given biological categorization, encapsulated by the fact that human beings are members of the same biological category: *Homo sapiens*. Even if true, this is but one interpretation of humanity, built on a scientific categorization that locates what is specific about the species through an understanding of genetic code. However, the very idea of humanity stretches back much further in time than the discovery of specific biological categories. When we cast our eyes back to Greek literature, we find a more philosophical understanding of what humanity may represent. Take for example Homer's *Iliad* and *Odyssey*, in which he acknowledges that what separates man from the gods is the mortality we all share, with the human condition characterized by "feebleness and misery" (Baldry 1965, 13). Homer also argues that there are specific characteristics of humanity that separate it from the beasts, namely the development of arts and language. His understanding of humanity is thus an attempt to define particular features of human beings that tie us together as humankind, recognizing that these can often be best understood through the fragility of being human. The ideas in Homer's work can be associated with the theories of Stoic philosophers of ancient Greek times, who began to conceptualize a world citizenship, whereby the world citizen is one who identifies with humanity alone (Ossewaarde 2007). The Stoic position thus asserts the idea that all persons possess an equal moral status due to the fact human beings share a common capacity for moral reasoning, which suggests, as a condition of the universality, that each individual has a primary moral affiliation with the rest of humanity as moral agents (Hayden 2005).

It is from this understanding of the equal moral capacity of all human beings and the corresponding assignment of a common moral "brotherhood" (Cicero 1998) that one can begin to discuss the role of humanity and the idea that each person whose life is at risk deserves equal consideration. Moving forward to more contemporary history, it is useful to also reflect on the way appeals to humanity have been specifically shaped by the "context of humankind entering upon a time of total war" (Mazlish 2009, 35). As German philosopher Theodor Adorno (2000) recognized in the aftermath of the Nazi atrocities, while people may still not agree on what is good, they can be clear on the question of what is bad and should thus be resisted. The attempts made by states to eradicate certain groups from the face of the earth reinforced awareness of what could clearly be defined as inhumanity, leading to the development of humanity itself as a legal concept. Humanity has thus been acknowledged in international law through references to "the common interests of all human beings," reflecting the increasing expansion of the idea of a moral community into practical initiatives (Coates 2006, 214). So one can point to the qualities of humanity as essential to the normative underpinning of both the UN Charter and the Universal Declaration of Human Rights.

Despite the often assumed neutrality implied by the concept, an understanding of how we can define humanity and what it specifically represents is still severely contested. Due to the almost limitless interpretations of what humanity consists of, it can often appear as though we should simply dismiss the concept altogether, as ultimately an empty signifier, for despite universal claims to its ability to encompass all human beings, it is in fact "so historically, geographically situated, as to have no meaning beyond its particular instantiation" (Feldman and Ticktin 2010, 2). Yet to completely dismiss the concept of humanity would be to fundamentally ignore how the concept has continued to shape our understanding around issues as diverse as climate change and mass atrocity crimes. This is best encapsulated by the language used around the concept itself. For example, former UN Secretary-General Kofi Annan (2001) spoke of a need to act "in defence of our common humanity." Similarly, President Barack Obama (2011) described the Libyan intervention as "necessary to protect common humanity." What these two examples support is the idea of humanity as a concept that must be considered worth defending and protecting due to its implied universal value. The decision by both diplomats and scholars to build arguments around the concept of our common humanity demonstrates an assumption that we all recognize what it represents and, furthermore, that acknowledgment of its value is implicit to that recognition. Thus, as Richard Shapcott (2010, 14) points out, despite there being clear divisions of humanity based upon "historically constituted communities," it is still possible to both identify with and have a moral concern for humanity.

Yet more often than not, it is unclear what moral values are being referred to and where the obligation to protect and defend humanity comes from. Moreover, one can often point to examples where humanity is taken up as an exclusionary concept for deciding who is to be shielded from harm, and who not (Fast 2016, 113). So there is a need to systematically unpack these assumptions and address claims made against the universal category of humanity. To that end, this chapter now puts forward two distinct interpretations of what is often being referred to when we talk of a common humanity.

HUMANITY AS HUMANNESS

Humanity can refer to the quality of being human, encapsulated as humanness. Humanity in this sense is the essence of what makes us human – an abstract property – rather than the human race or a set of individuals (Luban 2004, 90). In other words, certain basic values are considered inherent in all human beings. These values have most often been connected to "behaviours and dispositions that are congruent with the (moral) view of being humane," such as human capacities for friendship and empathy (Fast 2016, 116). This reading of humanity implies there is something fundamental to being human, and how we define that fundament has a profound impact on our understanding of the concept of humanity. As we begin to unpack this notion of humanness, it is vital to delve deeper into several contrasting philosophical interpretations of what this idea can signify. This will help us uncover specific human capacities that are seen to be universal.

For Ghanaian philosopher Kwame Gyekye (2004, 97), the concept of humanity stands in for a whole collection of characteristics and ideals that comprise an individual human being. Thus we can pinpoint certain basic values, norms, and ideals that are sure to be found in an individual who is a human being, one such being human dignity. Gyekye argues that the very possibility of a human society must be grounded in the reality of certain core human values, and thus human values must be considered universal (46). These core values are essential to our ability to flourish as human beings and thereby transcend the particularities of culture. Presenting humanity as a normative concept in this way is significant, for when we talk about a crime committed against humanity, we are suggesting that the very basic moral sensibilities that are instinctive to human beings are being challenged by that crime and that the foundations of human worth are therefore under direct attack. Humanity, then, is to be understood against a background of "the fundamental value and disvalue experiences of human beings" (97–8); these experiences are common to all human beings and make it possible to speak of a shared humanity.

The same line of argument is supported by the British political theorist Bhikhu Parekh (1999), who suggests that part of our understanding of who we are is based on the belief that we as human beings have several capabilities, which are unique to humans and thus reinforce a privilege we are deemed to enjoy over the non-human world. By acknowledging the fact of human uniqueness and superiority, we are able to formulate the concept of human dignity. Human dignity is thus essential to the idea of humanness; it follows that certain traits and characteristics are part of our common humanity. For Parekh, human dignity exists because humans "have capacities which non-humans do not and which humans consider being so significant, as to make them the basis of an appropriate moral practice" (147). Dignity here is a collective status, one that each of us holds because each of us possesses certain species-specific capabilities; thus, to say we have dignity is to say we must treat humans in a certain manner, not as inanimate objects (147). This interpretation places significant emphasis on the importance of human capabilities: humanity can only be understood in terms of what makes human beings different from other animals.

For Polish sociologist Zygmunt Bauman (2001), the idea of human dignity is also central. He understands morality as pre-social, in that humanity can be seen as intrinsically moral. Thus, individuals are deemed to have a moral capacity or impulse that is part of the essence of humanness. Bauman is therefore committed to the dignity of humanity, and this guides his belief in transcending the humiliations of the everyday to strive toward an alternative imagination that is fit for humanity (Bauman and Tester 2001). The realization of our humanity thus requires us to recognize cultural variety as critical to discussions of shared human values (Bauman 2001, 136). The universal nature of humanity must accommodate pluralism in order to best serve the cause of humanity; this will enable and encourage greater discussion around a shared conception of the good (140). Clearly, then, we must strive for the full realization of our common humanity through an appreciation of our shared capacity as human beings.

Our very ability to strive recognizes that we have an innate moral capacity to share in this experience and construct alternative ways of representing humanity. This understanding of common humanity therefore places a much stronger emphasis on the need for humanity to represent a common good, one that is inclusive of many contrasting interpretations of the good life. As such, the capacity to strive is provided by a universal moral disposition that is intrinsic to humanness.

It is possible to recognize the notion of humanness as stipulating characteristics that are intrinsic to all human beings and that exist naturally within us all, yet there have been some attempts to categorize these characteristics as created solely through our interactions with society. In other words, human nature can be viewed as a socially and culturally constructed concept that one does not uncover through abstraction. For example, the French philosopher Emmanuel Levinas (2005) directly questions the idea that humanness is an natural quality found within us. He argues instead that to be moral is not to be autonomous, but rather to be responsive and responsible for the other; thus, it is the recognition of suffering that creates obligations not to cause needless suffering (75). So if we are failing to respond to the needs of those who are suffering, then we are arguably succumbing to the "law of evil." Levinas's understanding of humanity is in this way tied to respect for the other: only through this connection with the other can we recognize and respond to evil. This suggests that humanity is distinctly connected to the concrete situations in which we find ourselves and is formed through lived encounters with other human beings.

Levinas rejects an explicit ideal of humanity that is innate, yet his focus on humanity as a responsibility to respond to human difference can still be interpreted as an appeal to universal human dignity. His approach to humanity is grounded in the infinite value of the other, which he upholds through an essentially Kantian construction, by stating the need to respect the other as an end in itself (Wu 2007, 11). In this sense, his understanding of humanity is still built upon an inherent human essence; he recognizes the notion of sensibility as integral to our common humanity.

But perhaps the most important means to understand humanness is by contrasting it with dehumanization. Acknowledging humanity's opposite, inhumanity, compels us to make explicit some of the assumptions we often take for granted when talking about humanity in a positive light. The logic that underpins the idea of dehumanization can thus be seen to assert that as human beings, we are all vulnerable to our status as humans being challenged or taken from us; this creates a need for all of us to defend it. So when we refer to dehumanization, we are explicitly embracing particular notions of what humanness must consist of. Put more plainly, we can learn a lot about humanity by examining how it can be violated. At this point it is useful to refer to the work of psychologist Nick Haslam (2006), who has examined how we can categorize humanness in relation to dehumanization. He draws from two separate conceptions: uniquely human (UH) characteristics, which relate to the boundary that separates humans from the related category of animals; and human nature (HN) characteristics, which are typically or essentially human but may not be the same ones that distinguish us from other species (256). HN characteristics are inherent to us; UH characteristics vary between people and cultures, for they are acquired rather than born. Haslam next posits that "different forms of dehumanization occur when the characteristics that constitute each sense are denied to people" (Haslam 2006, 256). Through these two categories, HN and UH, we can tease out specific concepts that are regarded as integral to humanness. For when HN characteristics are denied to a victim they are seen as "lacking in emotionality, warmth, cognitive openness, individual agency"; in contrast, when UH characteristics are denied to others, the victim is viewed as "lacking in refinement, civility, moral sensibility, and higher cognition" (257–8). This process of dividing up the essence of humanness provides a useful way to conceptualize the wide variety of human capacities we can view as integral to human beings.

But doing so also raises a number of difficulties when we attempt to speak of a universal form of humanness. If we view UH characteristics as relative, and thus reject the idea that these capacities represent an inherent natural quality, it may significantly alter how one views the relationship between mass atrocity crimes and humanity itself. It is then more difficult to claim that specific crimes against humanity directly damage fundamental human values we all share; instead, our understanding of the value that is threatened is potentially reliant on contrasting ideas of humanness. Nevertheless, one can argue that the ability to speak of unique human characteristics is still built upon a universal conception of human capacity, whereby the recognition of these features must first derive from a shared capacity to differentiate ourselves from animals, connected to our innate human nature. In this sense, we can still appeal to a universal harm that is created when a perpetrator refuses to recognize the unique human characteristics that separate us from animals. It is therefore argued that the ability to acknowledge uniquely human characteristics, and the concurrent ability to deny their existence to victims, provides a clear indication of the universality of humanness as a concept.

What links these contrasting interpretations of humanness is their ability to recognize that humans have at least the innate capacity or ability to foster a specific form of human essence, which can be viewed as unique to human beings and which defines what it means to be human. Often what is referred to as the core feature of humanness is some form of human dignity that qualifies us as members of a common humanity. This basic acknowledgment of a shared human dignity helps provide a universal human value that can be seen to transcend cultural divides and that must be respected and protected. In this regard, we must also think of humanity in terms of what it is *not*: denial of rights, persecution, and degradation of the person, "all of which imply the absence of respect and dignity" (Fast 2016, 115). Through this ability to recognize attacks on the unique value of humanness, we can make claims to the existence of both a distinct human community and our membership in a shared moral community. So when we attempt to categorize the harm committed by mass atrocity crimes, we must be able to acknowledge the potential impact this has on a shared universal notion of humanness.

HUMANITY AS HUMANKIND

Humanity can also be referred to as simply humankind, meaning the aggregation of all human beings. This requires us to accept that as human beings we all belong to a single collective group and that this allows us to have interconnections with human beings as a whole. Reinforcing such claims is scientific analysis related to the universal biological features human beings share and the similarities in every human being's basic needs and interests. The collective element of this understanding of humanity is based on the fact that we are all members of a human species, living on the same planet, and that we are both constrained and interconnected by this fact.

The concept of humankind can be split into two further categories. First, humankind can refer to every human person, treated collectively, albeit still conceived as a composite set of individuals (Macleod 2010, 293). Second, humankind can refer to every person, but thought of as a collective and singular body (292). In this latter sense, humanity is a single entity that has a conscience or interests on its own terms. To illustrate this distinction, one can acknowledge that rather than mass atrocity crimes staining the conscience of every individual human being, it is the group of humankind whose conscience is damaged. Such a reading recognizes that certain properties and values belong to the group in its own right, rather than being properties reducible to all members (297). When we discuss certain acts as staining the conscience of humanity it is difficult to argue that every single human being has had their conscience stained; but when we refer to humankind as a group, we can more easily construct the argument that a significant group representing humankind has been directly affected as a singular body. In this sense, humanity as sovereign or as a global community is shocked or offended by certain acts (Geras 2011, 49). Once we assume that a particular group can be assigned responsibility – or alternatively, be a victim of harm – we can view certain acts as violating key interests of a group – interests such as its culture or diversity (Macleod, 2010, 297). Thus, humanity arguably has an interest in maintaining its relative diversity and security. Insofar as individuals identify with humankind, then damage inflicted on a collective body also inflicts secondary damage against each of those individuals. Implicit in this understanding of humankind is the assumption that some form of universal moral value exists.

Directly related to the notion of humankind are ideas of human interconnectedness, which have been discussed at length by international relations scholar Andrew Linklater. He talks directly of an increased human interconnectedness, in the sense that humans have acquired more "universalistic structures of consciousness" in order to become more adept at interacting with strangers and outsiders (Linklater 2009, 482). He contends that as humans enjoy the benefits of increased global and intellectual exchange, we are able to identify more with distant people and to assist them by "drawing serious violations of human rights to the attention of a worldwide public" (490). This increased sense of interconnectedness with humans around the world also links back to his discussions of a global harm narrative; here, he argues that recognition of harm must be a key element of a universal global ethic (492). In his work on harm, Linklater's (2011, 5) central aim has been to understand whether the modern world has made progress in establishing the concept of harm as a key moral and political question for humanity. This is important, for it can be argued that the near universal recognition of the idea of harm can help unite those who disagree profoundly on many other matters (Hurrell 2012). He demonstrates how global interconnectedness and understandings of harm have changed over time, leading to a greater recognition of the impact of harm as an ideational concept employed within global politics. We will return to the concept of harm later in the chapter in order to emphasize its significant role in claims to a universal moral motivation to respect others as human beings.

What the ideas presented so far suggest, then, is the importance of acknowledging how the greater recognition of human beings as a collective entity drives the need for us to scale up social and political association (Linklater 2009, 493). This process can be directly related to the creation of the R2P, which is part of a growing trend toward redefining international standards of ethical behaviour, as well as establishing new mechanisms for reinforcing the notion of our common humanity. So when we discuss these ideas in relation to debates surrounding mass atrocity crimes, we can use Linklater's writings on human interconnectedness to explain how very different cultures are able to agree that genocide and crimes against humanity should be prohibited. Furthermore, one can expand the arguments based on increased human interconnectedness to claim that some crimes can in fact harm humanity itself, not just their direct victims. As Linklater argues, "the widening of emotional identification, has shaped long term trajectories that have come to affect humanity as a whole" (493). Through this increased understanding of the impact of harm and greater interconnectedness, one can begin to assume specific responsibilities attached to humanity as humankind.

It is important to note that defining humanity in this way places significant weight on the role of social relations that human beings have built up over time. Critical to a notion of humankind is thus the ability of individuals to relate to a collective entity, whereby something other than "material entanglements" can bind strangers together in recognizing harms committed against others (492). Thus, there is a need for greater ethical engagement with the "social consequences of interconnectedness" to counterbalance tendencies to privilege in-groups, to whom we may attach significant emotional meaning (493). Humanity is fundamentally attached to a growing and fluid understanding of changing global relations – an understanding that relies on the ability of individuals to recognize the collective and interconnected nature of humankind. In this regard, the ability to acknowledge the significance of the collective group of humankind is critical to forming a universal conception of harm created by mass atrocity crimes. Only through this acknowledgment can one begin to locate a moral imperative for states to act in defence of those threatened by such crimes.

CONCEPTUALIZING A DUAL UNDERSTANDING OF HUMANITY

While both categorizations are useful for breaking down different elements of what we often refer to as our common humanity, it is important to note that the two interpretations do not exist independently of each other. When people refer to humanity, they often interpret its existence as containing elements of both humankind and humanness. One can see this in a statement by lawyer and academic Geoffrey Robertson (1999, 220), who contends that crimes against humanity "diminish every member of the human race." Implicit in this claim is the suggestion that some crimes not only concern the whole of the human race but also, with regard to a collective understanding of humanity, directly challenge and diminish human essence, which is key to the idea of humanness. To explore the interconnectedness of these two interpretations, this chapter focuses next on a conception of humanity informed by the thinking of Immanuel Kant. This will highlight the importance of both reason and harm to the chapter's conception of humanity as well as emphasize the existence of a thin universalism. By drawing on Kant's theoretical claims regarding the concept of humanity, it will be possible to also ground the idea of human dignity in the status of human beings as creators of moral law. This will move us beyond humanity understood as biological, in terms of the distinction between human beings and other species, or as based solely in human capacities for rationality, and allow us to outline a more normative understanding of humanity, one that builds on the importance of both recognition and justification. This new conceptualization will then be utilized to reinforce the key relationship between common humanity and crimes that directly violate that concept.

First and foremost, Kant's philosophical claims regarding the concept of humanity can be seen as central to theorizing humanity as a limit on all other ends that can be pursued. In this sense, the formula of humanity put forward by Kant is used to pick out a negative requirement based on the intrinsic worth of humanity itself, as a supreme principle of morality (Kernstein 2006). As Christine Korsgaard (1996, 114) argues, the distinctive feature of humanity is its capacity to decide under the influence of reason that something is desirable and thus deemed important or valuable as an end in itself. Humanity is thus encapsulated in the capacity shared by humans to exercise reason in order to set ends. Based on this understanding, one can frame the concept of humanity in distinctly universal terms, allowing the theoretical recognition of universal harms to be more easily located and identified.

Central to Kant's approach to moral philosophy is the concept that one should always treat other human beings with respect as having ends in themselves; that is, the need to respect all human beings exists because all human beings possess absolute inner worth (Sensen 2009). Kant's supreme principle of morality is expressed in the categorical imperative, by which he acknowledges the duty to "act only in accordance with that maxim through which you can at the same time will that it become a universal law" (Kant 2002, 222). This duty applies to us unconditionally and is independent of any personal motive or desire. It thus requires that one's actions accord with universalizable maxims that respect all individuals as ends in themselves (Kant 2002). As Thomas Pogge (1998) highlights, central to Kant's moral philosophy is the idea that moral principles must be universal; in this sense a maxim can be adopted only if everyone is obligated to do so.

Building on this initial interpretation of the categorical imperative, Kant moves on to express the formula of "the end in itself" more specifically, by focusing on the concept of humanity. His second categorical imperative therefore states that one must "act in such a way that you treat humanity whether in your own person or in any other person, always at the same time an end never merely as a means" (230). This conception of common humanity can thus be seen to rest on the idea of human dignity, encapsulated in the notion of intrinsic worth, which Kant refers to as unconditional and incomparable (Merry and Ruyter 2011). Human dignity is thus used to describe the basic values people have irrespective of their own individual characteristics (Merry and Ruyter 2011). By placing greater emphasis on the unique value of human beings as requiring our ultimate moral respect, Kant provides a more personal understanding of morality.

This Kantian position thus makes it possible to recognize humanity as encapsulating appeals to both humanness and humankind. For example, one can read Kant's second formulation of the categorical imperative as referring to humanity as the species of human beings, by which each member of this class must be treated as an end (Hill 1980, 85). However, the second formulation is also a recognition that humanity is not represented by the collective of humankind alone; it can also relate to a specific set of characteristics that make persons human (Hill 1980). This formulation of the categorical imperative expresses a moral law that we must all respect humanity, as an intrinsic rather than relative value (Hayden 2005), based on a recognition of both humanness and humankind. For Kant, to act morally is always to act for the sake of the value of humanity in a person. In this sense, humanity is an end in itself, whereby "its objective value takes the form of its being an existent or self-sufficient end which has dignity or absolute worth" (Wood 1998, 171). This understanding of humanity is built upon the idea that all humans have a capacity to reason and that our ability to reason is integral to the creation of moral rules. Humanity is thus a value that grounds moral rules, providing a motive for obeying duties based on the dignity of reason as an absolute and unconditional value and an end in itself (Wood 1998, 177). Accordingly, humanity provides a reason to explain why we should abide by moral laws. However, the extent to which reason alone can fully capture and ground the moral status of human beings needs to be examined in greater detail.

THE FOUNDATIONS OF HUMAN DIGNITY

While the Kantian approach outlined above focuses specifically on the possession of reason as distinguishing us from animals, providing us with the ability to create ethical rules, it is also key to build on this approach to consider, alongside reason, the importance of recognition and justification in grounding the moral status of human beings. In this sense, humanity cannot be fully recognized through a purely rationalist logic of justification. Instead, the appeal to moral reason also demands responsibilities in terms of how we view and treat others. This requires first moving beyond focusing the idea of human dignity predominantly on the claim that all human beings can face suffering and thus deserve respect. In doing so there is a danger that we will see all humans as simply victims, in the process presenting victims as innocent and pure (Margalit 2007). The consequence of that is often the failure to show sympathy to certain groups who suffer when their moral purity or innocence is more contested or unclear. An understanding of the moral status of human beings must therefore move beyond this strict division between "us and them" and acknowledge the complexity of the relations we have with one another beyond suffering alone. As George Kateb (2011) rightly points out, "violations of human dignity have existential weight independent of suffering itself" (16) and thus suffering and harm alone cannot be seen to fully capture what it means to be treated as non-human. Moving forward, it is therefore critical to better understand human dignity in relation to our role as social agents. Underpinning this idea first of all is the human need for recognition, which must be understood as an essential part of constructing any form of social order. It is through engagement and interactions with others that humans can learn to locate and recognize the perspectives of others. The act of dehumanization is thus a clear example of how humans can fail to recognize the moral status of their victims and disregard "the subjective experiences of the victim as a factor that counts against his or her mistreatment" (Ruiter 2021, 16). Honneth (1995) has argued that the ethical development of society has been driven forward through historical struggles for recognition. Furthermore, the moral status of human beings is located not just in ideas of recognition but also in the interconnected right to moral justification and self-determination. As Rainer Forst (2011) highlights, to be a "law-giving member means not being disregarded when it comes to legitimizing moral action or social rule" (968), whereby one should not be marginalized by others and denied a moral right to justification. Human dignity is thus defined through both the struggle for recognition and the moral right to justification.

In contrast to this approach, there have been recent attempts to move beyond the idea of dignity or of defining the human in terms of a particular essence. Anne Phillips (2015) puts forward the argument that claims to be human are understood as claims for equality, whereby equality is "something that we establish when we treat one another as equals" (69). In this regard there is no need to provide foundations in abstract concepts; equality is instead seen to exist through the collective claim and commitment to it. Yet the extent to which a focus on equality can in fact fully capture what makes all forms of dehumanization wrong can be questioned. Dehumanization is thus about more than discrediting claims to equal treatment, it is also connected to a harm committed against a shared human status. So when we begin to apply this theoretical grounding to discussions of mass atrocity crimes, we recognize that these crimes affect humanity in a number of ways, not only through denying the humanity of individuals in terms of suffering or claims to equality, but also in terms of denying humanity itself and its range of identities (Anderson-Gold 2009, 197). One can then categorize crimes against humanity as attempts to directly exclude particular groups from their right to humanity, by which these acts are wholly contrary to the rights of future generations and thus concern all of humanity. Furthermore, such crimes must also be viewed as a threat to the capacity of human beings to develop the moral law in political communities. Taking this on board, it can be seen to feed into a key argument made by Kant (1998) that "a transgression of rights in one place in the world is felt everywhere" (440). This understanding again reiterates a dual understanding of humanity, incorporating the importance of both humankind and humanness. The next chapter will build on this theoretical understanding of humanity to outline the global harm generated by these acts. For now, it is still necessary to further clarify the strength of this conception of humanity in contrast to a number of theoretical approaches that have directly questioned the premise of a common humanity.

DEBATING THE EXISTENCE OF A COMMON HUMANITY

Many definitions of humanity are possible, as are many judgments of its relative importance as a concept. And many people still directly question the very existence of any shared conception of humanity and contest its relevance to debates about what moral responsibilities we owe to others. Focusing on communitarian and anti-foundationalist approaches, this section will outline the philosophical stances that have developed against appeals to a universal humanity. In responding to these claims, this chapter will ultimately focus on the need to highlight the implicit universal claims that continue to underpin these theoretical approaches, arguing that a recognition of the role played by the concept of humanity remains integral to our ability to fully locate why mass atrocity crimes pose a threat beyond the borders of states where they occur.

From a broadly communitarian position, we all share particularism – that is, "we participate, all of us, in thick cultures that are our own" (Walzer 1994, 83). Communitarians thus subscribe to a "particularistic moral culture" informed by shared norms, values, and meanings attached to a "collective history and identity" (Etzioni 2009, 114). It follows that moral norms are cultural rather than universal and thus morality is communal rather than global (Shapcott 2010, 51). For cultural relativists such as Charles Taylor (1993), embeddedness in a single culture is critical to social identity, for "outside of the reference points of culture, I would not know who I was as a human subject" (45). Culture is thus essential to one's ability to identify the self, without which one cannot develop characteristically human capacities. This is reinforced by Alasdair MacIntyre (1995), who suggests that "deprived of the life of [my] community, I would have no reason to be moral" (217). Thus, communitarian approaches to morality are deeply skeptical about substantive universalism and emphasize that the contextual origins of community and ethics override any abstract bonds between members of the human species (Shapcott 2010, 50). Furthermore, they are critical of cosmopolitan values, viewing these as a direct threat to cultural communities as the source of moral beliefs – indeed, to the very diversity of distinct cultures.

Thus, communitarians reject any notion of humanity as a motivator for us to act on behalf of distant strangers, for only the communities with which we identify can provide the moral motivation to do good (Kymlicka 2001). In this respect, obligations to those beyond our borders are extremely minimal and what happens in other communities should not generally concern us directly. Yet one must at the same time highlight that this need for communal belonging is in fact a universal statement based on the needs of all human beings as part of humankind; moreover, it also reinforces the existence of specific human capacities – for instance, the need to live within meaningful communal associations – as universal and key to humanness.

Regarding the threat to the diversity of culture, communitarians then claim that particular norms and cultures are fundamentally valuable and so must be protected (Taylor 1985) and that attempts to impose universal standards must be seen as a denial of the integrity of groups. However, the ability to give equal weight to the rights of all groups arguably rests on a universal principle of equality. Consequently, the need to protect communities that are directly threatened by harm must be viewed as critical to the concept of common humanity. An appeal to common humanity therefore inherently requires the ability to recognize the importance of diversity, for any attempt to threaten that diversity could be seen as an attack on the concept itself.

Consequently, if we can consider the domination and assimilation of communities as bad, then why should we view the same acts as acceptable *within* a given community? (Shapcott 2010, 82). Mass atrocity crimes that directly threaten diversity within wider communities must also be understood through a conception of humanity, in order to locate why such acts can be seen as creating a universal harm. In this sense, when we talk of a crime against humanity, we can understand its significance in terms of the perpetrator's desire to eradicate specific victims or its refusal to share the earth with them. The diversity that exists among us is universal – indeed, it is critical to the identity we share as a species. The only way to recognize the importance of this diversity is through a universal conception of the inherent worth of humanity itself. Communitarians like Michael Walzer

(1977) do recognize that some sort of minimal universalism must exist and that nation-states should therefore uphold universal moral duties in certain circumstances, such as genocide and mass violence. In this regard, Walzer upholds an approach that still acknowledges and appeals to an understanding of universal humanity, justifying humanitarian intervention in cases that "shock the moral conscience of mankind" (107). This again reinforces the need to adopt certain universal premises, such as equality and the universal importance of defending cultures, as part of a common humanity.

ADVANCING THE HUMANITY VERSUS SOLIDARITY DEBATE

For those who support a greater focus on the role of solidarity in informing our moral understanding of harm, debates about common humanity have revolved largely around the supposedly abstract quality of the concept. Because of the lack of theoretical consensus surrounding the concept of humanity, and its apparent misappropriation in political discourse, a number of theorists have attempted to move beyond the universal construction of a so-called common humanity. Appeals to a more easily definable concept of solidarity have been utilized in order to locate a different foundation for the ethics of intervention.

Anti-foundationalist scholars such as Richard Rorty (1989) have attempted to discredit the concept of common humanity, rejecting as meaningless appeals to a larger entity such as humanity. Rorty (1989, 196) opposes any attempt to ground universal moral imperatives in a concept of human reason and has developed a social theory of solidarity in place of a moral philosophy concerning the concept of humanity (Booth and Dunne 1999). He argues that nothing is prior to history or beneath socialization, which is "definatory of the human"; he points to the need to improve "greater human solidarity, which does not have to rely on the idea of an essential moral self that must be common to all humanity" (Rorty 1989, xiii). His approach can thus be categorized as an attempt to move beyond the debate between relativism and universalism. He appeals to human sympathy rather than to an abstract moral truth, rejecting the notion that human beings have intrinsic features.

In this regard, Norman Geras (1995, 54) has argued that Rorty's rejection of a common humanity can be viewed as an attempt to question the idea that something universally human can serve as a foundation for ethics. In Rorty's view, no specific human characteristics exist that can provide a moral framework to shape our understanding of moral obligations. Yet according to Geras one must question Rorty's argument that a shared human capacity for experiencing pain and suffering lacks roots in a common human nature. It can instead be argued that Rorty's notion of greater solidarity still aims to provide something common to us as humans – that he still relies on the existence of common characteristics in human beings, including our susceptibility to humiliation and our capacity for language (Geras, 1995, 89). Rorty's solidarity argument still has an essentially universalist basis; he does not fully escape the idea of a common human nature, he just more narrowly defines it. Thus, even while claiming to put forward an anti-foundationalist approach, he still holds on to essentially liberal values in conceding that all humans ultimately recognize the existence of pain and humiliation (Wheeler 1997, 22). Moreover, Rorty clearly invokes pain and humiliation as normatively "bad" and as in some way threatening the ability of people to be distinctively human. In so doing, he undermines his original premise: in attempting to move beyond foundational and universal claims to humanity, he *reaffirms* the integral nature of humanity.

In an attempt to build upon and further clarify Rorty's appeal to solidarity, Alex Bellamy (2002, 474) argues that in our search for a criterion to legitimate humanitarian intervention, we must locate a starting point for constructing a pragmatic solidarism. This acknowledges how hard it is to ground conversations in the abstract concept of common humanity. Such solidarism is "rooted in pragmatism which holds that human solidarity is based on sentimentality rather than common humanity" (489). He then argues that humanitarian intervention should be based not on universal moral principles but rather on "informed practice based upon the extension of values created within particular communities" (489). Bellamy is reluctant to base any legitimizing criteria for intervention on a universal concept such as humanity, yet arguably he is still appealing to a universal human capacity – here, to sympathy. In doing so he fails to recognize this trait as a specific part of our humanity, in that our capacity to feel sympathy for others and to acknowledge pain is only possible because a shared human capacity exists. As Geras (1995) has also pointed out, the very concept of humanity involves a relationship with solidarity: the two cannot simply be separated as opposing concepts. Sympathy and solidarity must instead be seen to also rely upon a willingness to sacrifice for the political project of common humanity; in this way, ideas of sympathy can help lead to a "more intense moral or practical commitment" to common humanity (98). This suggests there is a need to recognize a deeper connection between these two concepts.

German philosopher Jürgen Habermas also appeals to the concept of solidarity. He is likewise cautious about appeals to an inherent human nature, instead grounding his ethics in the "postmetaphysical realities of intersubjectively shared forms of life" (1990, 247). He appeals to a purely political conception of human beings, such that membership in an ideal communication community can help generate a "consciousness of irrevocable human solidarity" (248). Thus, for him, solidarity is grounded in the "realization that each person must take responsibility for the other because as consociates all must have an interest in the integrity of their shared life context in the same way" (244). Yet this statement still assumes that humans share the ability to locate solidarity. Furthermore, Habermas's intersubjectivity and deliberative model is Kantian by design, resting on a moral argument that human beings all share a rational and moral capacity, on a recognition that this capacity is fundamental to human coexistence and cohabitability, and on the idea that individuals ought to be members of this self-lawgiving global community (Habermas 2008). The argument put forward by Habermas is therefore built on the need to support solidarity; but rather than discredit the concept of common humanity as part of this process, he is seemingly able to acknowledge it as integral to recognizing the need for solidarity in the first place.

So it is vital to conclude that these two concepts, humanity and solidarity, are not mutually exclusive, and that when attempting to separate them we cannot fully escape from some form of universal conception of inherent human capacity. As Catherine Lu (2000, 256) highlights, the moral condemnation of cruelty must be translated to an obligation to uphold the concept of humanity, through a need to alleviate human suffering. Thus, reason and suffering are both common to human beings everywhere, and consequently they should be used to provide the basis for a "justifiable moral universalism" (Shapcott 2010, 47). This points to the importance of critically identifying the impact that suffering has on human agency and autonomy, whereby our ability to recognize concern for strangers comes from seeing them as human beings. Moreover, identifying with moral universals must be viewed as essential to any moral project committed to relieving human suffering (Falk 1992, 22). The concept of humanity allows one to identify the universal capacities humans have to recognize suffering as well as reason.

These contrasting discussions of humanity and solidarity demonstrate that though scholars often reject the notion of a universal concept of humanity or human nature, many continue to speak of features that are universal to all humans – to acknowledge capacities that ground us all collectively – when attempting to understand the harm created by mass atrocities. The connotations of the concept itself may be rejected, but completely rejecting what it means to be human is much more difficult. Clearly, then, there are shared moral assumptions that humans make claim to and explicitly appeal to, and these can be seen to ground moral expectations not just of ourselves but of states and political actors as well (Boucher 2011, 291). What humanity ultimately represents then is a vital acknowledgment of core human characteristics that are thought to hold value. It may be impossible to empirically prove the existence of an inherent human nature that exists within us all, but it is a step too far to thereby disregard the concept of humanity. When examining the moral language connected to the framing of our common humanity, one can highlight a shared experience that is created through the concept's social construction. This relationship is important, for it suggests that the construction of a universal human trait is now deeply embedded in our moral understanding. Despite the difficulty in defining the concept and its assumed abstract quality, humanity continues to be a concept that cannot be fully removed from the construction of moral language, and more importantly from the construction of international law.

HUMANITY'S INFLUENCE ON INTERNATIONAL PRACTICE

To further explore humanity's impact on the construction of moral language, this chapter focuses next on how this translates into international practice. First of all, the very fact that we raise the question of "should we act" in the face of mass atrocity crimes in the first place assumes that we have some moral ideals and principles by which we recognize and condemn certain acts (Luban 2002, 99). Absent some form of shared moral concept, the question of whether we should act in the face of mass atrocity crimes simply would not arise. This again relates back to a Kantian understanding of human capacities and the metaphysical idea of morality, by which moral agency is seen to stem from human existence within moral communities, through which we speak of moral actions in terms of people being either morally right or morally wrong (Brown 2009, 41). Kant argues that we all have a capacity for moral reasoning and that this represents a universal attribute of the human species. So one can highlight how the concept of humanity has been constructed through language to form an essential part of the moral decision-making involved in legitimizing practices such as protection of refugees or humanitarian intervention. Moreover, many punitive international laws are built upon an *a priori* assumption of humanity's existence, and thus it remains an essential value in the process of consensus building. Humanity therefore continues to be presented and referred to as a concept with an inherent value; furthermore, it is a concept that is seen to guide the framing of moral decision-making, due to its implied universal status. However, the extent to which it can also provide the key motivating factor for state engagement on such issues remains severely contested. Even so, it is clear that notions of humanity are still being used as appeals to reinforce the assumed moral good of certain actions.

To see how we have come to acknowledge humanity as a vital component of the practices we seek to justify, let us turn to its influence in international law and conduct. As Faustin Ntoubandi (2007, 42) argues, the process of creating laws or principles of humanity can be seen to support the existence of a transcendental form of humanity, which in turn defines how we consider specific acts. The idea of transcendental values and principles has served as the precursor to the modern notion of crimes against humanity (Ntoubandi 2007, 42). Indeed, even those who commit acts considered as against humanity frame their actions and motivations in terms of an understanding of humanity. They recognize that they are directly threatening humanity through a process of dehumanization – thus, their use of words such as "rats" (Holocaust) and "cockroaches" (Rwanda Genocide) to refer to their victims. This demonstrates how the language of humanity is deeply embedded in our understanding of specific mass atrocity crimes; that language is plain to hear not only for the potential rescuers but also for those who are committing the crimes in the first place. As Matthew Weinert (2015) argues, there is something stable about notions of human dignity, in that they "fundamentally imply living in a life worthy of being lived" (59). Without acknowledgment of such foundations, we would be unable to respond fully to the basic question of "what is wrong with slavery" (60). In this sense, the concept of humanity remains central to the language of mass atrocity crimes and protection; appeals to the concept are deeply embedded in our thought processes. Consequently, when we see mass atrocity crimes and label them as such, we are already believing in and acting on the concept of humanity, and thus we can argue that humanity in some form already exists. Yet the question remains: how can we give further substance to that humanity? This significant relationship between humanity and mass atrocity crimes will be further explored in chapter 3, which will highlight how the concept of humanity plays a critical role in defining the universal harm of certain actions and our understanding of moral "oughtness" that is attached to such claims.

CONCLUSION

This chapter has demonstrated that the concept of humanity must be understood as vital to an understanding of our shared global condition. The complete rejection of the concept would leave us theoretically impoverished as we attempted to discuss the challenges human beings face in coexisting on this planet. This is perhaps best underscored by the centrality of humanity to our ability to construct ideas of universal jurisdiction in order to prohibit the most heinous crimes against human beings, which at the same time can be seen to offend collective global sensibilities (Wilson 2010). By putting forward a distinct dual conception of humanity, grounded in the basic moral right to recognition and justification, it has been possible to reinforce the universal nature of our common humanity, which is arguably a critical starting point for locating the specific harms created by mass atrocity crimes. Humanity's conceptual value is thus much more connected to the identification of universal threats than it is to claims of an intangible global connection. Despite attempts to reject the idea of humanity a mere abstract turn of phrase, the idea of humanity remains integral to our ability to conceptualize the moral status of human beings and thus to reflect on the so-called bad life in terms of what basic rights must be owed to all. When we violate the dignity of others, we disregard the right to recognition and the moral right to justification, and this has an impact on the diversity of human experience. Humanity is thus both an abstract concept and a lived experience: it provides a way for us to conceptualize our shared capacities as human beings while also relating to the inherent interconnectedness of our species through narratives of harm. Humanity as an idea in practice "unfolds through an ongoing struggle of who is or is not a member and who has status – and to what degree" (Weinert 2015, 174). In this sense, tensions between the universal and the particular are usually brought out through the imposition of concrete policies that require us to act upon such moral claims. Moving forward, there is a need to explore in more depth how the theoretical claims outlined in this chapter have been transposed onto international legal frameworks to try and assess the extent to which knowledge of humanity's properties helps generate the potential for motivational compliance. This is crucial to outlining why such abstract ideas matter in practice and to reflecting on why their imposition has thus far been so uneven and inconsistent. The next chapter will therefore focus more specifically on the question of how can we categorize a crime as directly challenging a shared understanding of humanity.

3

Threats to Our Common Humanity: Why Humanity Matters

Why should mass atrocity crimes concern all states, and why do states insist that others should not commit mass atrocity crimes against their own populations? The responses to these questions, by both diplomats and scholars, are most often articulated through an appeal to our common humanity, but frequently without much further clarification. In this regard, by appealing to humanity, state leaders are implicitly arguing that the existence of a common humanity provides certain moral obligations for both states and individuals when mass atrocity crimes are committed. Yet one may also ask why common humanity matters, in that we have an international legal order demanding that states view such acts as being of international concern. However, one must also recognize that the strength of international law itself rests on the normative values that underpin them. As Coupland (2001) has rightly argued, clarifying humanity and its relationship to international law is not merely an academic pursuit; the word itself carries weight in "international legal and political discourse when armed violence, its effects or its regulation are under discussion" (972). So, while states do not actively challenge the idea that mass atrocity crimes are unacceptable state actions, this does not instantly mean that the implicit harm in such actions is not worth exploring. States have to weigh up a range of harms that are occurring globally, and decisions as to who should be protected are not simply a matter of narrow national interest; rather, they are a product of competing demands that include responsibilities connected to the idea of protecting common humanity. In light of other competing ethical demands on state resources, theorizing the harm that is created by these acts is thus critical, so as to emphasize what is at stake when states choose to place specific interests above responsibilities to humanity's protection.

We must first assess the strength of the obligations seen to be generated by the moral weight of humanity and the extent to which certain acts can be conceived as being against humanity. To that end, this chapter will outline how recent literature has attempted to conceptualize humanity as a key component of our understanding of why certain crimes generate international concern. This chapter's significant contribution will therefore be to move beyond claims that such crimes are simply "conscience-shocking" in order to present a more theoretically informed argument that addresses how we can conceptualize the impact such crimes have on the values and ideas that are argued to be essential to our existence as human beings. Building on the theoretical approach outlined in the previous chapter, it will be argued that such crimes can be seen to challenge a dual conception of humanity, in that they not only generate a harm against the diversity of humankind but also challenge our distinct humanness, understood through our ability to coexist as political animals as well as our capacity to reason and develop moral rules. This is critical, as when we discuss a lack of political will for addressing mass atrocity crimes, it is these values of diversity, coexistence, and reason that are at stake as states make political decisions to place these harms below other competing demands. Consequently, tackling and preventing mass atrocities represents a much broader goal than just stopping violence; it can also benefit longer-term goals of addressing poverty and supporting development, community cohesion, and gender equality. Before considering why states do not implement those laws and principles that reflect an underlying belief in common humanity, one must first theorize why humanity matters in the first place.

The chapter has three sections. First, it outlines the conceptualization of crimes against humanity, highlighting how notions of universal moral law connected to the concept of humanity have a long and significant history. It traces how the legal concept of crimes against humanity has gained acceptance and now forms a key part of international criminal law. Second, the chapter presents an extensive critical analysis of the current international law literature, analyzing contrasting conceptions of why certain crimes must be seen to concern all of humanity. Guiding this discussion is an assessment of how contrasting interpretations of humanness and humankind influence how scholars understand crimes against humanity. Third, the chapter presents the case for recognizing mass atrocity crimes as distinct global harms. It argues that humanity is the core concept underpinning the need to recognize a hierarchy of crimes and explains why mass atrocity crimes threaten a shared idea of our common humanity. The chapter reinforces this by outlining a new theoretical approach to conceptualizing crimes against humanity, one that builds on a dual conception of humanity, underpinned by the centrality of both moral reasoning and harm recognition, in order to fully capture the uniquely global harm of such crimes. The chapter concludes by laying out why the prevention of mass atrocity crimes must remain a critical goal for the international community and why such acts must concern all of us as human beings.

THE FOUR CRIMES OF R2P

Before moving on to discuss the historical conceptualization of crimes against humanity, it is critical to sharpen the focus of this chapter, especially regarding the decision to emphasize the category of crimes against humanity. In the R2P, crimes against humanity are viewed as just one of the four crimes; I argue, however, that this term can best capture what is egregious about all four mass atrocity crimes, beyond the narrow legal definition of each crime. To explain this argument, I will delve into the link between crimes against humanity and each of the other three crimes in turn.

Genocide

There has long been a strong historical link between genocide and crimes against humanity, due to their emergence in response to the Nazi atrocities committed during the Second World War. It was in this context that genocide was recognized as a *type* of crime against humanity, and that link has continued to be strongly reinforced in international law, as referenced in the 1997 Jelisić case at the International Criminal Tribunal for the Former Yugoslavia (ICTY 1999). In this judgment it was argued that "a crime characterised as genocide constitutes, of itself, crimes against humanity within the meaning of persecution" (ICTY 1999). What therefore makes the label of crimes against humanity so distinct is that its commission is regarded as an assault not simply on the victims involved but against all humanity (Wald 2007, 624). This idea of a harm to humanity remains strongly linked to the crime of genocide and is thus integral to how we conceptualize the overall harm caused by both these crimes. Yet it is still important to acknowledge that crimes against humanity and genocide do have different legal definitions and interpretations. Most noteworthy, crimes against humanity encompass discriminatory acts against a much wider range of groups than genocide, along with many other kinds of acts beyond the five that are listed in the Genocide Convention (1948). The act of genocide can thus be seen as much more restricted in its scope due to its focus on specific groups (racial, religious, national, or ethnic), as well as the need to establish the perpetrators' intent to destroy the group in whole or in part. Yet despite these differences, what the two crimes share most importantly is an acknowledgment that very serious offences "shock our sense of humanity" and therefore "constitute attacks on the most fundamental aspects of human dignity" (Nersessian 2007, 246). Consequently, unpacking and exploring this key claim will remain the focus of this chapter, underpinning the decision to categorize genocide as a type of crime against humanity.

Ethnic Cleansing

From a distinctly legal perspective, ethnic cleansing, understood broadly as the forcible deportation of an ethnic or religious group, has long been recognized as a crime against humanity. There is no formal legal definition of ethnic cleansing; however, it has been recognized as a crime against humanity under the statutes of both the International Criminal Court (ICC) and the ICTY. Furthermore, ethnic cleansing is also often recognized as constituting one of the foregoing genocidal acts, further reinforcing its important links to genocide and crimes against humanity (Sirkin 2010, 491). One can thus highlight that ethnic cleansing results in similar harms to those of genocide and crimes against humanity and can therefore be seen to derive from similar agendas (Sirkin 2010, 492). It makes sense, then, to understand the harms caused by ethnic cleansing under the term crimes against humanity both in a legal sense and in relation to the types of harms generated by the crime.

War Crimes

The central difference between the legal definitions of war crimes and crimes against humanity concerns the circumstances in which the crime is committed. War crimes are defined as criminal conduct that takes place in the context of armed conflict, whereas crimes against humanity can occur in war or in peacetime. As a result, some war crimes may not meet the threshold of crimes against humanity, in terms of being widespread or systematic in nature, and thus could simply constitute random acts of violence in the context of war. However, the hierarchical nature of war crimes was acknowledged by the International Law Commission (ILC), a commission established by the UN General Assembly with the specific goal of "making recommendations for the purpose of ... encouraging the progressive development of international law and its codification" as outlined under Article 13(1)(a) of the UN Charter (1945). The ILC's draft code of crimes against the peace and security of mankind, the latest version of which was adopted in 1996, made the assessment that only war crimes committed in a systematic manner or on a large scale could be considered crimes within the code. This hierarchical approach to identifying war crimes was reaffirmed in the wording of the Rome Statute when the ICC was established in 1998 (International Law Commission 1996; Frulli 2001, 335).[1] Consequently, it is still the case that actions such as inhumane treatment or rape can form the basis for charges of both war crimes and crimes against humanity (Wald, 2007, 631). As a result of this close connection between the harms generated by both crimes, it is increasingly the case that war crimes and crimes against humanity are charged together rather than under the single charge of war crimes (Wald 2007, 631). With this in mind, it makes sense to also discuss war crimes under the wider umbrella of crimes against humanity, when such acts are deemed to have reached the same threshold.

THE MOTIVATIONAL ROLE OF HUMANITY IN RELATION TO THE FOUR CRIMES

In reflecting on the harms caused by each of the four crimes, one must first acknowledge the central role humanity plays with regard to how state actors frame their moral concerns. The perceived emotional pull of these crimes does not come simply from the technical legal definition of the crime; it also arises from a crime's connection to the potential harm it may cause to a collective humanity. Thus, when it comes to the question of responding to such crimes, the motivation to do so is most often directly linked to an idea of humanity and its need to be protected, regardless of the eventual classification of the crime itself. To further clarify, while the crime of genocide may be perceived to represent the "crime of crimes" and thus may carry increased normative and motivational power, one can highlight how states and other actors still predominantly focus on and appeal to humanity as the central motivational force in such discussions. This is best exemplified by Kofi Annan's comments at the United Nations Millennium Summit, where he asked: "how should we respond to a Rwanda, to a Srebrenica – to gross and systematic violations of human rights that affect every precept of our common humanity?" (ICISS 2001, vii). Furthermore, motivational appeals in response to war crimes and ethnic cleansing can be seen to gain increased traction through a recognition of their close links to the broader category of crimes against humanity. One can therefore highlight the increasing practice of prosecuting crimes both under or in connection with crimes against humanity, thus helping reaffirm the shared global harms caused by these international crimes (Sirkin 2010, 491). Categorizing each of the four crimes under the umbrella of crimes against humanity thus makes it possible to focus on the most important element they all share, which is, the link to a collective threat underpinned by the idea of humanity.

As previously highlighted, the R2P's moral content begins from the claim that certain crimes are of so much global significance that they require us to provide an argument for the moral conditionality of state sovereignty, which can be suspended or superseded by events of a certain kind (Vernon 2002, 242). This implies that states and communities face certain legal obligations in regard to the protection of humanity, whereby the protection of humanity is not simply a legal figure of speech but must instead be acknowledged as a "metaphysical and practical identity of all human beings, as the supreme value for humankind, and as a species" (Chen 2013, 25). Humanity thus provides normative reasons to perform or abstain from certain actions, based on humanity representing the supreme value of human existence and on humanity being a species (Chen 2013, 26). On this reading, it can be argued that all four of these crimes have the potential to violate and harm humanity itself, which ultimately necessitates that the international community prosecute those responsible. Universal jurisdiction is thus predicated on the idea that these four mass atrocity crimes[2] offend the interests of *all* humanity and that prosecuting them is an *erga omnes* obligation (Hayden 2005, 115). *Erga omnes* obligations are those that apply to everyone and so must apply to the international community as a whole.[3] Thus it is crucial that these crimes also be applicable to a variety of legal systems and that no state be able to derogate them in any circumstances.

The concept of humanity is crucial to our ability to conceptualize the very worst crimes that humans can commit. As Hannah Arendt (1963) argued in "Eichmann in Jerusalem," what separates the crime of murder from the crime of genocide is that an "altogether different order is broken and an altogether different community is violated" (272). What Arendt is referring to here is that the crime committed is against a much broader community, namely humanity itself. By separating out this difference between domestic and international crimes, one can begin to assess what role the concept of humanity plays in our understanding of why states should bear a responsibility to save strangers from mass atrocity crimes. It is therefore argued that the concept of humanity is central to differentiating specific crimes from others and thereby advancing our understanding of the values that are threatened by mass atrocity crimes on an international scale. What is both significant and novel about acknowledging that a crime is against humanity is that the crime is being committed against a universal moral concept (that of humanity as a collective moral and legal entity) (Hayden 2005, 107). This abstract idea is thus central to the underlying moral imperative enshrined in the R2P, which this chapter explores in more detail.

THE LEGAL CONCEPTION OF CRIMES AGAINST HUMANITY

It is vital to begin by looking more closely at where the idea of a crime committed against humanity originated and how that original conception continues to influence how we value humanity. As Mohamed Badar (2004) rightly argues, "the contemporary status of crimes against humanity under international law cannot be understood or appreciated without reference to its history" (76). So before locating how ideas of humanity have come to influence states' interactions with international law in the twentieth century, it is important to acknowledge that notions of common humanity and universal moral law have an long history. This is visible in our capacity to recognize shared physical vulnerabilities, which strongly influenced a multitude of early cosmopolitan thinkers, from the Sophists to the Stoics. Furthermore, we can point to how, in the eighteenth century, the development of humanity as a "normative-legal idea" came to be underpinned by theories of natural rights – which had particular relevance for the anti-slavery movement in England (Zagor 2011, 269). Although engagement with these debates is beyond the scope of this book, it is vital to acknowledge here that ideas of humanity have a long history of spurring the development of both natural and cosmopolitan law perspectives as they relate to international harm. This influence is visible in the creation of crimes against humanity.

The law of crimes against humanity was first officially stipulated in the Nuremberg Charter. But as a concept, it had been acknowledged before then in international discourse, perhaps most notably in the 1907 Hague Convention, which made the first official reference to the "laws of humanity." However, arguably the most significant example before Nuremberg of state engagement with the idea of crimes being a direct violation of humanity was in connection to the Turkish massacre of Armenians in 1915, which was condemned as "a crime against humanity and civilization" (Vernon 2002). William Schabas (2009) writes that this constituted "the first use, at least within an international law context, of the term 'crimes against humanity'" (20). This case is also significant with regard to the reaction of the United States to efforts by Britain and France to prosecute Turkey for these crimes. At the time, the United States objected to the idea of "laws of humanity," arguing that this form of law had no specific content. Thus, the proposal to conduct trials of the Turkish perpetrators came to nothing. Clearly, humanity as a concept is rather new to international law, though for some states, it had considerable normative worth earlier than that. All of this reinforces the concept of humanity as a social construct: the phrase *laws of humanity* now embodies the idea that some humanitarian principles exist that *transcend* conventional law (Ntoubandi 2007, 42).

The modern notion of crimes against humanity was first codified in 1945 in the Nuremberg Charter by the four Allied powers of the Second World War, under the auspices of the International Military Tribunal. The Nuremberg Charter is of central importance to this chapter, for it officially recognized the value of humanity as a legal concept and at the same time stipulated that humanity itself can be challenged by certain acts. This acknowledgment of crimes against humanity as a distinct category of international crimes, understood in relation to the collective idea of humanity, was a significant moment in the development of international law. Perhaps most importantly, it was a critical step toward acknowledging the potential conditionality of state sovereignty in that it recognized that specific actions by states against their own people can create a legal right for the international community to prosecute those involved. The definitional development of this category of crimes throughout the rest of the twentieth century reinforced its ongoing relevance to how states understand the most extreme crimes humans can commit.

When we examine the theoretical development of the concept since the Nuremberg Charter, we encounter a number of significant clarifications with regard to its application. First, we note the move away from defining crimes against humanity as an extension of international humanitarian law applicable to war situations toward their eventual recognition as an "autonomous source of rights accrued to individuals in periods of peace as well as in war" (Badar 2004, 140). International humanitarian law is understood as a legal framework applicable to situations of armed conflict and occupation. It represents a set of rules and principles aimed at limiting the impact of armed conflict for humanitarian reasons. While the process of removing the conditional link between war and crimes against humanity was gradual, it was arguably accelerated by the 1948 Genocide Convention and later by the 1951 ILC Draft Code,[4] in that both recognized that such crimes could be committed in times of peace *or* war. This shift was connected to a broader trend: states agreeing to limit the ability of leaders to commit atrocities against their own people with impunity.[5] The creation of the R2P must be understood as part of this normative trend.

A second key development with roots in the original Nuremberg Charter was the move to recognize non-state actors as potentially able to commit crimes against humanity. In the 1951 Draft Code of Offenses against the Peace and Security of Mankind, the ILC updated the definition of crimes against humanity to recognize that both state authorities and private individuals may commit crimes against humanity (ILC 1951). By expanding the application of crimes against humanity yet again, it reinforced a clear acknowledgment that these crimes were not defined simply by the application of state power;

they must also be defined and understood in terms of their impact on the victims and humanity understood collectively, whether the state was involved or not (Hwang 1998). The move to apply crimes against humanity beyond individuals in control of the state reflects an ambition to cover the acts of terrorist groups or organizations that have the capacity to control territory without necessarily occupying it permanently. Again, this acknowledges the need to capture a greater number of crimes that may represent a challenge to humanity, as well as to expand approaches to identifying threats to humanity.

Finally, the development of crimes against humanity has further clarified the scope and characteristics of such crimes. In the 1993 UN Secretary-General's report on the ICTY Statute, it was argued that inhumane acts have to be "committed as part of a widespread or systematic attack" (UN 1993). This requirement of "widespread or systematic" was subsequently included in the definition of crimes against humanity for the ICTR as well as in the 1998 Rome Statute. This definitional element of crimes against humanity has since become central to distinguishing crimes against humanity from common crimes, which do not rise to the level of crimes under international law (Badar 2004, 109). This policy requirement reinforces the idea that isolated and random acts cannot amount to crimes against humanity and helps clarify the importance of having a hierarchy of international crimes (Chesterman 2000, 316). In this sense, crimes against humanity are those that are seen to "shock the conscience of mankind and warrant intervention by the international community precisely because they are not isolated, random acts of individuals, but instead result from a deliberate attempt to target a civilian population" (316). These criteria make it possible to draw a stronger conceptual link between the moral idea of a collective humanity and those crimes that directly threaten it. These parameters set critical benchmarks for how we can begin to theorize the international dimension of crimes against humanity and why the normative idea of humanity is so integral to our ability to categorize certain crimes as rising above those of national jurisdiction.

But we need to examine in greater detail two more philosophical questions: How can humanity itself in some way be threatened by these crimes? And why should states around the globe respond to these crimes? While legal definitions are a useful starting point in locating the significance of categorizing certain acts as international crimes, the normative and moral underpinnings of these crimes require further philosophical scrutiny in order to explain why they demand certain responses by states. The complexity of this debate is evident in the deliberations concerning the concept of "inhumane" contained in the original Nuremberg Charter, and those same deliberations have featured in subsequent discussions of international law. For example, Article 6(c) of the Nuremberg Charter refers to crimes against humanity as "inhumane acts," which one can conceptualize as offences committed against humaneness (a specific human characteristic). However, as a definition it has come under close scrutiny, as well as harsh critique, perhaps most significantly because it fails to set a high enough threshold for what can count as a crime against humanity (Bassiouni 1999, 330). There are many acts that we refer to as inhumane, but how many of them concern all of humanity? So we need to expand on what it is that differentiates crimes against humanity from, say, particularly gruesome acts of murder. The next section of this chapter will take stock of current debates about the moral and philosophical underpinnings of crimes against humanity. By assessing the relative strength of contrasting interpretations, it will be possible to develop a more comprehensive understanding of humanity's normative role in defining such acts. This chapter will argue for a dual understanding of humanity as well as demonstrate why certain crimes concern the whole of the international community.

CONTESTING THE PHILOSOPHICAL FOUNDATIONS OF CRIMES AGAINST HUMANITY

This section brings together a range of conceptualizations regarding crimes against humanity. Through these, we can explore why we should view crimes against humanity as threats to a collective understanding of humanity. This will help clarify why common humanity and its protection matter. The focus is not on defining what a crime against humanity is or its strength as a legal concept; rather, it is on theorizing the idea of collective harm by locating what values and beliefs are challenged by crimes against humanity, understood through the idea's moral capacity. While there have been a number of long-running legal debates over the definition of the term[6] as well as its legal application (Altman 2012), this section will focus on the need to theorize how notions of humanness and humankind comprise essential elements of our understanding of what harms are created by crimes against humanity and ultimately why such acts should concern states. All of this will make it possible to further conceptualize the international scope of such crimes and thereby reinforce the global community's moral imperative to protect individuals from these crimes.

THE INHUMANITY OF CRIMES AGAINST HUMANITY

Put most basically, crimes against humanity can be understood in relation to their opposition to humanity itself. The focus here is often on the inhumanity of the act itself, which ties its meaning directly to our understanding of what humanness *is* (Ntoubandi 2007). As emphasized in the previous chapter, humanness is understood as the essence of what makes us human; it acknowledges that all human beings hold certain basic values. It follows that crimes against humanity reject the values attached to humanity in favour of appeals to brutality or barbarity. In attempting to reflect this understanding in legal terms, Article 6(c) of the Nuremberg Charter referred to crimes against humanity as "inhumane acts," understanding such crimes as offences against specific human characteristics. However, it is vital to note that the very notion of inhumanity is subjective and requires further clarification when we attempt to scale up this understanding to the international level. Part of the difficulty in recognizing crimes against humanity as simply inhuman comes from the fact that a wide variety of crimes can in certain senses be regarded as inhumane. So in framing the specific harm of such crimes in terms of their inhuman nature, it fails to set a high threshold for what can count as a crime against humanity and, most importantly, how we can conceptualize such acts as international in scope. Many acts can be spoken of as inhumane, but how many can we claim concern the whole of humanity?

The decision to focus on the significance of humaneness in the original Nuremberg Charter was strongly criticized at the time by Hannah Arendt (1963, 275), who questioned whether the Nazis "had simply been lacking human kindness." Taking a similar line, Richard Vernon (2002, 238) argues that "we cannot suppose that the most inhumane results (however measured) reflect the most subjectively measured inhumanity." In other words, collating crimes against humanity with crimes of inhumanity places far too much emphasis on specific circumstances for us to trace directly the agent's moral feelings or lack of them (238). Christopher Macleod (2010) is also critical of attempts to understand crimes against humanity in terms of humanity representing the idea of an inherent human nature. He rejects the assumption that crimes against humanity are those that are in fact inhumane, and he is therefore skeptical of attempts to understand crimes against humanity as involving actions contrary to human nature. By such logic, given that many crimes can arguably be classified as going against our human nature, crimes against humanity would amount to "merely a particularly egregious enactment of a lower-order crime" (293). One must therefore further interrogate what differentiates crimes against humanity from particularly gruesome acts of murder. The language used in the Nuremberg Charter failed to create a holistic understanding of the "crime" that would help explain the need to recognize such acts as creating global harms.

A THREAT TO THE INTERESTS OF HUMANKIND

Expanding on this requirement to better conceptualize crimes against humanity as being of international concern, Macleod (2012, 297) argues that an action can be categorized as a crime against humanity if and only if it is a crime that damages humankind. In this sense, humanity is viewed as the victim of the crime committed; it is not that humaneness as a moral quality is being lost or denied, but rather that damage is being done to humanity as a collective entity (Vernon 2002, 238). As such, humankind is argued to be damaged when one of its interests is violated – for example, when cultural diversity is reduced so as to harm humanity as a whole, of which we are part (Macleod 2012, 203). This reasoning perhaps suggests why the global community should confront states that are committing mass atrocity crimes against their own people. When crimes are seen to damage humankind – in effect, citizens around the world – one can make the case that it is in the interest of the global community to prosecute those individuals on behalf of humankind collectively.

However, Macleod's understanding of humanity's interests is arguably underdeveloped. If humankind is the relevant object of protection, and if humankind therefore has the authority to recognize these crimes as illegal and as offences against humanity, then one must ask: in virtue of *what* are these crimes treated as offences against humanity? (Geras 2005, 169). What are the potential consequences of these crimes that can justify regarding them as an attack on all human beings? Macleod does not provide a conclusive response to this question and does not enumerate how certain crimes harm humankind and its values collectively. This failure to fully specify the harm created by crimes against humanity limits the usefulness of an approach that focuses so heavily on a conception of humanity as representing humankind.

LOCATING HUMANITY IN HUMANNESS

One way to more comprehensively locate the harm caused by crimes against humanity is to place a greater emphasis on the role of humanness. For Massimo Renzo (2012, 449), humanity is understood and defined as humanness, so a shared human value or human characteristic is violated when crimes against humanity are committed. This understanding is based on the idea that human rights are inherently tied to our humanity. That is, human rights are possessed by individuals in a pre-political state of nature, and the existence of human rights does not hinge on their embodiment in any political institution (450). Human rights are those we hold simply in virtue of our humanity; it follows that crimes against humanity are those that deny the status of the human being by violating these natural rights we all have (451). Crimes against humanity, then, are attacks on these fundamental natural rights, which are essential for a minimally decent life (453). This is a critical distinction, for it allows Renzo to reject the idea that all attacks on human rights constitute international crimes. Instead, he recognizes that certain basic rights represent a clear moral minimum and thus constitute reasonable demands that are held by all of humanity.

Renzo acknowledges that crimes against humanity directly violate our natural rights, but he rejects claims by other legal theorists, such as Larry May (2005), who suggest that humanity itself can be harmed in the process. For Renzo (2012), the wrongness of the crimes makes all members of the international community accountable for them. That is, we are accountable to all our fellow human beings by virtue of belonging to the community of humanity (457). Crimes against humanity fail to recognize the basic rights we all share as human beings, which means we can talk of a universal obligation to punish this specific crime. Renzo's accountability-based model emphasizes the accountability of the wrongdoer rather than a specific global harm caused by such acts; it also attaches responsibilities to our identity as human beings. This idea is very much founded on the concept of human dignity, which is the value that explains why all humans are said to have human rights; furthermore, human dignity is understood as the value that human rights are meant to protect. Thus, Renzo's theory suggests a need to recognize certain human characteristics and values as universal in order to articulate why crimes against humanity should be of global interest. This requires a strong belief in the idea that we are all members of the international community and so must all be answerable to this community when crimes are committed that directly attack human dignity.

This same argument is supported by Antony Duff, who draws a similar conclusion to that of Renzo. Duff (2009, 20–1) rejects any notion that mass atrocity crimes such as genocide actually harm or victimize humanity as a whole; instead, he views certain crimes as wrongs that properly concern the whole of humanity. As such, he believes that perpetrators must answer not just to a specific political community but also to humanity itself. This concept is built on the idea of humanity representing a moral rather than political community, whereby certain wrongs are everyone's business simply because of our shared humanity with both their victims and the perpetrators (Duff 2009). Crimes against humanity thus do not depend on the existence of the state or on any system of rules or conduct; they are instead a form of natural law that creates the obligation not to commit such crimes, based on being a human being, not simply a fellow citizen (Renzo 2012). A key criticism of this humanness approach to understanding crimes against humanity is that both Renzo and Duff broaden our understanding of the concept to include a greater number of crimes.

Because he focuses on individual violations of human rights, rather than solely on violations that have a collective dimension, Renzo is forced to recognize any case of murder as a crime against humanity. So there is an argument to be made that while many crimes may attack certain human characteristics of the victim, a focus solely on humanness still does not help us fully capture why states may have moral obligations to the international community to acknowledge and respond to such crimes. Renzo and Duff suggest that the perpetrators have a responsibility to answer to humanity for their crimes, but neither scholar places significant emphasis on the impact the crime may have on humanity as a metaphysical entity. This is significant, for our intuitions of the harm created by mass atrocity crimes are often framed in language that relies on the idea of humanity itself being directly threatened or on the creation of a global harm. Thus, crimes against humanity may threaten more than the individual rights of the victims. In this sense, one can argue that we need to be clearer and more systematic when trying to understand what makes crimes against humanity so different from, say, acts of murder. By broadening out the concept of crimes against humanity, we may downplay the reason why that category of crime was created in the first place. An entirely different order is broached when a crime against humanity is committed rather than a single murder. So we must not lose sight of the need to maintain a hierarchy between domestic and international crimes.

Moving forward, it is vital to locate the ethical underpinning of a wider global harm in order to explain why certain acts can be of so much significance to those living thousands of miles away from where the crime was committed. This arguably requires a greater emphasis on the idea of humanity as also representing humankind. Furthermore, it is important to underscore that both Renzo and Duff leave unattended the extent to which we as citizens and members of the international community collectively should have a responsibility or obligation to help prevent crimes against humanity and protect those who are threatened by them. In the legal philosophy literature outlined earlier, the emphasis is placed on the responsibility of the perpetrator as directly accountable to humanity. The humanness approach put forward by Renzo and Duff is unable to conceptualize what should drive a state to intervene on behalf of humanity when in theory state security cannot always be described as under threat from these actions. In other words, if we do all have natural rights, why should the global community have a responsibility to protect them? And in what circumstances should they be protected?

COMMUNITARIAN APPROACH TO CRIMES AGAINST HUMANITY

To articulate how we can differentiate crimes against humanity from crimes such as murder, it is crucial to locate other values and ideas that are challenged by crimes against humanity. One approach is to place greater emphasis on the group-based element of crimes against humanity. This is particularly important in communitarian approaches, which place a significant moral worth on the idea of groups and argue that embeddedness in a single culture is critical to social identity (Taylor 1993, 45). A group-based understanding of crimes against humanity underpins Larry May's (2005) international harm principle, which focuses on why group-based violations concern the international community. Just as domestic crimes are seen to harm a particular national community, crimes against humanity can be seen to harm the world community. This is reinforced by May's belief that a key interest of humanity is for its members not to be harmed; thus, it is argued that when a crime against humanity occurs, the harm is caused by an entity standing in for a particular community. Here, a harm to humanity is understood as based on non-individualized characteristics of the individual; so it is group-based harms that should be of interest to the international community, for they are "more likely to assault the common humanity of the victims" (May 2005, 83). The international community and humanity itself are therefore harmed when "the perpetrator of a crime does not react to the individual features of a person, but rather to those features that the individuals share with all, or very many others" (83). This argument acknowledges that humanity itself is a victim when the intentions of the perpetrators are to harm individuals on the basis of group characteristics rather than individual ones. Crimes against humanity thus harm all of us due to the shared solidarity we feel for others based on our common vulnerability to harm.

It is important to note here that May's conception of the international harm principle is conditional on what he calls the security principle. This principle is premised on the idea that if states "fail to provide physical security and subsistence of its subjects, then that state has no right to prevent legal bodies from justifiably infringing that state's sovereignty," an idea that has many parallels with the R2P principle (68). However, other states only have an obligation to prosecute the perpetrators of such crimes when there is also a direct harm to the international community understood through the international harm principle. Together these two normative concepts attempt to provide a more complete answer to the question of why some entity might legitimately cross the borders of a sovereign state to protect victims, and more significantly, why the international community has an interest in what is going on within a particular state's borders.

Thus, what makes group-based violence significant for May is that it creates harms that are of direct interest to the international community: first, because group-based harms are more likely to assault the common humanity of the victims, understood as the need for social belonging, and second, because they are more likely to create issues around borders and damage the broader international community (83). However, there are a number of significant objections to May's group-based conception of crimes against humanity and of the perceived direct threat these crimes pose to our common humanity. As May argues, the rationale behind the international harm principle is that humanity is harmed when "the sufferer merely stands in for larger segments of the population who are not treated according to individual difference" (85). However, Alejandro Chehtman contends that the justificatory work is being done by the fact that the victim is a member of a vulnerable group or persecuted minority. The victims of these acts are chosen because of their affiliation with a specific vulnerable group, and thus it is the group that is harmed by the crimes, not humanity representing humankind (Chehtman 2010, 98). This point is supported by Andrew Altman (2006, 369), who argues that the form of religious hatred that leads to antisemitic genocide hinges on the notion that Jews are different from the rest of humanity, and that it is this difference that leads to their selection as targets from among all humans. May ignores the specific rights individuals hold regardless of group affiliation. This is significant, for we need to understand humanity as representing more than group affiliation; indeed, we need to understand it as representing the rights of every human being.

Altman (2006) also takes issue with the construction of May's domestic and international analogy, which stipulates that crimes at the international level harm the global community in much the same way that crimes at a domestic level harm the national community. It is argued that the international situation is different, in that the absence or ineffectiveness of a state would not condemn individuals to lives of horrific insecurity in the same way the absence or ineffectiveness of a domestic state would impact individuals in a particular territory (370). In highlighting the Rwandan and Cambodian genocides, Altman argues that these events did not affect the interests of Australians in the same way that domestic murders in their country would, as such genocide and crimes against humanity can be seen to not directly challenge the vital interests of most humans. Such an argument implies that states should not view mass atrocity crimes as a significant security issue if these crimes are taking place beyond their borders. Yet one must also ask whether values are being challenged by mass atrocity crimes that go beyond simple issues of security and have an impact on the metaphysical idea of humanity in ways that are more concerning to humankind at large than Altman is willing to acknowledge.

EXPANDING HUMANKIND: THE ROLE OF DIVERSITY

Moving away from the communitarian-based approach put forward by May, a range of theoretical arguments significantly emphasize humankind even while recognizing the role that ideas of humanness need to play in our understanding of crimes against humanity. One example is Hannah Arendt (1963), who provides a more nuanced conception of what humanity's values are and what is directly at stake when crimes against humanity are committed. Arendt (1963) claims that genocide is a crime against humanity, one that directly offends the human status. Here, humanity is more than just the human race as a whole; it is also a property that everyone holds by virtue of belonging to it (Vernon 2002, 239). A crime against humanity is thus intended to "eliminate certain races form the face of the earth"; the perpetrators are refusing to share the earth with certain people (Arendt 1963). In other words, crimes such as genocide represent an attack on human diversity; they signify an attack on a characteristic of the human condition without which the words humanity or humankind would be devoid of meaning (261). Arendt (1963) argues rather than focusing on the impact of suffering or the number of victims involved, we should focus on the threat to human nature and the organized attempt to eradicate the concept of the human being – *that* is the defining feature of crimes against humanity. Diversity is thus conceptualized as characterizing elements of both humankind and humanness, based on an anthropological and normative universal that acknowledges diversity as a core dimension of humanity. By this understanding, "an attempt to annihilate one group should be understood as an attack on the condition of human plurality" (Bilsky 2010, 206). Thus, crimes against humanity are not only attacks on the bodies of those victims but also crimes against humanity itself, understood through its diversity and plurality.

This understanding of the critical importance of diversity to our common humanity is echoed by Michael Ignatieff (2001), who argues that "what defines the very identity we share as a species is the fact that we are differentiated by race, religion, ethnicity, and individual difference." Based on this understanding, an attack on any of these differences can be regarded as an attack on the "shared element that makes us what we are as a species". Elaborating on this point, Ignatieff argues that the value of our humanity lies in the ability it gives us to honour and recognize difference, in that this difference is a common inheritance we must all defend when anyone is attacked for manifesting it. Both Arendt and Ignatieff suggest that killing off a whole human grouping would harm all of humanity because as a species we are characterized by our abundance of groups; our awareness of difference is central to what it means to be a human being. As such, crimes against humanity are understood through the defining feature of group diversity.

Yet one must ask: why would humanity be devoid of meaning in the absence of diversity? Implicit in this formulation of crimes against humanity is the assumption that local identity, displayed through the diversity of cultures and nations, must be regarded as a key element of our common humanity (Gaita 2005, 164). Arendt (1963, 262–3) therefore argues that if these crimes go unpunished, then no "people of earth" will be able to feel assured of their existence, which is ultimately tied to the security of the space they share. As such, the denial of space to any group is a crime against humanity, one that harms and endangers humankind.

Yet in practical terms, how we define a "group," or even diversity itself, has major implications regarding who is part of a common humanity and therefore essential to protect (Brown 2009). If we take the UN 1948 Genocide Convention as an example, the only groups alluded to in this document are "national, ethical, racial or religious groups" (UN 1948). As Anthony Lang (2005) notes, the UN convention defined these groups as having special significance in social and cultural life; yet one can equally question how we can justify singling them out for protection. It is argued that these groups "contribute more essentially to social structure and life (collective and individual) than others" (10). Because of their essential contribution, humanity would be radically diminished if they were made the target of crimes against humanity. As the genocide convention outlines, in attempting to recognize group diversity as an essential aspect of humanity we run the risk of ignoring the value of individuals outside of the groups to which they belong (Luban 2004, 116). This is especially apparent when we consider that the value of certain groups will always be contested, as demonstrated by the language utilized in the genocide convention. The implications of this distinction are therefore considerable, particularly when one is assessing how the concept of humanity can impact states' decisions to intervene and stop atrocities. Based on this argument, the significance of a group's cultural output is what dictates whether humanity is metaphorically damaged by such acts. Those who reject the cultural importance of a certain group are in effect denying its relevance to humanity. How we decide on this relevance will always be plagued with political implications. So it remains vital to look beyond mere group diversity and recognize an individual element to the value of humanity. This makes it possible not to be constrained by debates that solely concern the value we place on some groups relative to others.

Norman Geras (2005) has also been critical of Arendt's formulation of crimes against humanity as acts attacking the human status of their victims. He rejects the implication that crimes against humanity suggest that "mankind in its entirety might have been grievously hurt and endangered" (Arendt 1963, 276). For Geras (2005, 173), in empirical terms, "it seems that we are able as a species to survive successive genocides, the loss or the huge depletion of entire peoples, and just carry on." This raises a question: if humanity, represented as humankind, can continue to exist despite the continuation of mass atrocity crimes around the globe, then how can one argue that they threaten us all? Certainly, on an empirical level this is a far too extreme take on the threat these crimes pose. Yet this argument by Geras seemingly underestimates the variety of harms caused by crimes against humanity and the potential impact that attempts to eradicate elements of human diversity may have on our ability to maintain space for politics and human plurality. What Geras underestimates, then, is the potential for crimes against humanity to significantly reconfigure who is or is not deemed to be recognized as human and the negative impact this has on the ability of human beings to coexist on our planet. So it is crucial to recognize the impact such crimes have on the long-term sustainability of human existence.

THE POLITICAL NATURE OF HUMANITY

In beginning to address some of the concerns highlighted here, David Luban (2004) questions whether group diversity should be regarded as the defining feature of humanity. While he accepts that the diversity of human beings, as well as human groups, is a natural fact, he argues that focusing solely on group diversity implicitly ignores the value of individuals apart from the group to which they belong (Luban 2004, 116). For him, crimes against humanity assault both individuals and groups; it follows that this distinction ignores the possibility that groups pose an existential threat to individual identity (115). It is in the sense of attacking individuals on the basis of their group membership and targeting groups through their individual members that we can understand crimes against humanity as assaulting humanness.

The defining characteristic of human beings is that we are political rather than just social animals: we all require some form of artificial coercive organization (110). Yet these very organizations simultaneously threaten our well-being and perhaps even our survival. As Luban goes on to state, it is because we cannot live without politics that we are forced to live under the permanent threat that the "institutions of organised political life will destroy us" (90). Crimes against humanity are the worst of these threats, for they assault this particular aspect of being human, that is, our character as political animals. Accordingly, all of humankind shares an interest in repressing these crimes, for we all must exist in politics. Note that Luban is not suggesting that our status as political animals is purely metaphysical speculation; rather, that status can be classed as naturalistic and anchored in observation. He views human beings as self-aware individuals with their own interests who ultimately have a natural need to live in groups. In this sense, humanity matters because when we threaten it, we are attacking the very principles that make it possible for us all to survive.

But there is something more visceral and instinctive connected to the harm of crimes against humanity that Luban does not fully capture. Robert Dubler (2008) contends that Luban's explanation cannot fully explain the instinctive reaction that many have to the "evil that accompanies a crime against humanity" (97), suggesting that viewing such crimes solely as attacks on our character as political animals does not sufficiently capture the essence of such atrocities. Thus, if we are to capture the full range of harms created by such crimes, we need a deeper explanation for why crimes against humanity are perceived as conscience-shocking. It is useful to consider besides how crimes against humanity may also create a more significant psychological harm that goes beyond politics, a harm more shocking and visceral than is often realized.

THE TERROR OF CRIMES AGAINST HUMANITY

So far, this chapter has developed an overall conception of how humanity as a whole can be threatened. But we have yet to examine how crimes committed against humanity can harm us all more directly. One approach to addressing this is offered by Norman Geras (2005, 171–2), who suggests that fundamentally, crimes against humanity are committed against the human status of their victims: such acts are harmful to the key interests of human beings, threatening severe or irreversible damage to their well-being. But for Geras, a more important question is this: can we conceptualize these crimes as having a direct impact on our common humanity as dwellers on this planet?

Addressing this question, Geras (2005) contends that crimes against humanity "terrorize us all." The logic behind this statement is based on the idea that our "psychological well-being suffers from the sight of atrocities by fellow human beings" (Robertson 1999, 331). Geras applies this understanding of psychological effects, representing the harm caused by crimes against humanity, to support the idea that humanity is collectively the victim (Geras 2005, 175). However, the terrorizing element of crimes against humanity can hardly be considered universal, for not all human beings are terrorized simply by viewing or reading about these acts. Metaphorically speaking, these acts may be seen to shock the conscience of humankind, but it is much more difficult to argue that humankind is the direct victim of crimes against humanity. Geras can only tentatively conclude that "the psychological well-being of some significant proportion of human beings is somewhat worsened by crimes against humanity" (176). His argument highlights how difficult it is to locate a universal principle of harm that is committed against all of us. It is easy enough to conceptualize how these crimes represent an almost universal conception of the wrong; it is far harder to take the next step – that is, to demonstrate their threat to a collective humanity. This difficulty in theoretically capturing a threat to a collective harm thus leaves room to apply more empirically focused approaches centred on the role of the state in maintaining international peace and security in relation to common humanity.

A THREAT TO THE INTERNATIONAL COMMUNITY – A STATIST APPROACH

Yet another way of conceptualizing the harm created by crimes against humanity is to understand humanity in relation to the international community as a whole. If we assume that humanity refers to a community of nations and, furthermore, that it relies on that community for security, then it can be argued that crimes against humanity threaten the peace and security of humankind, or the peace of the world (Robertson 1999, 331). In other words, these acts matter to all states because they threaten peace and foment conflict. The idea that mass atrocity crimes threaten international peace and security has served as a legal basis for establishing such tribunals under Chapter VII of the UN Charter (Boot 2002, 610). Rwanda and the former Yugoslavia are two examples. This demonstrates how a state's ability to conceptualize the harm caused by such crimes is still closely intertwined with the UN's legal framework. This conception of humanity attempts to de-emphasize the impact on persecuted individuals in order to focus on the state's central role in protecting humankind. Arguably, this situates the international order itself as most in need of protecting.

However, this heavily statist approach to conceptualizing humanity has a number of key deficiencies, most significantly with regard to the impact these crimes have on the international system. To start, this approach assumes that crimes against humanity such as genocide directly threaten world peace and security. However, genocide that is potentially limited to a national territory and left to run its own course would not necessarily threaten anyone beyond the target group (Geras 2005, 169). Indeed, one could even argue that attempts to intervene or prosecute the crimes committed could jeopardize international peace more seriously than non-intervention would. Contrastingly, it is still important to highlight that if the community of states consistently failed to intervene to halt mass atrocity crimes it would in many ways be extending permission to such acts. In this sense, decisions by states to intervene to protect those threatened by mass atrocity crimes play the critical role of acknowledging that such acts will not be permitted within the community of states. Furthermore, it is still vital to recognize that even when mass atrocity crimes are confined to a specific geographical area, their impact often results in a significant number of civilians fleeing from the conflict, thus placing substantial strains on the surrounding states in the region.

But when we view the harm created by these crimes solely as a threat to traditional readings of international peace and security, we fail to locate harms that have so often been ignored by states acting under a more rigid understanding of their responsibility for maintaining international peace and security. To understand the motivation to create a moral and political concept such as the R2P, we must acknowledge that past state responses have often failed to prevent or react strongly enough to serious instances of international harm. Thinking of humanity as being represented solely by the international community of states severely limits our ability to discuss how individuals react to these crimes or the moral wrong committed by the perpetrators. In many respects, the interests of humanity in such cases are viewed as interchangeable with state ambitions for securing peace and security.

By assessing a wide range of approaches to theorizing the harm generated by crimes against humanity, from both legal theorists and political philosophers, it has been possible to highlight the centrality of the concept of humanity to such debates. Clearly, though, we so far lack a systematic understanding of the link between crimes against humanity and the moral reasoning behind the responsibility of states to respond to threats to humanity, be it through intervention or assistance. So to reinforce why states have responsibilities to those threatened by these acts, we require a more expansive theorization of the harms created by crimes against humanity.

RECONFIGURING A DUAL APPROACH TO OUR UNDERSTANDING OF GLOBAL HARM AND HUMANITY

This final section of the chapter brings together some of the key arguments previously broached in order to lay out a "dual approach" to understanding crimes against humanity. This will help us identify the specific role humanity plays in locating a responsibility for states to prevent such crimes and protect populations from them. Building on the dual conception of humanity outlined in chapter 2, it will be argued here that crimes against humanity threaten both the characteristics of humanness and a collective understanding of humankind. Key to this argument is recognizing the impact that a failure to respond to crimes against humanity can have, not simply on international peace and security or specific human characteristics, but also in terms of specific global harms that directly threaten a collective idea of humanity that must be defended by all human beings.

This approach also draws upon the key roles played by both reason and harm recognition for our understanding of humanity. This will help us reflect on the impact that crimes against humanity have, not just on our ability to create the appropriate social and political conditions to construct moral rules, but also in regard to the visceral nature of violence that connects these crimes back to our shared capacity for empathy and recognition. This discussion will enable us to conceptualize how this new theoretical approach can address the current gaps in the literature outlined earlier, thus helping us move beyond the humankind-versus-humanness dichotomy. The next stage of this process requires a more thorough assessment of how the moral ideas relating to harms against humanity have so far affected states' behaviour at the international level.

LOCATING GLOBAL HARMS

To grasp why states should concern themselves with populations threatened by mass atrocity crimes, we must do more than revisit the sovereign rights held by states; we must also acknowledge the global harms such crimes generate and the impact they have beyond the management of peace and security. To demonstrate the importance of recognizing crimes against humanity as specific global harms, we must first explain why this categorization is required and what it can tell us about the normative motivation for states to respond to these crimes. That in turn means recognizing crimes against humanity as challenging a dual conception of humanity: as humankind and as humanness. Regarding humanness, we need to understand crimes against humanity as assaulting a fundamental quality of being human, and we must do so in a way that allows us to differentiate them from other acts that also attack human qualities but are to be understood as domestic rather than international crimes. The ability to differentiate domestic from international crimes against humanity is integral to locating why certain crimes can transcend borders.

Arguably, it is David Luban (2004) who has provided the most comprehensive account so far of why crimes against humanity threaten both humankind and humanness. Here I will outline how we can expand his criminal prosecution–focused understanding to reinforce the recognition of crimes against humanity as global harms. As noted in earlier, Luban (2004, 159) defines crimes against humanity as an affront to our human nature as political animals and thus to our natural need for the society of others. For him, this characterization of crimes against humanity is what underpins why humanity has an interest in criminalizing atrocious violent persecution by organized groups against civilians (160). In expanding this conception of crimes against humanity to encompass debates about states' normative responsibility to prevent such crimes and to protect populations from them, we must further conceptualize the impact on the international community of the failure to ensure the overall survival of political communities. The responsibility to prosecute such crimes is one thing; the decision to intervene or respond to such crimes is a different thing and is often heavily reliant on locating a more immediate global threat. This has led to an overemphasis on security narratives to define state responsibility, as demonstrated by May's (2005) focus on the security principle (see above).

So we need to somehow recognize crimes against humanity as distinctly global harms. Doing so will help reinforce the idea that the responsibility to respond to such crimes, on the basis of humanity, requires states to recognize not just the threat to the international order or security but also the harm caused to a collective idea of humanity when individuals represented as a group are under threat. Focusing on harm thus captures a threat that is underemphasized when we focus too strictly on security and order. As Luban (2004) argues, this harm is to a core characteristic of human beings, that is, to the social nature of our political belonging. In this sense, our humanness is defined in terms of our status as political animals; crimes against humanity threaten this distinctly human status, violating the individuality and sociability of victims in tandem (120). The threat to political life, indeed its potential destruction, reinforces a collective need for humankind to repress these crimes and ensure that sovereignty cannot serve as a shield against culpability.

Arguably, there is another vital element besides to normatively conceptualizing crimes against humanity as global harms, one that is underplayed in Luban's account. That is, the harm must be understood in relation to the visceral nature of the violence used by perpetrators against specific groups. Very often it is that violence that defines crimes against humanity and becomes the driving motivational force for building both moral empathy and the recognition that collective state action is required. Zagor (2011) has argued that "an effective principle of humanity both incorporates and necessitates a sentiment of empathy" (290). This reality is most plainly expressed by the standard description of crimes against humanity as "conscience-shocking." That wording can be viewed as an attempt to capture the extreme level of violence the perpetrators apply as they inflict particular harms on individuals in a particular group. In this regard, moral aversion to such crimes does appear to tap into an essentially human response to this form of violence, most often a shared outrage or shock that humans are capable of committing such crimes.

Central to this moral outrage is the potential destruction of political life. But also central to it is the extreme violence that apparently flows from the perpetrators' will to choose who can remain part of our common humanity and who cannot. Furthermore, this violence often takes the form of specific actions that seek not just to kill or injure its victims but to destroy their status as human beings by engaging in extreme violations of their human dignity. This has often included acts such as torture, rape, sexual slavery, and extermination on considerable scales. In this sense, such crimes represent moves to normalize forms of dehumanization that directly challenge our collective understanding of human status and work to severely undermine ideas of bodily integrity and human recognition. The whole of humankind therefore has an interest in limiting the powers of anyone who would choose violence as a tool to butcher humanity and the social groupings within which human beings exist.

Yet as this chapter has highlighted, the connection between empathy and the shock of extreme violence does not entirely capture the global harm meted out by crimes against humanity. When describing crimes against humanity as global harms, we must understand these acts as an affront to our collective human nature as political animals and thus to our ability to generate moral rules by which to live; we must also acknowledge how this sort of violence not only destroys political association but also dictates who has the opportunity to exist in groups and who does not. Such violence aims directly to disfigure the individual human status of its victims.

Conceptualizing crimes against humanity through this dual approach makes it possible to acknowledge the significant implications such global harms have for the international order resulting from the breakdown in political association, as well as the potential longer-term effects of legitimizing practices of dehumanization that attempt to radically alter shared conceptions of human dignity. It is through this reasoning that we can stake the claim that all states need to offer protection on behalf of a common humanity to whomever is threatened, wherever they may be. Allowing certain states and organizations to use violence to expel specific groups from humankind, thus directly challenging central characteristics of humanness, would fundamentally threaten not only the diversity of humanity but also the continued existence of group association as a universal and distinct human characteristic shared by us all. It is this understanding of crimes against humanity that makes it possible to define these acts as truly global harms. Consequently, this chapter has reinforced the complexity of the threat created by mass atrocity crimes, a threat sometimes underplayed in the current literature. When states are forced to weigh which responsibilities to prioritize, be it in terms of their own specific national interests or other humanitarian causes, there is more at stake than simply averting the direct violence of mass atrocity crimes. This provides further justification for why political will should still be invested in the R2P, which needs to be recognized as a morally valuable agenda vis-à-vis other moral norms and responsibilities (Pattison 2018). By applying a dual conception of humanity, supported by appeals to the centrality of reason and harm recognition, it is possible to highlight the importance of acknowledging interconnected harms that generate moral obligations to not just prosecute these crimes but to prevent them and protect others from them as a matter of urgency.

CONCLUSION

This chapter has demonstrated the significant values placed on the concept of humanity and has articulated a clear theoretical and normative understanding of how these values can be threatened. As Luban (2004) originally argued, "the central questions for any theory of crimes against humanity are how these deeds violate humanness, and why they offend against all humankind" (90). The distinct dual approach to conceptualizing crimes against humanity outlined in this chapter provides a useful way to emphasize the centrality of political association for conceptions of humanness; it also highlights a collective threat to humankind that arises when we allow the perpetrators of extreme violence to decide who can coexist as individuals, based simply on group affiliation. This dual understanding of crimes against humanity as an attack on humanity, understood through both humanness and humankind, provides a comprehensive reply to the question of why humanity matters and ultimately why states have a responsibility to respond to crimes against humanity beyond their borders. We thus need to locate the harm of crimes against humanity, not simply as enforced by a collective solidarity between peoples in regard to a shared aversion to suffering, but also as part of a broader collective ambition to limit harms that challenge the ability of humans to coexist (Linklater 2011). However, while there may be a critical moral link between crimes against humanity and states' responsibility to respond, the complexity of this relationship requires further examination.

As this chapter has shown, without greater philosophical scrutiny of our understanding of mass atrocity crimes and their connection to humanity, we cannot fully draw the link between the legal and moral rights of intervention. The arguments in this chapter have provided the foundation for understanding why certain crimes must be seen as challenging our common humanity. In developing this argument further, I next examine how moral appeals to humanity and its application in international law, founded in concepts such as crimes against humanity, have impacted the political decision-making of UN member-states as they respond to mass atrocity crimes around the globe. This will be crucial to exploring the impact the introduction of the R2P concept is having on this process, in particular, to assessing its role in supposedly strengthening the moral obligations that are created by our common humanity. If appeals to humanity remain integral to the normative justification for action, then to what extent can humanity be seen as generating sufficient political will to persuade states to fully respond to mass atrocity crimes?

4

Humanity and the United Nations

Central to the conception of the R2P is its perceived role as a moral imperative derived from our common humanity, thus arguably providing a normative justification for why states should change their behaviour in order to address mass atrocity crimes. But to what extent has the R2P been able to shift state behaviour when it comes to recognizing shared responsibilities for responding to such crimes? To address this question, we need to examine first how appeals to humanity's emotional pull factor have shaped states' behaviour at the institutional level, namely within the two key UN organs: the General Assembly and the Security Council. For supporters of the R2P principle such as Anne Orford (2013), the UN and its organs have begun to derive "jurisdiction to police the conduct of governments not only from state consent, but also from their role as executive agents of an international community that represents our common humanity" (104). Yet as this chapter will explore, ambitious claims to the growing influence of humanity appear to run counter to recent UN practice and state behaviour. This chapter will argue that there has always been significantly uneven development in how states acknowledge the specific harm generated by mass atrocity crimes and how they frame their responses. Moreover, there appears to also be a growing challenge to the moral authority of humanity claims in an increasingly divided international community.

To chart this reality, this chapter will focus specifically on debates surrounding the issue of international peace and security and threat expansion, in relation to how the UNSC categorizes the threat posed by mass atrocity crimes. This will enable us to trace how the challenge of expanding the focus of the UNSC in terms of threat identification has ebbed and flowed, so as to highlight the complex role humanity has played in such discussions and challenge claims to its linear and teleological impact. This historical analysis will demonstrate the lack of a consistent pattern in the way both the UNSC and individual states have categorized mass atrocity crimes, despite consistent rhetorical claims to the distinct threat they are argued to pose to our common humanity. In this sense, notwithstanding the creation of the R2P concept and the political agreement to acknowledge four specific mass atrocity crimes, outlined in the 2005 WSOD, the threshold for dictating the point at which consensus can be forged in order to avert mass atrocity crimes remains highly contentious. This suggests that the moral cause of humanity and calls for its protection have not directly reinforced the role of the R2P as a distinct motivator for "converting a shocked international conscience into decisive collective action" (Thakur 2015, 23). Consequently, it remains critical to explore how normative arguments concerning the motivational qualities of humanity feed into current debates about the R2P's implementation gap and how these may be better addressed moving forward.

This chapter begins by outlining the role of the UN Charter and making the case that it remains a critical site for exploring how moral claims made in support of humanity and the R2P interact with competing geostrategic and national interests. The chapter then traces the relationship between sovereignty and the UNSC's interpretation of threats to international peace and security, focusing on how ideas of humanity and human protection have helped forge new approaches to categorizing threats and thereby further challenged traditional interpretations of sovereignty. In light of this shift, it will be critical to also reflect on the previous colonial legacy of intervention for humanitarian purposes and the extent to which the R2P's attempt to reinterpret sovereignty is ultimately a product of Western power rather than a move to protect a common humanity. Following on from this analysis, the chapter will assess the role the R2P has played in shaping recent debates in the UNSC about threat identification, focusing on the cases of Libya and Syria. It will be argued that rather than understanding recent developments in threat expansion as part of a fixed linear progression, one defined by a continual increase in state response to human suffering and the protection of a common humanity (Tietel 2011), the interactions among humanity, sovereignty, and more traditional conceptions of threats to international peace and security have continually ebbed and flowed. The chapter after this one will analyze more closely the limits of humanity as a motivating principle and the extent to which a focus on the motivational function of humanity has led to an oversimplification of the complex processes behind state practice when deliberating on mass atrocity crime prevention and protection.

THE UNITED NATIONS

This chapter is framed around the workings of the United Nations – more specifically, the UN Security Council – and its interactions with state actors in constructing shared agendas and normative goals. The justification for this focus is twofold. First, the UN as a whole arguably represents "the most vocal and visible space in which the contesting claims of universality and particularity in our globalized world find expression" (Mazlish 2009, 12). In this sense, it is the central forum for states to debate their responsibilities to others. Mazlish (2009, 86) argues that the UN Secretary-General in particular has taken up the moral authority to speak for humanity. In tandem with the Secretary-General, the UN Charter is integral to shaping international consensus on so-called rightful conduct. Second, the UN, most notably the Security Council, is where the complexities of the relationship between the R2P concept and the normative power of humanity are played out. According to the ICISS (2001), the UN has "the capacity (if not always the will) to deal with the whole spectrum of peace, security and human protection issues" (48). Thus, the UN is a key point of reference for examining how state decisions and actions regarding prevention and intervention practices have evolved over time. This in turn means we can trace the R2P's development within the UN alongside its relationship to competing normative interpretations, which have continually shaped its construction and application.

This chapter focuses largely on the interactions between the UNSC and the R2P concept, more specifically on how the R2P has challenged states to adjust their understanding of threats to international peace and security. These interactions go to the heart of a much broader debate over the UNSC's role in the global system, which seems increasingly different from the one first set down in the 1945 UN Charter. Central to the R2P's project is the need to forge greater consensus on the responsibilities and obligations that states and the international community must now manage in order to better protect human dignity and our shared humanity. As the previous chapter highlighted, these values are progeny of the post-Holocaust era, in which states have begun to consider – albeit often inconsistently – the wider implications of mass violence and grave human rights abuses for the maintenance of international peace and security (Weinert 2015). The R2P is central to this movement to redefine the behaviour and actions of states within the international system. As Orford (2013) argues, one can view the creation and emergence of the R2P principle in recent decades as an "insight into the place that moral arguments now occupy in internationalist debates" (84), in that moral appeals to concepts such as humanity have generated greater enthusiasm for reforms to global institutions and laws. In analyzing this relationship between humanity and state conduct, we can challenge key assumptions regarding the impact the R2P principle has had on addressing the dual question of when sovereignty can be overridden and what acts constitute legitimate grounds for such action.

The UN Charter

The central purpose of the UN is outlined in the very first line of Chapter 1 of its Charter: to maintain international peace and security. Reinforcing this goal, Chapter 2 outlines the key principles of the organization – most importantly, that "all members shall refrain in their international relations from the threat or use of force against the territorial integrity or political independence of any state" (UN Charter 1945). The use of unilateral force by states is thus prohibited, except for self-defence, as recognized in Article 51 of Chapter VII. However, the UNSC's powers under Chapter VII of the Charter also outline its crucial collective security role, whereby the council holds the authority to sanction force in order to avert a threat to international peace and security, as outlined in Article 41. The prerequisite for taking collective coercive action, under Article 39, is the determination that a situation amounts to a "threat to the peace," "breach of the peace," or "act of aggression" (UN Charter 1945). In addition, the council is also able to initiate "measures not involving the use of force," including economic sanctions and/or the breaking of diplomatic relations, to help maintain international peace and security.

Note that the council need not resort to non-forceful measures in the first instance; rather, the council has the discretion to decide when force is required. It is recognized that the UNSC has the primary responsibility for peace and security; the General Assembly plays a residual role in this. So if the council fails to address a specific threat to international peace and security, the General Assembly can take up a "Uniting for Peace" resolution, enabling it to recommend to its members collective measures to maintain, or restore, international peace and security (UN 1950).

As this chapter will show, humanitarian crises, which may include one or more of the core R2P crimes, have at times been judged to have reached a threshold deemed to threaten international peace and security. It is at this stage that two responsibilities emerge: to restore peace and security and to prevent mass atrocity crimes. While these two responsibilities may at times be in sync with each other, it is also the case that responding directly to mass atrocity crimes is not always viewed as compatible with protecting international peace and security. Moreover, as Gehring and Dörfler (2020) have argued, the extent to which the R2P has a direct impact on UNSC actions on peace and security has been overstated in parts of the R2P literature. So it is critical to emphasize that the R2P itself does not obligate council members to accept atrocity crimes as automatically constituting a threat to international peace and security.

In this sense, it is not simply that states may disagree over who bears the responsibility to act in such situations; it is also that they often fundamentally disagree on which cases should draw international attention in the first place. As a result, agreement among states regarding which crimes should be enshrined in the R2P principle (i.e., the four core crimes) has not brought an end to debates over *when* domestic incidents of mass atrocity crimes constitute threats to international peace and security and thus meet the moral threshold. So while the R2P reinforces the need to legitimate "intervention in cases that are not of an inter-state character," the process of authorizing such intervention remains the same (Oellers-Frahm 2014, 186) – indeed, it is underscored by the procedures laid out in Article 27 of the UN Charter. Article 27(3) states that "decisions of the Security Council on all other matters shall be made by an affirmative vote of nine members including the concurring votes of the permanent members." Permanent members thus have the power individually to veto a resolution

(Gifkins 2021, 4). The idea behind the veto is twofold: to ensure that the great powers continue to be committed to the UN, and to avoid great power conflict. The recent high-profile uses of the veto in mass atrocity crime situations, such as Syria, have generated a strong movement for veto restraint initiatives (see the next chapter).

The R2P, then, does not introduce any new legal obligations, nor does it attempt to rewrite UNSC procedures concerning the imposition of coercive action against another state by the international community. Because of this, the R2P is in fact better understood as a distinctly moral imperative rather than a legal one (Tacheva and Brown 2016), with the moral imperative grounded most strongly on the concept of a common humanity (Welsh 2008, 105). Understanding the normative dimension of the R2P in this way thus opens up the question as to what extent the R2P, underpinned by the motivational capacity of humanity, has directly shaped debates around locating threats to international peace and security. This question remains unanswered in the R2P literature and needs to be addressed in order to clarify the scope of the R2P's influence on UNSC action, as well as the role the concept of humanity plays in underpinning the motivation for such behaviour.

MANAGING INTERNATIONAL ORDER: SOVEREIGNTY AND THREATS TO INTERNATIONAL PEACE AND SECURITY

Before assessing the role of concepts such as humanity in influencing an expanded conception of what constitutes a threat to international peace and security, it is vital to briefly clarify the relationship between sovereignty and the management of international peace and security. This is important for a number of reasons but most significantly because, despite the development of the R2P principle, it is still the framework of threat identification, outlined in the UN Charter, that shapes when sovereignty may be overridden and coercive intervention authorized by the UNSC for humanitarian purposes. In this regard, while R2P advocates have focused predominantly on the importance of reframing sovereignty, the introduction of a broader understanding of sovereign responsibility does not automatically address the issue of when internal acts by a state threaten international peace and thus require the engagement of the UN Charter. The principle of non-intervention is contained in Article 2(4) of the UN

Charter and is further supported by Article 2(7), which prohibits the UN from intervening "in matters which are essentially within the domestic jurisdiction of any state." A clear qualification to this principle is then contained in Article 24, which confers responsibility for maintaining international peace and security on the UNSC. The justificatory mechanisms for agreement on coercive action for protection purposes, leading to the bypassing of state sovereignty, are thus closely tied to how the UNSC decides what constitutes a threat to international peace and security. However, it is vital to qualify at this point that the idea of justifying humanitarian-motivated action through this process is relatively new and only began to gain traction in the final decade of the twentieth century.

Yet while the formal legal practice of authorizing intervention through this method is relatively new, we must also reflect here on the past practices of states in justifying intervention for humanitarian purposes and the colonial legacy attached to many of these actions. First and foremost, those states involved in carrying out operations in support of the R2P most often once had colonial empires; the UK, in particular, has a highly selective and hypocritical record when it comes to humanitarianism, given the abuses it carried out as a colonial power (Newman 2021, 19). The colonial legacy of the major powers has thus generated much concern over the true motivations behind the R2P's creation and its efforts to redefine sovereignty. This contestation is ultimately shaped by the fact that weak states have long viewed the principle of sovereignty as a shield against intrusive actions by more powerful states; so it can be argued that the shift to "sovereignty as responsibility" opens the door to a return of "colonial habits and practices" (Chimni 2002, 104). Furthermore, much of the concern of smaller states is that the R2P decision-making process, which is dominated by powerful states on the Security Council, creates an opportunity for the major powers to intervene in smaller states based on their narrow strategic interests. However, as this chapter will later outline, criticism of the Libyan intervention and its motivation by non-Western states has ultimately had the knock-on effect of making Western states much more risk-averse when it comes to intervention, and has at the same time further divided the Security Council on matters of international peace and security. Before examining this particular example in more detail, the chapter will discuss the evolution of the UN's relationship to human protection.

The Broadening of Peace and Security (1945–1999)

Understandings of what constitutes a threat to international peace and security remain fluid and have been influenced by a wide range of moral, political, and legal claims over the past seventy years. For much of its history the UNSC has held a restricted conception of threats to international peace and security. Fassbender (2002) contends that the UN's founders took the idea of international peace and security to essentially refer to the prevention of another major war that could "shake the foundations of the established state system and threaten the survival of humankind," as opposed to the protection of civilians from inter-state violence. Thus, the creation of the Charter was an attempt to maintain the status quo by averting further large-scale inter-state wars (Fassbender 2002). The five permanent members of the UNSC were therefore given veto rights on the UNSC; at the same time, though, they were burdened with a special primary responsibility for maintaining international peace and security. Given the overriding responsibility of the P5 to maintain peace, it was not originally thought that the USNC's actions would be guided by "universally shared values such as the protection of human lives and human rights" (Nasu 2011, 391). However, in the post–Cold War era, there has been a significant shift in global security objectives. This has been caused in part by a decline in outbreaks of inter-state wars, an increasing need for the UN to manage the impact of civil wars on the international order, and the growth in human security initiatives.

As Weinert (2015) contends, we might now consider it a central aim of the UNSC and the UN to "try and counter dehumanizing realities by encouraging forms of responsibility that deliver on the promise of protection" (91). Nevertheless, the extent to which the UNSC has been willing to accept the increasing expansion of threats to international peace and security, in particular those to human suffering, has been vehemently contested. In part, this is because, while the UNSC can create legally binding resolutions, authorized by the UN Charter, on matters of international peace and security, at the same time, as Doyle (2015) highlights, it is also a "political body, authorised to decide based on its own judgement of what constitutes threats to the peace" (116). This combination has significantly challenged the UNSC's ability to act consistently on the multitude of security threats it is now compelled to consider. But before one can begin to examine how the current procedural workings of the UNSC currently function, it is vital to trace how the concept of threats to international peace and security has developed over time and how the UNSC has adapted to this changing global reality. Later, on this basis, we can highlight the limitations of viewing the R2P as a distinctly new approach to building consensus on the authorization of measures to prevent mass atrocity crimes and to protect those threatened by them.

The Cold War that followed the creation of the UN Charter continued to be defined by what one might view as a negative or traditional reading of international peace and security. The UNSC was generally indifferent to the internal actions of states, which were seen as purely domestic matters (Buchan 2013, 100). So the UNSC most often eschewed jurisdiction over internal conflicts and human rights abuses if involvement would infringe on actions that had no clear international repercussions (Manusama 2006, 57). Even so, on a number of occasions the UNSC did review its definition of international peace and security, perhaps most importantly in the case of South Africa and Rhodesia in the 1960s and 1970s.

The Cold War years were defined not just by major power confrontation but also by decolonization struggles. It has been suggested that the UNSC's decision to challenge South Africa's attempts to export apartheid to Southern Rhodesia represented a significant move by the UNSC to begin responding to "human welfare and dignity" (Weinert 2015, 101). As Weinert notes, this was one of the first times the UNSC was prepared to "expand the parameters of the meaning of international peace and security by including in its calculus systematic violations of human rights" (100) and thus expand its focus so as to encompass the domestic impact of state actions. Consequently, Resolution 221 was adopted by the UNSC, which implemented sanctions on the basis that the situation in Rhodesia represented "a threat to the peace" (UN, 1966, S/RES/221). For Weinert (2015), this case represented a distinct move by the UNSC "toward advancing a conception of human dignity" (103). However, it is important to highlight here that the UNSC's engagement of Chapter VII in relation to Southern Rhodesia was also strongly driven by "a desire to protect the territorial integrity of the sovereign state and the UK" (Buchan 2013, 103). Furthermore, writes Fassbender (2011), these actions were very much situated in "the special context of the fight against colonialism and racial discrimination" (3) and not as direct action against the violation of human rights and international law. Nevertheless, this incident is an early example of the emergence of a "nascent international community" beginning to form, one that was potentially more responsive to the threats posed by violence, abuse, and human suffering (Buchan 2013, 103). Furthermore, as Dunne and Staunton (2016) point out, examples such as this demonstrate how "international peace and security was increasingly being understood in ways that were only intelligible in relation to claims about the justice and protection of peoples" (48). The Southern Rhodesia case in particular was a significant precursor to a distinctly post–Cold War turn toward greater recognition of the human element of security policy.

The end of the Cold War brought about a new verve for redefining the parameters of the UN's responsibility, underscored by new thinking around the limitations of the UNSC's traditional interpretations of international peace and security and the idea that strict adherence to this more negative reading of the UNSC's responsibilities could, in fact, be harming human rights (Fassbender 2011). This was perhaps best articulated at a UNSC meeting on 31 January 1992 during which heads of state acknowledged changes to the nature of international peace and security. It was declared that the "absence of war and military conflicts amongst states does not in itself ensure international peace and security" and that "non-military sources of instability in the economic, social, humanitarian and ecological fields have become threats to peace and security" (UN 1992a). The interventions of the 1990s thus clearly demonstrated a move toward including the threats posed by "failed states" and ethnic conflicts as part of a shared understanding of global security threats. This was part of an attempt to broaden the legitimacy of the use of force in such situations (Del Sarto 2006, 508). However, as Yamashita (2007) highlights, the UNSC at this time still viewed grave human rights violations and humanitarian crises as in some way "unique" and requiring "exceptional measures" (567), demonstrated by resolutions on the situations in northern Iraq and Rwanda. The use of such wording was particular to this type of threat, which suggests that the idea that human rights abuses threatened international peace and security had not yet matured and thus lacked fully fledged recognition as a legitimate ground for Chapter VII action (Yamashita 2007, 567). Illustrating this is UN Resolution 688, which focused on the repression of the Kurdish population in Iraq. That resolution expressed concern about the magnitude of human suffering; but it also clearly identified the "massive flow of refugees towards and across international frontiers" (UN 1991) as a threat to international peace and security. Similarly, the UNSC, while referring to the situation in Rwanda in 1994 as "a unique case," sought to limit its scope as representing a threat to regional rather than international peace and security (UN 1994). As Hurd (2012a) notes, both these examples highlight how the UNSC was beginning to adapt its language in an effort to legitimize humanitarian problems as part of the international peace and security architecture.

Yet in contrast to these two cases, the UNSC was sometimes able to detach the more traditional security threats caused by mass atrocity crimes, such as refugee flows across borders, from the harm posed by grave humanitarian suffering as a threat in and of itself. This was perhaps best demonstrated in the case of Somalia. After President Mohammed Said Barre was ousted in 1991, the country fell into civil war and heavy fighting erupted in the capital, Mogadishu. In response to the escalating violence and human suffering, the UNSC passed Resolution 794 in 1992, declaring that "the magnitude of the human tragedy caused by the conflict in Somalia, further exacerbated by the obstacles being created to the distribution of humanitarian assistance, constitutes a threat to international peace and security" (UN 1992b). While the Somalia situation was somewhat unique in that the government had completely collapsed, thus placing the UN in an unofficial trustee role, it was nevertheless a significant moment: here, the UNSC recognized the threat that grave human rights abuses can pose beyond the territorial space in which they are conducted (Buchan 2013, 112). The unanimous adoption of the resolution was thus a landmark in the development of state understandings of threats to international peace and security, in that for the first time the UNSC viewed human suffering as a distinct threat and authorized action under Chapter VII accordingly (Glanville 2013, 184). However, the decade was also defined by a number of serious failures by the UNSC, most significantly the UN's response to the Rwandan genocide in 1994, which cast lasting doubt on the sustainability of this initial progress toward recognition of human suffering. As the 1999 independent inquiry into the UN's failure in Rwanda would conclude, "there was a persistent lack of political will by member states to act or to act with enough assertiveness" (UN 1999a). Governments with the capacity to act at the time clearly prioritized other interests and thus avoided committing resources to protect Rwandans from genocide (see chapter 6).

The unique and inconsistent nature of the Security Council's response to outbreaks of mass atrocity crimes throughout most of the 1990s played a part in shaping the much quicker unilateral approach taken by NATO forces to the humanitarian crisis that unfolded in Kosovo in March 1999. Notably, no legal right to intervention was invoked in this case; instead, the moral argument of a shared humanity requiring protection underpinned much of the rhetoric favouring action. For example, the concept of humanity provided a critical motivating focus to the comments that President William Clinton (1999a) made in a direct address to the people of Kosovo, in which he stated that "all of us – Americans, Europeans, Serbs, Kosovars – must join together to stop driving wedges between people simply because they belong to different ethnic groups and to start accepting that our differences are less important than our common humanity and our common aspirations." Clinton (1999b) would later also suggest that the actions taken by NATO had reaffirmed a commitment "to a common future, rooted in common humanity." The NATO bombing campaign therefore raised pressing questions as to the current deficiencies of international law and the principles of the UN Charter, which ruled out such actions if they were based solely on humanitarianism. While such action was clearly in violation of international law, the moral case for intervention, in light of the evidence of crimes against humanity taking place, did gain support from a majority on the Security Council. This was notably expressed through the council's blocking of a Russian resolution that requested an end to the strikes, which was rejected 12 to 3 (UN 1999b). It seems there was now a greater willingness among states to rethink the connection between morality and law and to open up space to promote humanity as a guiding principle and motivation in debates around why mass atrocity crimes were a shared and universal concern for the international community.

Overall, during the early post–Cold War era, states gradually because more receptive to idea that mass atrocity crimes and extreme human suffering had the potential to directly threaten international peace and security. Those same years also saw interventions by the UNSC that further eroded absolute conceptions of sovereignty and demonstrated that in some circumstances "local actors claiming to uphold national sovereignty" could be overridden (Cater and Malone 2016, 279) Underpinning this shift was an growing emphasis on the responsibilities states had to a collective humanity, with humanity playing an increasingly important role as an identificatory and reflective concept. In this sense, states had begun to identify distinct human harms that required the UNSC to rethink how it might best address such acts moving forward.

The Creation of the R2P and Its Impact on Threat Identification

The actions of NATO forces in Kosovo drew attention to a significant dilemma, which was how to reconcile the UN's foundational principle of member-state sovereignty and the accompanying primary mandate to maintain international peace and security with the growing emphasis on the interests and welfare of people within those states (ICISS 2001). In UN Charter terms, this required finding a way to "save succeeding generations from the scourge of war" while at the same time sufficiently protecting "we the peoples of the United Nations" (UN Charter 1945). In response to this challenge, the Government of Canada represented by politician Lloyd Axworthy assembled a commission of diverse actors to help forge new common ground on the issue. In 2001, this group tabled the International Commission on Intervention and State Sovereignty (ICISS) report.

The ICISS report recognized that the UNSC was taking an increasingly expansive view of international peace and security. It proclaimed the rise of an "emerging guiding principle of the responsibility to protect" that recognized "state practice in regard to reconciling a state's obligation to peace and security and humanity" (ICISS 2001, 50). This statement is important, for it was a clear attempt to establish a further responsibility for UN member-states to live up to. Thus, the R2P would need to do more than simply redefine threats to international peace and security; it would also have to set out a clear responsibility to a collective humanity that might at times be separate from the UNSC's primary responsibility (i.e., to maintain international peace and security). The idea of humanity itself being under threat was also implicitly suggested in how the document framed its understanding of peace and security. It argued that in some situations, there may be significant loss of human life but no "direct or imminent threat to international peace and security in the strict sense" (ICISS 2001, 52). In this regard, the report called for states to recognize threats to humanity that fell outside the previously drawn boundaries of international peace and security.

The motivation to expand this understanding must be understood in relation to the concept of humanity. The argument here goes that mass atrocity crimes pose the most serious threat to the very ideals on which humanity is built: "Nothing has done more harm to our shared ideal that we are all equal in worth and dignity, and that the earth is our common home than the inability of the community of states to prevent genocide, massacre and ethnic cleansing" (ICISS 2001, 75). Glanville (2012) notes that while the ICISS report did not offer a legal argument, it made a *moral* argument, which it expressed in terms of our common humanity, calling for "practical protection for ordinary people, at risk of their lives" (10). The report stated a need to "strengthen the prospects for obtaining action ... in response to conscience-shocking situations of great humanitarian need" (74). This reinforces the idea that the moral principle of humanity is at the core of the R2P concept. It follows that preventing mass atrocity crimes and responding effectively to their outbreaks must be a universal goal for the international community, based on the importance of human dignity to the management of international society. This is critical to the significant moral claim made in the proposition that the R2P offers the best way to ensure no more Rwandas (viii). In this sense, the ICISS report "articulated a moral appeal to elevate the prevention of, and end to, human suffering above the principle of non-intervention in the UNSC's determination of threats to international peace and security" (Fraser 2014, 205). Here, the ICISS was proposing that states consider the impact of mass atrocity crimes on our collective humanity, in order to move beyond the deadlock caused by restrictive interpretations of peace and security. The R2P must "help stimulate support for action by reminding states of their common responsibilities"; preventing major atrocities in the future was going to require states to place the demands of a common humanity above narrower debates over the categorization of threats to international peace and security.

In contrast, the eventual 2005 WSOD can be viewed as part of a process to "bend the meaning of international threats to peace and security," as understood in Chapter VII, by broadening the standard for authorizing the use of force while at the same time restraining its application to four core crimes, namely genocide, crimes against humanity, war crimes, and ethnic cleansing (Doyle 2015, 144). This was meant to address the UNSC's past failures to adequately protect those threatened by mass atrocity crimes, by building further consensus on the legitimacy of force to protect populations and underscoring the need for states to consider the potential impact mass atrocity crimes on their ability to maintain international peace and security. In the past, states had inconsistently conceptualized what constituted a threat to international peace and security. The WSOD set out to try and rectify this by drawing clearer parameters as to when they could interfere forcefully in the sovereignty of other states. Arguably, this would help states define their political responsibilities both to their own populations and to the international community at large, in part by making the threat of mass atrocity crimes central to the P5's primary responsibility, which was to maintain international peace and security (Doyle 2015, 144). The 2005 WSOD thus created a politically driven agreement asking states to consider from now on how domestic-based crimes could directly threaten international peace and security; but it did not place any new legal obligations on states that would demand a more consistent response to mass atrocity crimes.

Importantly, the 2005 R2P agreement expanded the political scope for identifying threats to international peace and security even while rejecting the idea that specific harms to the collective idea of humankind and common humanity constituted sufficient grounds for intervention. Thus, that agreement narrowed the possibilities for implementing collective responsibility; it was "no longer the challenging framework of common humanity which creates the moral responsibility, but rather the specific political commitment of states to act through the UN to address potential or real atrocities" (Welsh and Banda 2010, 225). Waldorf (2016) therefore argues that the 2005 WSOD has shifted the focus from "moral judgments about what shocks the conscience of humanity (ICISS 2001) to legal determinations about what violates international criminal law" (56) and has replaced "subjective moral judgments (and selective political decisions) with something more consensual and more consistent."

However, while this was clearly an attempt to establish the parameters of accepted intervention practice within the framework of the four core crimes, the mechanisms for implementing protection forces still relied on a process of political debate, which ultimately concerned the moral hierarchy of identifying threats to international peace and security. Thus, the 2005 agreement must be understood as reinforcing existing, but fragile, state agreement as to the potential of mass atrocity crimes to threaten international peace and security, rather than an attempt to create a new responsibility founded on respect for human dignity and common humanity. The R2P agreement does not therefore demand that states recognize the core crimes of R2P as always constituting threats to international peace and security, but it does add to the political pressure on states to consider such crimes on a case-by-case basis. As Brown (2013, 440) has acknowledged, "states do not simply clear their in-trays and abandon all other considerations when faced with gross violations of human rights." In this sense, the UNSC's primary responsibility remains the maintenance of international peace and security, whereas the R2P mainly provides enhanced legitimacy for mass atrocity crimes to be viewed as direct threats to peace and security.

The UNSC's ability to activate responses remains premised on a "political assessment of what constitutes a threat or breach of peace and security," and this has contributed to the ambiguity surrounding the ability of the R2P to remain impartial and consistently operationalised (Tacheva and Brown 2015). In this regard, it makes sense to view the R2P as representing a distinctly pragmatic framework of protection, defined by a "duty of conduct" that at a minimum generates a "responsibility to consider" the appropriate action concerning all incidents of mass atrocity crimes (Welsh 2013a). While this more pragmatic interpretation of the R2P is clearly an attempt to shrink down the influence of moral obligations, the framing of a theoretical "responsibility to consider" must also be understood and interpreted through the language of common humanity, which informs our ability to recognize why we should consider the harm of mass atrocity crimes in the first place. As this chapter will further outline, the R2P agreement places the pressure for change not on a new legal expectation but on the normative force of our humanity. Consequently, what the 2005 R2P agreement has left open is whether the UNSC is expected to take action "if it finds that national authorities are manifestly failing to protect their population from mass atrocities even without making a finding of a threat to the peace" (Nasu 2011, 413). At the core of R2P debates since then has been contestation over when atrocities committed domestically should trigger the Security Council to recognize such actions as a threat to international peace and security.

WHEN TO PROTECT HUMANITY – CONTESTING THE EXPANSION OF THREATS

To what extent has the more formal recognition of an expanded understanding of what constitutes a threat to international peace and security, as articulated in the WSOD agreement, affected state identification of mass atrocity crimes and action to address them? In considering this question, it is vital to analyze how the concept of humanity has become increasingly integral to the perceived motivating capacity of the R2P, as advocates attempt to challenge past collective failures to protect. It will therefore be argued that the 2005 agreement has so far had a relatively limited impact on the UNSC's willingness to more consistently expand its understanding of threats to international peace and security. Despite the unanimous agreement achieved by states regarding the 2005 WSOD, there has been pushback against the implications of that document by major states in the years since, most significantly with regard to the scope of international peace and security.

One can highlight a notable example of this pushback in the Russian response to a 2008 UNSC meeting on Peace and Security in Africa, concerning the potential imposition of sanctions on Zimbabwe, following the violence and human rights atrocities committed by the Mugabe regime. Russia spoke forcibly against recent attempts by member-states to highlight threats, viewing these as beyond the UN Charter's understanding of international peace and security. Russian ambassador Vitaly Churkin argued that "we have of late seen an increasingly obvious attempt to take the UNSC beyond its UN Charter prerogatives and beyond the maintenance of international peace and security" (UN 2008). This line of attack was challenged by a number of other UNSC members at the time, including Panama, which stated that "in today's globalized and interdependent world, the concept of threats to international peace and security has evolved to include situations in which there are serious and widespread violations of human rights" (UN 2008). The imposition of sanctions was subsequently blocked by both Russia and China (alongside elective members South Africa, Indonesia, and Libya), following claims that the situation in Zimbabwe did not threaten international peace and security and must be recognized as a domestic issue (UN 2008). Russia and China's pushback against expanding the application of the UN Charter reinforces the idea of a hierarchy of threats to peace and security. Both these countries argue against a blanket expansion of threats to peace and security; in their view, serious human rights abuses are but one potential threat to peace and security, not part of an overriding principle that would compel states to protect in all cases, bypassing state sovereignty. In this regard, while the 2005 R2P agreement formalized a political responsibility to recognize mass atrocity crimes as threats to international peace and security, it did not place a definitive moral obligation on the major powers to always put threats to humanity and human suffering above other pressing security concerns.

In light of the ongoing disputes over the identification of threats to peace and security, and the potential deadlock within the UNSC on this matter, the UN Secretary-General reopened the debate over the UNSC's primary obligation. In the Secretary-General's 2009 report, "Implementing the Responsibility to Protect," he argued that the UNSC has the *primary* responsibility for maintaining peace and security but not the *sole* responsibility (Ki-moon 2009). That is, where the "perpetration of crimes relating to the responsibility to protect may not be deemed to pose a threat to international peace and security," the UN General Assembly "can then address such issues when the UNSC fails to exercise its responsibility with regard to international peace and security because of the lack of unanimity among its five permanent members" (Ki-moon 2009). This refers back to a key principle in the ICISS report: that the UN should be able to seek support for military action from the General Assembly. When the UNSC is divided, an "Emergency Special Session" can be called under the established "Uniting for Peace" procedures; the General Assembly can then, with a two-thirds vote in favour of action, confer legitimacy on a possible intervention and encourage the UNSC to rethink its own position. This does not create a legal right to use force, but it did bestow some legitimacy on any subsequent action and thus represents a direct criticism of the veto power (Gallagher and Ralph 2013). The Secretary-General's return to this principle reflects an ongoing battle within the UNSC regarding its ability to forge consensus on threats to international peace and security as well as the ambition that "we can, and must, do better. Humanity expects it and history demands it" (Ki-moon 2009). This debate thus reflects the ongoing struggle between our common humanity and the limited political will among states to drastically change their behaviour on moral grounds. To explore this debate, we now turn to two of the most significant R2P cases since the principle was formally adopted.

Libya

Despite the often hostile reaction to attempts aimed at expanding the application of threats to peace and security after the 2005 R2P agreement, the 2011 intervention in Libya was heralded as a moment of clarity for R2P advocates: here, the R2P had made good on its promise of protection, compelling states to intervene collectively on behalf of the international community, with much fanfare (Thakur 2011a; Weiss 2011). Chesterman (2011) writes that perhaps more notable about the resolution was that the UNSC chose not to include language that characterized the situation as "exceptional" or "unique" in order to try and persuade skeptical states to support the use force in Libya. Instead, the resolution directly enforced the broadening of the UNSC's international peace and security mandate (280). The resolution plainly characterized the evolving crisis in Libya as "a threat to international peace and security" (UN 2011b). Yet even though the UNSC did not use the language of exception, conditions in Libya were in fact rather unique: there was a clear threat of mass atrocity, a short time frame, and agreement from regional actors (Bellamy 2011, 263–9). That the violence was imminent and bore some relation to previous mass atrocity incidents strengthened the case for action. For example, to help ratchet up concern and create pressure for an immediate response, the United States explicitly warned that Libya could become "another Srebrenica" (Adler-Nissen and Pouliot 2014, 901). Moreover, past failures to prevent mass atrocity crimes had significantly influenced Western leaders' motivation for involvement, most notably in the case of David Cameron (Blitz 2011). The framing of these moral arguments in terms of past historical examples was key to legitimizing NATO's actions; it also played down the R2P's role in such debates.

Despite the UNSC's gradual expansion of Chapter VII's definition of threats to international peace and security, up until 2011, states had not declared categorically that "a domestic mass atrocity is sufficient for authorising force"; rather, there needed to be "tangible evidence of a threat to international peace and security – meaning [a] cross-border dimension" (Graubart 2015, 207). Moreover, while the reference to the R2P within the 2011 Libyan Resolution 1973 reflected a move to address this lack of clarification, the appeal to Pillar I of the R2P was used mainly to reinforce the host state's responsibility to deal with such atrocities, and can therefore be seen as an attempt to *reconfirm* state autonomy and responsibility rather than that of the international community. As Dunne and Gifkins correctly point out, linking the R2P to Libya's responsibility as a sovereign state, instead of invoking the international community's collective responsibility, emphasized the continued controversy that surrounds the R2P principle. In the aftermath of the intervention, the decision to rely on the imminent threat of mass atrocity crimes, rather than the cross-border threat to international peace and security, remained contested, and this led to further friction in the UNSC regarding the limits of threat expansion (Graubart 2015, 215). The intervention itself thus displayed some similarities with the way unique and exceptional situations had motivated action against mass atrocities in the pre- R2P era.

As Hehir (2013b, 137) correctly points out, while the UNSC decision to adopt Resolution 1973 on Libya reflected the normative ambition and spirit of the R2P, it must be understood as part of a much broader "trajectory of Security Council responses to large-scale intra-state crises that predate the emergence of R2P." Thus, "the response to the situation in Libya is better understood as an aberration rather than the product of a new disposition and the harbinger of a new era" (158). Moreover, as Morris (2013) points out, "states did not cite R2P in the debates over Libya simply because it did not figure significantly in their thinking" (1273). In this sense, it marked only that the R2P had "become part of the context of UNSC deliberations" (Byers 2015, 113). It remained unclear whether the expansion of threats to international peace and security in this specific case would herald more consistent practice by the UNSC when it came to identifying mass atrocity crimes as clear threats to peace and security.

In the aftermath of the Libyan intervention, consistent opposition and skepticism continued regarding the application of force under Pillar III of the R2P. This emanated from a number of major powers, including Russia, South Africa, China, and India (Beresford, 2015; Bloomfield 2015; Averre and Davies 2015; Lee and Chan 2016). As the Syrian case will highlight, it seems that instead of clarifying how threats to international peace and security were to be identified, the Libyan example further divided states as to the parameters of threats, thus putting into question the limits of moral appeals to the motivational cause of protecting a shared humanity.

Syria

As anti-government demonstrations swept across the Middle East in early 2011, the Syrian government launched a violent crackdown on protesters, sparking a civil war. In August 2011 the UNSC expressed its concern about "the deteriorating situation in Syria." Months later, states began calling out the direct role of Al-Assad's forces in many of the attacks on Syrian civilians (UN 2011c; UN 2012a). Soon after, President Barack Obama in his 2012 State of the Union Address reinforced a stark message to Assad that he would "soon discover that the forces of change cannot be reversed and that human dignity cannot be denied." Tragically, this would not prove to be the case: the conflict escalated at an astounding rate, with millions of Syrians facing the threat of mass atrocity crimes. In contrast to Libya, the crisis in Syria was plagued by UNSC deadlock, with no agreement as to whether the situation represented a threat to international peace and security.

Despite a multitude of accounts of crimes against humanity and grave human rights abuses in Syria (UN 2014a), China and Russia both steadfastly supported the need to fully respect "the sovereignty, independence and territorial integrity of Syria." For them, defending these rights was essential to maintaining "peace and stability in the Middle East region, rather than complicate the issue" (UN 2012b). The position taken by Russia and China was harshly attacked by other members (UN 2012b), yet it was consistent with the 2005 WSOD, according to which, while states were required to consider mass atrocity crimes as potential threats to international peace and security, the ultimate responsibility for action remained within the UNSC's overall primary responsibility to maintain international order. That location allows states to prioritize traditional security threats over mass atrocity crimes and the alleviation of human suffering. A number of states did however directly question the positions taken by Russia and China, leading Germany to argue that the UNSC had "again failed to assume its responsibilities and to live up to its mandate to maintain international peace and security" (UN 2012b). The so-called failure of the UNSC is best defined as a moral and political one, in that no direct legal obligation had been broken; instead, the states' own normative positions had clashed, resulting in contrasting readings and interpretations of how best to meet the UN Charter's demands.

The confrontation over whether the Syrian situation amounted to a specific threat to international peace and security crystallized a growing division within the Security Council. At its heart, the question was about when peace and security trumped humanity and the protection of human beings from mass atrocity crimes. Newman (2016, 37) has pointed out that many of the states now rising in power and influence – China, Russia, India, Brazil, South Africa – are "markedly more conservative in terms of the balance between international order and individual justice." Rising powers are beginning to demonstrate rather forcefully that they will not be happy simply to be socialized into the existing international order – that is, they are not "norm-takers"; instead, they are ready to contest and resist certain interpretations of human protection norms as well as Security Council practices (Newman 2016). This changing international order has further complicated the R2P's normative progress as well as, indirectly, the cause of humanity that lies behind the principle's initial ambition.

Research into the rhetorical debates that shaped the Security Council actions on Syria clarifies this divide between competing visions of international order. States such as China and Russia that rejected intervention or any coercive measures against Syria sought to frame the conflict, including debate over it in the UNSC, as outside of human rights concerns and appeals to humanity (Medzihorsky et al. 2017). At various times, a number of members forcefully called out these tactics. In particular, Rwanda during a 2014 debate argued that "all of us must commit ourselves to putting action for humanity above inaction for interests. That is the only way we can honour the Syrian victims and show to a sceptical world that we, the members of the Security Council, have learned lessons from the past" (UN 2014b). This division was framed in similar terms by France during the same debates as one that ultimately required "overcoming our differences in order to focus on the aspect of our humanity we all share" (2014b). Such claims speak to the perceived self-interest and purposeful obfuscation that was argued to be driving the position of both Russia and China. Moreover, the disagreement between the P5 states concerned divisions beyond just the Syrian conflict; they must be seen as speaking to a broader normative confrontation between global conflict management and the prevention of mass atrocity crimes (Medzihorsky et al. 2017). Whatever the pros or cons of intervention in Syria, the council was most often divided on whether the atrocities taking place there were in need of any response by the UNSC.

One must highlight here how the case-by-case basis for implementation stated in the R2P often generates clashes between states over the best way to maintain international peace and security. As Welsh (2013b) acknowledges, "a form of inconsistency is built into the very text as a recognition that the UNSC is a political body and must deliberate, and various calculations will come into that decision." In other words, the very possibility of disagreement between the permanent members of the UNSC and their capacity to veto a draft resolution is "a core structural part of the Security Council" (Chan 2013, 881). Thus, while the 2005 WSOD agreement was central to reinforcing a political agreement between states to formally expand the identification of threats to international peace and security, it did so through the institution of the UNSC, which means that the implementation of the doctrine will always compete with a range of other factors when states are weighing the maintenance of international order.

However, in contrast to the lack of consensus in the UNSC concerning the situation in Syria, the UN General Assembly was able to pass a number of resolutions (UN 2012c; UN 2014c) emphasizing the threat the conflict posed to international peace and security, reminding the UNSC of its "primary responsibility for the maintenance of international peace and security and to take measures to put an end to all serious violations of international humanitarian law." The contrast between the two institutions further reinforces the complexities of the UNSC's primary responsibility to maintain international peace and security and the limitations to its ability to fundamentally shift its focus toward a more human-focused security outlook. Alongside the actions of the General Assembly, the UN Human Rights Council remained active, launching a commission of inquiry to examine failures to uphold the R2P (Welsh 2019, 67). The way international threats are weighed in the UNSC has since caused many to question its decision-making process, which has so often placed the impact of mass atrocity crimes and human suffering below more traditional state-centric security threats. As Fraser (2014, 212) has argued, the lacklustre international response to the Syrian crisis can be seen as "symptomatic of the general inconsistency with which the UNSC refers to R2P in its determination of international peace and security." This has led some to suggest that "the R2P does not have any implications for the decision-making in the SC" (Oellers-Frahm 2014, 206). Such claims speak to the challenges the R2P has faced in its attempts to alter the decision-making process of states when it comes to identifying potential threats to international peace and security.

Summary

The two examples discussed here highlight how Russia and China, in particular, have often perceived core international crimes as not always needing to constitute a central focus for the UNSC (Botte 2015, 1036). Some may argue that the cases highlighted here represent critical national interests, and as such, potential military intervention may have only made the situation worse. But it is still important to remember that the resolutions vetoed by Russia and China on Syria "did not call for anything approaching military intervention" but instead were meant to "impose economic and political sanctions" (Hehir, 2016, 177). Decisions to address threats to international peace and security do not always have to involve the imposition of force; a number of other coercive options that are part of R2P's Pillar III would not threaten state sovereignty as directly. Accordingly, the contestation over the Syria cases speaks much more to the limitations of moral advocacy when it comes to limiting humanitarian harm; military intervention is not always in play in such discussions.

For prominent R2P advocates such as Simon Adams (2015), Executive Director of the Global Centre for the Responsibility to Protect, the Syrian crisis in particular has been a significant failure for the UNSC, due for the most part to the UNSC's failure to sufficiently recognize the Syrian government's actions as direct threats to international peace and security, this despite the later consensus over Resolution 2170, adopted to recognize ISIL and Al-Qaeda affiliates as threats to international peace and security. This same point is highlighted by Ainley (2015, 42), who acknowledges how consensus was relatively swift in regard to undertaking airstrikes against ISIL, which were justified as anti-terrorist measures. Yet this remains in sharp contrast to the reluctance of states to forge agreement on action to alleviate humanitarian suffering in Syria. These points draw attention to the current formulation of the UNSC's hierarchy of threats to international peace and security, in which threats in relation to grave human suffering and mass atrocity crimes continue to be far down the list of motivating factors for action. This has led to the suggestion that the R2P is now "at odds with the complexities of the decision-making process of the UNSC and in particular, with the powers of the veto" (Cannizzaro 2014, 213). This in turn has reignited a number of normative debates concerning the moral influence of common humanity when it comes to the issue of Security Council veto restraint. As Hehir (2016) points out, the logic of veto restraint, and the concept of R2P itself, both rest "on the premise that the P5 can be convinced to change their foreign policy priorities so that they give more consideration to the protection and promotion of human rights" (175). Debates thus take on a circular logic in which the failure of humanity to drive sufficient consensus for action is met with further calls to change the decision-making process in order to reinforce respect and support for our common humanity and the need to act in its defence. This current situation brings to mind previous comments made by Wheeler (2002) in regard to humanitarian intervention, in which he argued that "changing the decision-making mechanism will not eliminate the challenge of balancing the moral imperative to use force to rescue imperilled humanity against the pragmatic question of whether force will succeed and do more good than harm" (134). All of this leads one to re-examine the limits of the motivational power of humanity. The concept remains integral to our understanding of mass atrocity crimes and to our capacity to reflect on and locate global harms; its ability to motivate shifts in state behaviour and action is arguably much more limited. Chapters 5 and 6 will discuss these matters in more detail, in theorizing the scope of humanity's current role in the process of negotiating responses to mass atrocity crimes.

While it is vital to recognize the R2P as a work in progress – a point that Gallagher (2015, 268) argues must be accepted by advocates and critics alike – there remains a surprisingly repetitive logic to the way debates about the R2P have continued over the past two decades. As disputes concerning the identification of threats to international peace and security have demonstrated, fierce disagreement continues over how to apply the UN Charter, which the normative motivational force of humanity has made only limited inroads in changing. How states interpret threats to international peace and security and what actions they choose to take is a function not just of narrow national interests but also of what Morris (2015, 420) views as "fundamentally different interpretations of the social obligations which P5 states hold," particularly in terms of how to manage the international order. This division further complicates the R2P's ability to generate institutional consensus within the Security Council; it also raises more complex questions concerning how to motivate the collective responsibility of the international community.

CONCLUSION

UN Security Council practice has evolved significantly over the past twenty-five years. What *has* been consistent throughout this period is that international crimes are not always considered threats to international peace and security. This is partly because, despite the normative and conceptual expansion of notions of what constitutes a threat to international peace and security, the UNSC still operates under the same rules that resulted in their failure to respond adequately to the massacres in both Rwanda and Srebrenica (Fraser 2014, 212–13). While the UN has clearly acknowledged a wide range of interlinked factors affecting security, many of these are viewed as generating traditional security threats only to the extent "that they indeed have an impact on 'security,' both conceptually and empirically" (Del Sarto 2006, 509–10). This is despite claims by advocates that the R2P has confirmed the expanded UN powers to support coercive measures, so that there is no need for "further clarification [as to] the Security Council's power to make such a decision" (Evans 2009). UNSC practice clearly draws a more complex picture than this. Over the past three decades, its members have at times chosen to expand their interpretation of threats to international peace and security, yet as this chapter has demonstrated, the creation of the R2P has not sufficiently solidified this practice. States are still selective regarding when to expand (and shrink) their responsibility to identify threats, instead of pursuing gradual and consistent expansion, and this challenges the often teleological understanding of the R2P's development. Furthermore, notwithstanding critics' fears that the broadening of responsibilities within the UNSC "would fundamentally alter the relationship between non-Western states and international institutions" and thus "undermine the UN" (Chandler 2004, 68–73), the R2P has not forced through significant change in UNSC procedures.

Where the R2P remains most contested, however, is in terms of how states recognize their responsibilities to others, in particular how they weigh the hierarchy of threats to international peace and security. This chapter has demonstrated how despite the general expansion of threats to international peace and security over the past few decades, the R2P has so far been unable to reinforce state adherence to a more expansive interpretation of threats to peace and security. The assumption that the R2P has put an end to debates concerning the parameters of threat identification in the UNSC is still wishful thinking on the part of advocates. Moving forward, the mixed performance of the UNSC in responding to mass atrocity crimes since the adoption of the R2P suggests that the challenge of generating sufficient political will remains a considerable obstacle to protection, in that states have continued to contest the moral and geographical scope of their responsibilities. Consequently, while the concept of humanity has remained integral to the R2P concept and its fight to change state behaviour, it is becoming increasingly limited in its ability to generate political will in response to mass atrocity crimes. As the next chapter will examine, while appeals to common humanity are often central to helping determine what we ought to do in a particular situation, the concept is not always sufficient to motivate us to actually do it. Thus, while the potential for change rests heavily on the normative credentials of humanity, the R2P's moral progress will be constrained, particularly in regard to building consensus for coercive measures under Pillar III.

5

Assessing the R2P's Motivational Capacity: The Role of Humanity

In his final report on the R2P as UN Secretary-General, Ban Ki-moon (2016) focused specifically on the ongoing challenge of mobilizing collective action to protect populations from mass atrocity crimes. Reflecting on a period of "retreating internationalism, diminishing respect [for] international humanitarian law and a growing defeatism about promoting ambitious agendas like protection," he made a final plea to member-states to "show greater resolve in defending and upholding the norms that safeguard humanity, on which the responsibility to protect rests" (18). At the core of his plea to member-states was the concept of humanity as an overriding moral imperative; states, he emphasized, have a moral obligation to generate consensus in situations of mass atrocity crimes.

As the last chapter examined, appeals to the concept of humanity have long been a consistent part of attempts to motivate responses to atrocity crime situations, with vastly inconsistent results (Zolo 2002; Zehfuss 2012). So there is a need to examine more closely the role played by that concept when efforts are being made to generate a consensus for humanitarian action.

This chapter begins by exploring the role of humanity as the key moral imperative behind the R2P project, examining the philosophical arguments that link humanity as a concept for locating universal human harms to its role as a moral imperative for motivating the prevention of such global harms.

The chapter's second section is structured around three contrasting hypotheses of humanity's role in the R2P conversion process. Here, humanity is conceptualized as either (a) as a rhetorical tool with no motivational qualities, (b) a means to redefine and humanize sovereignty in order to motivate support for the R2P, or (c) a motivating principle that diminishes in influence as the R2P principle is diffused into action. I then argue that the impact of humanity as a motivational factor diminishes throughout the R2P conversion process, which points to how state interests and identities have failed to directly internalize the cause of humanity when it comes to the question of how to respond to mass atrocity crimes. Thus, we can understand the diminished influence of humanity in such discussions by examining how states often appeal to competing moral and political responsibilities when attempting to address the broader question of how to respond. This suggests that the concept of humanity does not easily transpose itself from framing harm onto framing a response to harm. Put another way, the strength of humanity is currently found in its ability to locate moral harm rather than in its ability to motivate action.

The simplicity of the moral debates surrounding the idea of an R2P conversion process has so far led to an exaggerated presumption as to the motivational qualities held by the concept of humanity. As a consequence, many advocates of the R2P continue to focus on the need to remove the last remaining barriers to consensus, which would allow the concept of humanity to function effectively through the R2P framework. But as this chapter will highlight, it is not simply sovereignty or veto rights alone that diminish the sense of obligation created by the R2P; it is also the lack of imperatives associated with appeals to humanity. So if the R2P continues to be predominantly understood as a moral norm, one that relies heavily on the motivational capacity of humanity, then its ability to fully transform how the international community responds to mass atrocity crimes will remain severely limited. The chapter concludes by arguing that in order to move forward discussions regarding the limits of the R2P as a mobilizing principle, there must be space for a more critical approach to conceptualizing the constraining realities of international decision-making and the recognition of humanity as an increasingly contested source of moral responsibility.

MOTIVATING HUMANITY

Most often, the R2P literature simply assumes humanity's normative status and value, and/or leaves it unexplored. Because of this oversight, those who attempt to explain the process whereby the R2P can motivate state response to mass atrocity crimes have continued to fall back on the concept of humanity as the underlying moral imperative, without sufficiently theorizing its motivational capacity and impact. As R2P advocate Ramesh Thakur (2015, 23) argues, humanity functions as the source of the R2P's international responsibility and "demands an acceptance of a duty of care by all of us who live in zones of safety towards all those who are trapped in zones of danger." This idea of an interconnected global population, in which people owe obligations to one another, is presented as integral to the R2P project. Thus the R2P is conceptualized as "the normative instrument of choice for converting a shocked international conscience into decisive collective action – for channelling individual moral indignation into collective policy remedies – to prevent and stop atrocities" (23). In this sense, the R2P serves as a tool of conversion, one that helps the UN Security Council harness the collective will of member-states, thereby transforming moral outrage into timely and decisive action whenever mass atrocity crimes are being committed. One can flesh out this idea so that the focus is directly on how the emotional and moral concerns generated by the outbreak or potential outbreak of mass atrocity crimes can spur collective action by UN member-states. In this sense, the conversion process takes place when the moral indignation felt by states develops into an agreement to take appropriate action in defence of specific moral goals. The R2P is argued to streamline this conversion process by removing barriers to agreement among states.

It has long been assumed that this idea of the R2P as a moral norm for building support for protection practices at the international level is central to its very existence (Evans 2008a). As Jennifer Welsh (2016a) argues, the R2P was built on the principle that "by building and invoking a sense of common responsibility – shared by states and other international actors – more concerted efforts to prevent and respond to atrocity would be undertaken" (985). Also integral to this process of converting moral sentiment into collective action is the notion that the R2P has been constructed to reduce previous barriers to generating international consensus on responding to mass atrocity crimes (see chapter 1). In this sense, the R2P provides a framework within which the moral cause of humanity can be fully utilized to mobilize and galvanize the international community (Evans 2008a, 65). However, this rather simplistic normative framing of a distinct R2P conversion process overstates the presence of a clear moral lineage – from the conscience-shocking nature of crimes, to the implementation of action – whose purpose is to avert global and universal threats. Thus, states *may* accept in certain situations that mass atrocity crimes are of international concern yet still prioritize other factors over the potential harm to humanity caused by those crimes. As a result, there is still a distinct lack of engagement as to the critical dual function of humanity as a normative concept that can help both to locate moral harm and to drive protection practices. So we need to focus more attention on the complex interactions among morality, politics, and law in national decision-making.

PROTECTING THE IMPERATIVE OF HUMANITY

To begin to assess the motivational qualities of the concept of humanity, we must first address the significant link often made between the moral obligation on states to address and respond to mass atrocity crimes and the role humanity supposedly plays in underpinning this responsibility. From a cosmopolitan standpoint, it is argued that the acknowledgment of a common humanity translates "ethically into an idea of shared or common moral duties toward others by virtue of this humanity" (Lu 2000, 245). The idea that each person has an equal moral status thus grounds appeals to humanity and justifies humanity's protection. Yet appeals to humanity are most often invoked without delineating the elements of humanity that are worthy of protection and, furthermore, how the concept of humanity can generate specific responsibilities so to recruit actors to undertake human protection.

At its core, the R2P should be understood as relating to two sets of internal claims: one around the responsibilities of states to protect their own populations, and another around the roles and responsibilities of the international community to assist and respond (Bellamy 2015c, 162). However, as Welsh (2014b) has noted, the "source of the international responsibility was not clearly defined. Did it derive from law, or from broader precepts of morality?" (127). Welsh suggests that owing to the lack of legal obligations expressed in the ICISS report, the R2P is predominantly a moral imperative derived from our common humanity, and thus it is humanity that underpins the essential moral obligation of the international community to provide sufficient protection to those threatened by mass atrocity crimes (127). The R2P, it follows, does not focus simply on the need to better recognize the "intimate connections between systematic and widespread violations of the rights of civilians and the breakdown in international order" (Annan 1999b). It is ultimately a moral imperative built on the premise that there is something fundamentally significant about mass atrocity crimes that creates the need for us to appeal to a higher moral obligation, as well as to acknowledge that atrocity crimes cannot be simply contained and managed. Here, humanity is being used to ground the concept of a wider international community, one that is able to recognize "that community is equally relevant internationally as it is domestically" (Bulley 2010, 7). In this regard, continuing outbreaks of mass atrocity crimes are a reality that is fundamentally damaging to a collective value of humanity. Thus, as chapter 3 explored, it is not simply individual lives that are directly threatened by atrocity crimes; so too are collective universal values, which must also be protected. The global harms created by crimes against humanity thus constitute an attack on the shared concepts of humanness and humankind that enable humans to coexist. The concept of humanity, then, is central to the argument that states have a moral responsibility to act against such crimes.

What the R2P and those who promote and study its influence have so often failed to examine is the extent to which these claims to the importance of protecting the moral category of humanity can provide not just a way to reflect on the harm caused by atrocity crimes (Macleod 2012), but also a sufficient motivation for states to seek to convert moral outrage into appropriate action. As Kok-Chor Tan (2006) has argued, the R2P seems to take for granted the existence of a default responsibility to protect, with the only obstacle to this responsibility being the principle of non-intervention. However, one must recognize here that permissible is not the same as, and does not necessary lead to, obligatory (88). In taking for granted some sort of default responsibility, advocates seem to have overlooked the complexities of the moral debates that are integral to conceptualizing the R2P conversion process. In this sense, the concept of humanity plays a critical role as a moral frame, one that allows states to reflect on the collective harm of mass atrocity crimes while at the same time acknowledging a motivational force that demands action.

As Catherine Lu (2006, 191) has emphasized, part of the controversy around the previous norm of humanitarian intervention arose from "disputes about the claims of common humanity itself." In this sense, while in the R2P literature there remains a general presumption about the "widespread acceptance of the moral community of humankind"[1] along with appeals to the moral universalism of rights (Coates 2006, 75), contestation regarding how the motivational power of humanity interacts with and functions in relation to international law has long been a particular point of contention. This was highlighted most notably by debates surrounding the 1999 Kosovo intervention by NATO forces, in which the idea of a "higher law articulated by our conscience" was seen to identify justice with moral standards (Bain 2010, 35). But despite the development of the R2P concept, one can still point to debates over the extent to which the higher moral power of humanity should more closely guide Security Council decision-making and thus at times require states to embrace a more expansive understanding of the UN Charter. This came to the fore most notably in the UNSC discussions over Syria (see chapter 4).[2] The current R2P landscape today reflects a clear and ongoing disconnect between the moral sentiment expressed by states when mass atrocity crimes occur and the motivation for supporting collective action to address such crimes. One is left to question, still, whether the idea of a common humanity can be a "practical motivating force in a divided world" (Lu 2006, 91). So if we are to fully understand the barriers that remain to building consensus on converting international moral indignation into more effective responses to atrocity crimes, we must better understand humanity's role in this process and the extent to which the R2P interacts with, and is constrained by, competing normative values and interests.

DEBATING THE MOTIVATIONAL ASPECTS OF HUMANITY

There are three broad ways to hypothesize the motivational aspect/capacity of humanity and its relation to the R2P: (a) as a rhetorical tool with no motivational qualities; (b) as a concept that redefines and humanizes sovereignty in order to motivate support for the R2P; or (c) as a concept that is important to framing the impact of mass atrocity crimes but whose role is diminished as the R2P principle is diffused into action. I will ultimately argue that while humanity remains an integral moral concept for framing the harm of mass atrocity crimes, its motivational capacity can best be conceptualized as a diminished force, in that its ability to generate a clear moral obligation is undermined as it moves along the process of fostering consensus for action.

Humanity as Rhetorical

There have long been efforts to rebut appeals to humanity as morally inconsistent, from Carl Schmidt's (2007, 54) famous critique that "whoever invokes humanity wants to cheat" to more contemporary challenges that suggest appeals to humanity are applied in ways that "obscure[] that lives are valued differently" (Butler 2009, 50). All of this has often reinforced a basic assumption among skeptics of intervention that references to common humanity by member-states and their diplomats are mere rhetorical flourishes and that the concept not only lacks any sort of real motivational power but also does not reflect the ways in which individual actors interpret and internalize the impact of mass atrocity crimes on the international system as a whole. This apparent disconnect between rhetoric and reality has become a common theme in R2P analysis as scholars attempt to explain the often-conflicting universal support for the R2P through language and rhetoric, as well as the widely inconsistent application of its stated aims by member-states.

One possible way to explain all this is to simply conclude that the concept of humanity does not generate strong motivational drivers for R2P-type responses. As Gallagher (2016) explains, "states are made up of human beings and political elites may even invoke concepts such as humanity when constructing international agreements but this does not mean that common humanity exists" (349). In this sense, when we reject the idea of any deeper human connection generating solidarity between humankind, we are left to question the premise of the R2P conversion process as well as the very idea that shared moral outrage can drive collective action to protect. A rejection of humanity ultimately places greater emphasis on the need to isolate the R2P outside of moral and normative debates in order to fully assess the contradictions that currently exist between state rhetoric and action, and to focus on the underlying political factors driving state policy. I now examine this realist-focused approach to understanding the relationship between humanity and the R2P in more detail, before partly refuting it.

The starting point for theorizing such an approach is to acknowledge the power politics at play beneath the slogans (Gallagher 2016, 351) and to recognize that "the idealistic tone in some normative advocacy of R2P is mainly political: a discourse to shape political decision-making" (Harrison 2016). In this sense, the R2P's ability to build agreement for action in mass atrocity crime situations must be understood exclusively in terms of the political, with the normative concept of humanity functioning solely to legitimate political motivation; that is, it cannot be grounded as a moral goal to be put into practice. The motivation for acting is thus fundamentally understood in terms of the interests of powerful states, "who are themselves not subject to the 'universal' ethic of responsibility" (Moses 2013, 133). Moreover, the idea of the R2P as a neutral or anti-political concept is rejected alongside claims that state decision-making can be significantly "controlled by vague notions of an 'international community' directed by the conscience of humanity" (132–3). Consequently, the belief that the R2P is dominated by the underlying power politics has continued to be controversial; questions arise over the extent to which it has allowed states to dress themselves up in the language of protection and humanity as a means to implement strategies in support of their own interests (Hurd 2012b).

As Christopher Hobson (2016, 438) has highlighted, the revival of classical realist thinkers, Morgenthau, Hobbes, and Schmitt, has influenced new approaches to the R2P that firmly reject the concept's ability to supposedly "transcend politics." Political realists such as Matt Sleat (2016a) have called for a greater focus on the way "practices of politics work" in relation to the R2P, acknowledging that "almost any political decision will generate unintended consequences" and thus "acting with the best intentions of preventing evil in mind is no guarantee that we will not end up doing more harm than good." In response to this political reality, Sleat (2016b, 78) has argued that the R2P should not be understood as an attempt "to put a universally justified or justifiable moral programme into effect, but as the attempt to create very localised centres of legitimate stability and order in complex conditions of chaos, violence and disorder." However, in reducing the R2P to a purely political transaction involving the transformation of violent chaos into order and stability, this approach arguably overlooks how the concept of humanity is central to grounding the four major crimes of the R2P and our understanding of why certain acts are universally understood to constitute the most shocking of "international crimes." In other words, without an acknowledgment of the moral concept of humanity, we cannot fully conceptualize the full harm of mass atrocity crimes, particularly in regard to populations that have no choice but to experience and live with the consequences of such acts. Thus, as Papamichail and Partis-Jennings (2016, 87) have argued, there is a need to recognize that mass atrocity crimes have "a symbolic dimension as well as a practical one"; it follows that a normative understanding of humanity is key to any aspiration to "transcend the radically divisive and dehumanising aspirations of genocidal action." This requires us to recognize the need to separate the meanings we place on the concept of humanity, not simply as an appeal to the imposition of universal actions of protection at the expense of the underlying political dynamics, but also as an essential moral force for global harm recognition during discussions of implementation.

In this regard, humanity's relation to the politics of intervention practices is often set out in terms of a diversity of legitimate but potentially conflicting ethical considerations (Lu 2007, 945). That, however, does not equate to the idea that humanity should be thought of as devoid of value or merit. State decision-makers are often forced to choose between competing moral duties to a range of international norms, and this can result in "countervailing moral claims" overriding appeals to protection (Vik 2015, 22). However, whether or not we have a shared ideal of unconditional common humanity or agree on the actions performed in its name, the fact that we continue to ask "Should we act?" against the threat of mass atrocity crimes in the first place assumes that we do have some moral ideals and principles by which we choose to recognize and condemn certain acts as inhuman (Luban 2002, 99; Souter 2009, 46). In this sense, the recognition of a shared moral concept remains integral, for without it, the question of whether we should act in the face of mass atrocity crimes simply would not arise. Thus, appeals to self-interest and inconsistency do not automatically change the underlying moral sentiment merely because they may be exposed as self-interested and inconsistent (Papamichail and Partis-Jennings 2016, 94). It can therefore be argued that attempts to reduce the concept of humanity to a rhetorical cover for political self-interest significantly underplay the importance of humanity's role in reinforcing the assumed moral wrong found within the actions of the perpetrators of atrocities. However, the extent to which the concept can provide more than a reflective point of reference for locating universal harm remains much more contested.

Humanizing Sovereignty

It is often argued that the R2P redefined state understanding of sovereignty by connecting it to an idea of compliance to specific universal duties, thus demanding that states extend their responsibilities to others. This was meant to create a more "inclusive community of humankind" (Linklater 2016, 392). As a consequence, the construction of the R2P has been framed as a direct solution to past barriers to forging consensus for protection practices, by acknowledging that responsibility can transfer from the state to the international level based on the severity of the atrocity (Welsh 2012, 106). This has enabled today's states to claim a "higher authority than the merely selfish claim to a 'right of intervention,' and thus reinforces the idea of humanitarian protection as a higher normative goal of the international community" (Cunliffe 2010, 81). In this sense, the international community is now "answerable to a higher authority, that of morality," so as to reject the absolutism of traditional sovereignty (Hopgood 2014, 190). To challenge sovereignty, then, there is a need to "tap into a profound source of collective belief about the capabilities and duties of humans" (Mitchell 2014, 40). This suggests that humanity is a concept requiring protection and that the threats made against it create a state of exception requiring human agents to challenge such violence. In this regard, it is argued that the concept of humanity is what largely drives the desire to address the real or potential threat of mass atrocity crimes, making it possible to overcome the tension between sovereignty and the protection of human life (43). This theoretical position has led R2P advocates such as Anne Peters (2009a) to argue that

> conflicts between state sovereignty and human rights should not be approached in a balancing process in which the former is played off against the latter on an equal footing, but should be tackled on the basis of a presumption in favour of humanity. [513] ... It is my claim that sovereignty has already been relegated to the status of a second-order norm which is derived from and geared towards the protection of basic human rights, needs, interests, and security. [544]

In reference to the R2P, Peters (2009b, 155) therefore highlights this recharacterization of sovereignty as implying a now inherent responsibility to protect, thus further emphasizing the role played by humanity as the ultimate normative source of international law.

This argument suggests that humanity has fundamentally redefined the normative construction of state obligations under international law, with the result that sovereignty now works in favour of protection. Peters (2009a) has referred to this process as the "humanization of sovereignty," arguing that sovereignty should now be seen to "exist only in function of humanity" (513). However, as has been previously highlighted, the 2005 WSOD, which enshrined the scope of the R2P, was specifically constructed to "fortify existing legal commitments, as opposed to an attempt to transform international law or create new legal obligations" (Tacheva and Brown 2016, 442). So it is vital to acknowledge that in some circumstances the R2P can also help strengthen traditional state sovereignty claims. The R2P sought to bridge the principles of humanitarian intervention and state sovereignty, thus helping reject the idea that both must be in constant confrontation or that one simply trumps the other (Glanville 2013, 191). In this sense, the R2P can be viewed as an attempt to provide a more flexible negotiation between the demands of sovereignty and the protection of humanity, both of which have moral and legal justifications.

As Ban Ki-moon (2008) has argued, the R2P must be understood as an "an ally of sovereignty, not an adversary"; thus it seeks to "strengthen sovereignty, not weaken it." This point has been further emphasized through the increased link between the R2P and state capacity building, which is used to reinforce the sovereign power of states and their ability to provide protection to their citizens (Roach 2016, 408). The concept of humanity thus has a much more complex relationship with the R2P than has previously been highlighted: more traditional appeals to maintaining international peace and security through the reinforcement of state sovereignty can often be much more powerful motivators for the goals of protection and prevention. Humanity in this sense is not always the central normative component in the motivational process of implementing R2P responses, even if it may be essential as a reflective guide to locating universal moral harms in the first place.

However, there is a need to also challenge the perceived dichotomy between sovereignty and the protection of humanity, whereby from the early stages of the R2P's normative construction, it was sovereignty that was understood to constitute the key barrier to intervention. This led to claims that "states are resisting the implementation of the R2P on the same basis that they have baulked at previous intervention theories: that it presents a challenge to sovereignty" (Martin 2011, 156). However, as noted so far, the conditionality of sovereignty existed long before the creation of the R2P, and thus in many ways the explicit focus on sovereignty has often led to an exaggeration of its deleterious impact on intervention practices. Moreover, as Glanville (2013) has also highlighted, sovereignty was never meant to encompass absolute freedom of the state and has always been understood to entail legal and moral obligations (Glanville 2013). In this regard, Martha Finnemore (2008) reminds us that "sovereignty has hardly proved an insurmountable barrier to intervention and, in fact, has always been malleable and conditional in a host of ways" (207). Consequently, despite the decision to place the R2P under the collective security framework of the UN and the authority of the UNSC, the continued contestation regarding Pillar III practice suggests that sovereignty has never been the main barrier to the acceptance of the R2P principle, as is often assumed. This is perhaps best highlighted by the varied voting record of the BRICS states when it comes to endorsing the UNSC's authority to use force to contain the atrocities in Côte d'Ivoire, Libya, and Mali (Lee and Chan 2016, 185). Thus, while states may rely on sovereignty to rebut the application of the R2P in certain circumstances, that rebuttal is not necessarily because states believe sovereignty to be an absolute principle that cannot be challenged, but more because it has been legitimized as a concept that can be used to stand in for other interests – for example, maintaining balance-of-power interests – as well as for concerns over failed states and terrorism. As Michelle Bentley (2017) acknowledges, state actors appeal to sovereignty mostly because it "provides the best way of achieving their aims as opposed to normative adherence in the conventional sense" (568). As a consequence, there has continued to be a strong focus on the maintenance of sovereign authority, demonstrated by the growing consensus around the first and second pillars of the R2P.

This may ultimately signify that there are still often times when order takes precedence over justice within the international system, so that states privilege national interest and independence over the rights of individuals (Garwood-Gowers 2015, 316). In this regard, due to the ongoing suspicion of the R2P's Pillar III, for the most part relating to fears surrounding "attempts to impose a certain conception of justice on states," a more pluralist conception of international order has continued to also hold traction, directly challenging the idea of humanity's protection as the now overriding normative responsibility (316). Thus, rather than being part of a distinct process of humanizing sovereignty, the R2P is in fact working to both reinforce sovereignty in certain cases and challenge traditional interpretations of sovereignty in others.

As the UNSC is currently formulated, its resolutions referencing the R2P usually focus solely on Pillar I of the doctrine, that is, on the primary responsibility of member-states to protect their populations from mass atrocity crimes. This further emphasizes the centrality of sovereign power to address such crimes. However, as James Pattison (2015) has argued, the creation of an international responsibility to protect must be understood as the "most important and value-added element of the responsibility to protect doctrine" (193). Hence, the R2P can be seen to have generated significant discussion around the responsibilities states should share as defenders of both international peace and security and protectors of "our common humanity." The concept of humanity is therefore still integral to reinforcing this added moral claim that the international community has a responsibility to protect those threatened by mass atrocity crimes and not just their own populations, along with the idea that in certain circumstances, sovereignty must be challenged and overruled. As William Bain (2010) points out, "a theory of obligation is required to connect sovereign as responsibility with the international responsibility to protect" (26). Appeals to such an obligation are in this way enshrined in a belief in the higher authority of humanity, so as to demand certain actions irrespective of shifting state interests. Consequently, while the R2P seeks to strike a balance between supporting and reframing state understanding of sovereignty, at its core it also refers to "global responsibilities that can only be met by sacrificing national interests" (Ralph 2017, 45). This idea of sacrifice can thus be linked back to protecting the dual conception of humanity outlined in chapter 3, which reinforced the core global harms generated by crimes against humanity. Yet while the R2P has clearly attempted to expand the UNSC's circle of empathy by broadening its focus beyond the state so as to encompass the protection of individuals, it also remains the case that this belief has not been deeply institutionalized, especially on the national level, and thus "many of us still don't see a moral relationship to a distant other" (Marlier and Crawford 2013, 413). If the R2P is to address occasions when host states remain indifferent to or complicit in mass atrocity crimes, it is important to motivate the member-states of the international community to rethink their immediate national interests.

As this section has outlined, the relationship between humanity and sovereignty in supporting the R2P concept remains distinctly fluid: the R2P has not simply redefined sovereignty through greater appeal to specific obligations generated by the concept of humanity. In this sense, rather than see the R2P simply as igniting a debate that plays off claims in support of humanity's protection against those of state sovereignty, it is much more the case that the complex layers of responsibility contained in the R2P principle reinforce distinctly separate normative claims in different situations. Furthermore, as Melissa Labonte (2016) argues, it has never really been the case that "sovereignty and non-interference" pose the "predominant obstacle to saving strangers – political will has" (142). Thus, it remains critical to highlight that while a strong commitment to principles of human protection is in theory not incompatible with territorial sovereignty, the ability to motivate states to respond to atrocity crimes beyond their borders still requires a clear acceptance of moral sacrifice – an acceptance that continues to be hard to generate. Thus, the R2P has so far struggled to fully reinforce the principle of humanity as a consistent motivational component reshaping state decision-making at the international level.

The Diminished Impact of Humanity

One of the most important ways in which the motivational force of humanity is seen to function is in regard to its role in securing a "moral bite." The idea of "a moral biting point" was referred to in the 2001 ICISS report, in which it was argued that "getting a moral motive to bite means, however, being able to convey a sense of urgency and reality about the threat to human life in a particular situation" (71). Put another way, a moral biting point assumes there is a direct and consistent relationship between shock and the motivation to respond, in which a certain threshold can be reached at which point the R2P overcomes competing state obligations and reinforces states' responsibility. This is reflected in the appeal made by John Roth (2016), in which he suggests that for the R2P moving forward, improving the odds that moral motives will bite "depends significantly on respecting and heeding the conscience-shocking calls for action" (160). However, as Bain (2010) has argued, the problem "is not found in the challenge of connecting the urgency and reality of particular situations with an appropriate (moral) motive [but in] an over-emphasis on 'responsibility' which, for all its attractiveness, cannot bear the weight placed on it" (45). Subsequently, when one examines the later stages of the process whereby states go about generating the required consensus to take action, this most often involves a complex web of empirical and structural concerns rather than a singular overriding moral threshold that begins to dictate such decision-making (Hehir 2016). As the UNSC's (2014b) deadlock in addressing the Syria crisis exemplifies, several initial statements called for action for humanity to be elevated above inaction for interests, but appeals to the higher moral goal of protecting humanity became increasingly muted as geopolitical realities and the complexities of dealing with the situation on the ground took hold (Ralph and Gifkins 2017). This suggests that the concept of humanity plays a significantly reduced role in framing the motivation for such discussions and that its influence on proceedings is limited by a range of competing constraints on state interests and behaviour. Thus, the moral bite of humanity arguably does not hold for particularly long and is loosened by many other factors.

This is clearly reflected in the metaphors we use when conceptualizing the moral decision-making process for generating consensus in situations of mass atrocity crimes. As George R. Lucas (2014) highlights, the metaphors most commonly used to explain the moral motivation for protection usually take the form of a "Good Samaritan" scenario in which a victim in dire need is brought to our attention, "promoting a felt need to render aid as the only moral decent response" (42). However, Lucas goes on to argue that such metaphors fail to capture the moral complexity of the most pressing cases of mass killing associated with genocide, which can be better theorized in relation to the domestic analogue of watching a neighbour suffer spousal or child abuse. Here, a clear feeling of discomfort and outrage generates a felt need to override the "sovereignty of the home and family in the interests of justice" (42). Yet despite this clear moral obligation to take appropriate action, we often wrestle with questions such as *how* the domestic intervention is to be carried out and *whether* we should avoid taking sides. We may thus let competing considerations override our belief in the clear moral wrong of the actions we have witnessed, due in part to the complexity of dealing with the situation effectively and the possibility that structural factors will result in further harm being done. Lucas also points to the longer-term issue of whether those intervening have "either the right or the requisite expertise to restructure the neighbour's family in order to prevent future violence" (42). This metaphor goes far to explain how, on its own, our felt humanity for those suffering horrific crimes does not instantly override other pressing concerns.

Consequently, despite the reformulation of language and the normative focus brought about through the introduction of the R2P, the barriers to motivating consensus for action remain constrained by the same limits that have so often thwarted humanitarian causes in the past. In this sense, the political dynamics that condition when and where states may choose to respond to atrocity crimes mean that humanitarian norms are "still generally honoured more in their breach" (Labonte 2013, 157). Thus, as Linklater (2016) argues, "emotional responses to inactivity in the face of distant suffering remain weak" (403), with the result that the link between moral indignation and practical implementation is still fundamentally contested. Thus, the demands we place on the concept of humanity as an overriding motivational force can at times lead us to oversimplify moral decision-making. This is perhaps best encapsulated by Barnett's (2002) comments about the UN's failure to avert the Rwandan genocide: "Because the UN and other bodies cannot aid everyone, they must develop rules that tell them who they should care about and when they should care. They have to be selective Samaritans. Yet, all such rules are supposed to vanish in the face of crimes against humanity and genocide, at such instance moral distance should be horizonless" (18–19). What Barnett captures here is the clash between our moral aspirations and the limitations of the concepts and institutions we build to try and achieve the lofty ambition of "never again." In this regard, the very premise of the R2P conversion process, in which the moral threat posed to a common humanity is transformed into collective action, needs to be understood in the context of the moral limits of political life itself. As Finnemore (2008) argues, interventions are not just "difficult technically or logistically" (218); they are also difficult normatively, in that apparent normative progress "does not make dilemmas go away" (223). The R2P doctrine has thus been presented as a formula for responding to all cases of mass atrocity crimes around the globe in which the only barrier now faced is the reach of our collective humanity.

Yet in practice, the very belief in the power of humanity to override other interests and structures continues to undermine the R2P; belief in a supposedly uncontested moral principle has led to dramatically polarizing results. It is vital then to reflect on how universal ethical constraints are not simply moral; they are also deeply political and "dependant [*sic*] on the political will of states to ensure their effective implementation" (Boucher 2011, 358). Consequently, as Hobson (2016) responds, "there is value in seriously reflecting on the way vulnerability and violence operate in world politics and coming to grips with our limited capacity to understand and respond to it" (454). In this sense, by rejecting the R2P as a potential expression of humanity and an embodiment of linear moral progress, one can begin to disentangle the complexities of humanity's role in underpinning the central normative content of the R2P, while at the same time recognizing the limitations of humanity's motivational influence on the process of state decision-making.

The R2P may have been built on the premise of a common responsibility to generate more concerted efforts to prevent and respond to atrocities; yet just over ten years after the concept's adoption, UN Secretary-General Ban Ki-moon (2016, 8) was forced to admit that, "although Member States have repeatedly emphasized their support for the prevention of atrocity crimes, this has not been sufficiently translated into concrete support for preventive strategies." While we can often get bogged down in smaller debates concerning how states interpret specific elements of the UN Charter or the ineffectiveness of the current international legal architecture, the ability to address the deeper issue of political will has much more to do with the strength of the moral principles we emphasize so strongly. Thus, the fact that genocide and crimes against humanity trigger our moral attention and offend our sense of responsibility, yet so often do not translate into effective and timely response, cannot be understood as solely a failure of political institutions. Instead, it suggests a limit to the efficacy of moral outrage generated by mass atrocities to fully motivate us to negate other pressing moral responsibilities. As Vik (2015) explains, "despite the universal agreement that 'something must be done,' we continue to accept excuses based on a pluralist limited understanding of moral responsibility to stand idly by while genocide unfolds" (142). This leads one to reflect on the limits of the moral concepts in which we place our faith and on the complexities of attempts to realize such goals in the world of international politics.

CONCLUSION

Many critics view the R2P as having failed because it is either too expansive, thus too much of a challenge to sovereign integrity, or too minimalist, thus reinforcing the status quo (Welsh 2016a, 985). Debates continue over such themes, with scholars contesting whether the R2P has failed to be fully institutionalized since its adoption by the UN (Roff, 2013, 200) or whether the way the R2P has been institutionalized imposes onerous limits on its potential influence (Ercan 2016, 146). However, such analysis of the R2P's limitations arguably overlooks the bigger picture. For those trying to generate consensus for protection, the underlying dilemma is how to explain *why* states should respond to mass atrocity crimes. The concept of humanity has for centuries underpinned the normative and moral responses to this question, yet a simple belief in the moral righteousness of the concept does not effortlessly translate into the motivation to enforce prevention and protection practices. In light of the recent emphasis on the importance of mobilization, it has been important for this chapter to challenge the key assumptions surrounding that process for building consensus for action under the R2P framework. This is significant, for the assumptions made about the motivational qualities of humanity do not just impact abstract theoretical debates; they also frame and support practical claims in terms of our response to mass atrocity crimes. In this sense, if the concept of humanity is to remain an essential part of the language used by both diplomats and academics to support and justify specific decisions, then the salience of these claims must be sufficiently interrogated. Consequently, what is required moving forward is a greater understanding of how moral claims translate into quotidian political decision-making.

What this chapter has therefore brought to attention is the divide between the moral aspirations supposedly embedded in the concept of humanity and the extent to which humanity can function as a motivational rather than merely reflective concept. By rejecting claims that humanity is simply a rhetorical concept of no specific value, along with the assumption that humanity's motivational influence has redefined the role of sovereignty in relation to the R2P principle, I have argued that humanity can best be understood as a relatively diminished factor in the motivational process, whereby competing moral and structural factors undermine the apparent higher and singular goal of humanity's protection. This suggests an ultimate disconnect between the moral aspirations and obligations we assume are embedded in the idea of humanity and our belief that by constructing concepts that limit the influence of sovereign self-interest, the international community will become more effective in its averting and responding to mass atrocity crimes. Consequently, it is argued that there are clear limits to humanity's power that extend beyond competing claims of sovereign rights. Thus, addressing the issue of R2P mobilization requires us to move beyond the assumed dichotomy between sovereignty and humanity and re-examine the central tensions in the process of motivating humanitarian action.

This chapter has sought to reignite such critical reflection on the concept of humanity in order to better inform our understanding of the complex interactions among morality, law, and politics and their impact on state adherence to the principles of the R2P. Moving forward, this conclusion raises several pressing concerns as to the future trajectory of the R2P project. Perhaps most significantly, it raises the question as to how we can now best conceptualize the R2P's core function and purpose. If the R2P is fundamentally limited in its ability to function effectively as a motivating principle for galvanizing action when mass atrocity crimes break out, then what role can it play in terms of influencing how states respond to mass atrocity crimes? This will be the focus of chapter 6.

6

The R2P's Key Added Value: Rethinking Implementation and Reform

If the R2P has a limited ability to function as a motivating principle that can galvanize action in response to mass atrocity crimes, then what role or added value can the R2P provide in relation to the overall challenge of preventing mass atrocity crimes and protecting those who are targeted by them? Furthermore, what might this claim mean for how we understand ongoing debates over R2P reform initiatives moving forward? In response to these questions, this chapter offers a new conceptualization of the R2P's key added value while also challenging the current focus of reform initiatives. In doing so, it reaffirms the case for a renewed focus on the role of political will and its interaction with moral and ethical concerns in a changing global order. Central to this chapter's core argument is the claim that appropriate mechanisms for addressing mass atrocity crimes are available to UN member-states yet their application has been inconsistent as well as at times contradictory. This suggests that the international community's ability to respond effectively to mass atrocity crimes is most often connected to a lack of consensus for generating sufficient moral sacrifice in light of other competing national interests,[1] rather than to direct procedural concerns that create a divide between how states wish to respond and the realities of upholding the UN's institutional framework. Any action taken individually or collectively by states to address mass atrocity crimes is in part an acknowledgment of a responsibility to others beyond their own borders. Such action may place at risk a country's resources and even the lives of its own soldiers. Because a response always entails some form of sacrifice, states must weigh competing moral, political, and legal questions when deliberating how to respond. However, while states have over time developed a body of laws and institutions designed to generate duties for states to respond to mass atrocity crimes, enforcement is left either to individual states or to the even less specific "international community." Consequently, the duty to respond is left open, with no state or group of states designated as having the overall responsibility. The result is that competing moral, political, and legal pressures coalesce to determine whether any action does takes place. Why, then, do certain competing duties dominate others? Answering that question will help us find better ways to strengthen the normative ambition to protect common humanity from the global harm of mass atrocity crimes.

The argument in this chapter has four sections. First, I examine a range of competing approaches from the current literature that seek to locate the key added value created by the R2P concept. Debates concerning the R2P's added value have been framed largely around how the principle has changed specific aspects of state behaviour over time, whether as a distinct rallying cry or as an evolving policy agenda focused on prevention. In challenging these two broad approaches, this section highlights the need to recognize the limits of a developing international collective will and the ongoing complexity of constructing new, prevention-based initiatives. The second section puts forward a new theoretical conceptualization of the R2P's key added value, with the concept understood as predominantly a "negative accountability claim." It argues that the R2P provides a moral framework within which states can more easily trigger debates over the question of "why we aren't protecting." Underpinning this new conceptualization of the R2P's added value is thus an assertion of the critical importance of humanity as a benchmark for universal claims to protection, reflected in the language and tactics used for challenging the failure to respond. Despite the R2P's function as a trigger for discussion, it has at times been sidelined as an approach for spurring action when mass atrocity crimes break out. Thus, I argue that the R2P works mainly by increasing moral and political pressure on state actors to consider a response to mass atrocity crimes, in this way reinforcing limited accountability claims on other states to at least try to do something. The R2P has struggled to generate further compliance pull on state actors, and this has left a significant gap between rhetoric and action.

In light of this assessment, the third section of this chapter assesses the implications this has for R2P reform initiatives and the emerging security dynamics of a changing global order. Most of the reform initiatives put forward by R2P supporters and critics have focused mainly on the UNSC's decision-making procedures and the challenge of addressing the trade-off between humanitarian objectives and state sovereignty. It will be vital to interrogate how moral imperatives interact with political and legal pressures to influence the motivational consensus for generating sufficient political response. In this sense, the current limitations of the motivational pull of humanity can be seen to have significant implications for those trying to explain the current R2P implementation gap. That gap is generated not simply by the failure to design and construct effective laws and institutional arrangements but also by the complexities of state decision-making, which are influenced by a range of competing demands and normative impulses in mass atrocity crime situations.

In its fourth and final section, this chapter focuses on the need to rethink the idea of political will and its relationship to state mobilization. It will argue that we must appeal to a more expansive understanding of political will that is more conscious of how a variety of humanitarian protection norms interact and compete with one another and the impact this has, not just on the R2P concept understood in narrow terms, but also on the goal of protection and prevention more expansively. This requires states to work collectively in calling out the hypocrisy of narrow state interests when it comes to addressing a range of humanitarian challenges. This is particularly crucial during a time of change in which liberal and cosmopolitan values are increasingly being challenged in a more polarized and contested global order (Ikenberry 2018). For humanity to be defended, states must assert more effectively the costs of inaction and work collectively to better link the prevention of mass atrocity crimes to a wider conception of national interest. This chapter, then, argues that we must develop a more ambitious approach to the challenge of mobilization, one that moves past the sovereignty-versus-humanity debate. In doing so it will be possible to more closely reflect on the way humanity, law, and politics interact at the global and national levels. The final chapter will focus on how we can then begin to develop practical drivers and initiatives for change.

DEBATING THE R2P'S "ADDED VALUE"

As the previous chapter highlighted, a key perceived strength of the R2P is often thought to be its ability to help "trigger international action" (Thakur 2011b), a process defined by the R2P's ability to convert moral shock into policy action. This line of argument was strongly supported by one of the R2P's original founders, Gareth Evans (2008b), who declared that the R2P "was devised as a new rallying cry" whose language of responsibility would help generate more effective, consensual responses to extreme, conscience-shocking cases. In this sense, the R2P needs be utilized to "elevate a particular crisis above the crowd of normal international political issues and demand some form of response" (Bellamy 2014, 68). Through this process of threat elevation, convergence can then be built between competing advocacy groups so as to support and mobilize decisive action (Lanz 2011, 241). According to Evans (2015), the R2P was established to "energise effective collective action by generating a new consensus reflex among international policymakers" (16). This view of the R2P as a catalyst for action is thus framed in opposition to previous incidents of state inaction in the face of mass atrocity crimes, in that the future success of the norm must now be measured in terms of the decisiveness of the global response to the "next conscience-shocking case of large scale killing" (Evans 2008a, 53). This interpretation suggests that the R2P works best as a bespoke answer to the challenge of motivating global protection practices, in that the threat of mass atrocity crimes has been elevated above the noise of everyday politics, creating an environment in which the politics of exception can be allowed to drive action and response. In this sense, mass atrocity crimes must be seen as not part and parcel of international life but as exceptions requiring a different type of response.

However, this idea of the R2P as a signifier of political exception has proven to be relatively ineffective as a tool of motivation. While challenging the moral consistency of the R2P's claim to convert shock and outrage into collective humanitarian action, this book has directly challenged the arguments made by both Evans and Thakur in particular concerning the R2P's central purpose. Both authors recognize that simply because intervention would be permissible or legitimate does not mean it will automatically occur, or even that it should occur, yet they still trace the motivation for the initial response back to the connection between humanity and the R2P. Consequently, as argued so far, the ability to locate universal human harms does not directly reinforce and reify the motivational capacity to take action on behalf of our common humanity. As the last chapter concluded, this divide in our understanding of humanity and its relation to the R2P requires us to rethink how to conceptualize the purpose of the R2P moving forward in light of this conclusion. It is vital, then, to also address the range of approaches put forward by other prominent R2P scholars who do not fully subscribe to Evans's and Thakur's "rallying cry" theory.

The R2P as a Policy Framework for Prevention

In rejecting the rallying cry thesis put forward by Thakur and Evans, Alex Bellamy (2009, 4) has argued that the R2P can have the most impact as a broad policy agenda increasingly focused in the area of atrocity prevention. Bellamy (2013) has argued that the R2P is a habit former and that it has been able to contribute to "changes in the interests and identities of states" (346) as they begin to internalize the goals of the R2P within their own domestic and international views. Through this long process of internalization of community standards, states eventually take it for granted that the protection of populations from mass atrocity crimes ought to be a matter of global concern, thus helping reshape international affairs (Bellamy 2014, 72). It is important to recognize here that Bellamy's interpretation of the R2P as a distinct policy agenda is directly at odds with attempts to categorize the R2P as a catalyst for action. He argues that the R2P has "little utility in terms of generating additional international political will" and thus the R2P must be employed as "a diplomatic tool, or prism, to guide efforts to stem the tide of mass atrocities" (Bellamy 2010, 166). Based on this argument, the primary goal for the R2P must therefore be the prevention of mass atrocity crimes in the first place; moreover, the key long-term test is "whether there are fewer cases of mass killing to respond to" (Bellamy 2010, 162). In this sense, the R2P is being asked to do more than simply galvanize political will when mass atrocity crimes break out; its aim, rather, is to fundamentally shift how states conceptualize the impact of such crimes on their own values and conceptions of human security.

Bellamy believes that the R2P has so far had little impact as a catalyst for action in part because of specific political and contextual issues that surround decision-making when mass atrocity crimes break out. It is argued that despite the plausibility of the arguments put forward and subsequent appeals to shared normative obligations, it is most likely that "contextual variables" will exert greater effect regarding whether consensus on intervention will be achieved or not (Bellamy 2013, 342). The suggestion, then, is that the internalization of the R2P by states will eventually lead to a world where the need to drum up motivation in light of a crisis will become a consistently less frequent occurrence. This for Bellamy is the best way to mitigate the complexities of multiple state obligations and interests that have to be managed in crisis situations. Those complexities can severely limit the ability of the international community to generate consensus for appropriate action.

Yet perhaps Bellamy is significantly overestimating the complexity of prevention itself and the idea of it being much less controversial than other humanitarian responses of protection. In this sense, it has often been argued that given the major difficulties inherent in attempts to generate responses to atrocity crimes as they occur, a focus on prevention will help bypass the significant challenges of competing interests and contestation over authorizing protection practices. However, as Welsh (2016b) has rightly emphasized, "prevention is in fact a controversial practice" in spite of the "universal rhetorical commitment to its prioritisation" (216). One can highlight the political contestation surrounding such practice in reference to the case of outbreaks of violence in South Sudan, where Western states demonstrated a significant reluctance to directly confront "local actors over escalating inter-communal hostility and serious human rights violations" (Welsh 2016b, 225). Moreover, even R2P "success" cases such as Kenya were never discussed formally on the agenda of the UNSC, thus demonstrating how atrocity situations are still often presented as "an internal matter for that state, and not a legitimate concern of the international community" (Welsh 2016b, 225). Furthermore, as Melissa Labonte (2016) argues, a shift in focus toward "prevention and capacity building, early warning, and international assistance may well obscure rather than strengthen the regulative effect of the R2P" (144–5). In this regard, it is often assumed that "norms of prevention and response are mutually exclusive" and thus both can be seen to "exude strong compliance pull among state and non-state actors" (145). However, this underestimates the challenges prevention creates in terms of the inherently intrusive character of certain preventive strategies, which can exacerbate domestic tensions through increased international involvement, as well as the difficulties of trying to locate causal patterns in how atrocities unfold. As Aidan Hehir (2015a) suggests, simply highlighting that potential triggers exist in a society "does not in itself catalyse action." (86). It can thus be argued that Bellamy's approach still relies heavily on the role of contextual variables, despite such factors being integral to his original concerns regarding Evans' rallying cry thesis.

Overall, both Evans and Bellamy underplay the challenge of motivation and the extent to which the R2P has struggled to bypass many of the previous obstacles to prevention and protection. Evans (2008b) argued that the decision to embrace the new language of the R2P was all it should take to start generating effective consensual responses in a way that the previous language of "right to intervene" could not. Yet taking stock of the analysis highlighted so far, it is clear that the shift in language has not created a pathway through which states can now avoid the constraining impact of long-term debates over the how, when, and why of intervention practice. Likewise, for Bellamy, the move to reinforce a need for greater involvement in prevention has not been a silver bullet for success. More recently, Bellamy (2020) has conceded that the track record of the past decade has shown that governments have consistently failed when it comes to adopting measures needed to prevent mass atrocities. As Ban Ki-moon (2016, 8) reminded states in his final R2P report, "although Member States have repeatedly emphasized their support for the prevention of atrocity crimes, this has not been sufficiently translated into concrete support for preventive strategies — even when there have been credible assessments of imminent threats to populations." The crux of the problem remains the difficulty in motivating change in state behaviour and an inability to successfully conceptualize how the R2P can function as a motivator for this change. States have thus remained cautious, particularly when it comes to decisions to spend tax revenues or place their own soldiers at risk, about helping to protect populations in other states from mass atrocity crimes. What is required to address this reality is a more macro understanding of the R2P's critical added value, which would better reveal the concept's current limitations and weaknesses.

The R2P as Constraining and Constituting Interests

In response to Bellamy's strict focus on the role of prevention and Evans's emphasis on the R2P as a rallying cry, a number of R2P advocates have conceptualized the role of the R2P in much broader terms. Most prominently, former R2P special adviser Edward Luck (2010) has acknowledged that when prevention does fail, the R2P must succeed in "generating the will and capacity to respond effectively to the failure to prevent" (351). Luck claims that the two functions need not be incompatible and that the R2P should be able to function as both a policy agenda that can help reinforce state prevention practices and a rallying cry for action during the immediate outbreak of atrocities

(357). Yet in highlighting the need for the R2P to be both preventive and reactive, Luck ultimately fails to move much beyond the positions so far highlighted by Evans and Bellamy and thus doesn't advance the debate very much.

In contrast, regarding the R2P's key added value, Jennifer Welsh has taken issue with Bellamy's strict focus on prevention. For Welsh (2014b), one of the R2P's core functions is to "emphasize what is appropriate and to shine a spotlight on what is deemed inappropriate" (136). Based on this, she then argues that Bellamy takes an "overly minimalist view of the norms function" by defining R2P as a policy agenda rather than a rallying cry for action (136). She continues that the strength of the norm must also be measured "by the degree to which notions of protection are invoked by international actors during real or imminent crisis" (136). In this sense, the R2P must also be able to function as a catalyst for debate. What type of action follows from such debate will always be contested, but what Welsh (2014b) emphasizes is the duty for states to consider how the R2P framework might apply to such situations (136). This idea of a duty of conduct was fleshed out in a 2019 article by Welsh in which she argued that the international community must both identify when mass atrocity crimes are being committed or are imminent and deliberate on how a range of actors should respond. Captured in this idea is an area in which the R2P has been able to have some impact, in that even the staunchest of critics now suggest that it has become somewhat harder for states to justify inaction.

A similar idea is picked up by Luke Glanville (2016a) who has argued strongly that the R2P "has a very real and readily observable impact on the behaviour of states" (185). That impact, he contends, is most observable in the way in which states are now forced to make "tactical concessions and adapt their arguments to alleviate pressures to comply" (187), thus demonstrating that the norm has some validity; states are now beginning to view R2P issues as a matter of routine. Glanville has also argued that the current focus of debates, concerning whether the R2P is best framed as a rallying cry to action or whether it is working to reshape the identities and interests of actors, is ultimately misplaced. He argues that the R2P is in fact working in both these ways at the same time and thus "constraining the interests of some actors and constituting the interests of others" (187). His evidence for this claim is supported mainly by the Libyan example; here, he argues that states' decisions to adopt rather than block the resolution could in large part be explained by the ideals the R2P reinforces, that is, the idea that "the international community should do what it can to protect populations from mass atrocities" (193). The R2P, that is, forced states to reconsider how they framed arguments relating to atrocity crimes and how they went about challenging or supporting R2P-related proposals in the UN.

Both Welsh and Glanville assume to different degrees – and thus fail to engage with further – the role of moral imperatives, such as humanity, in providing the normative component underpinning the R2P. To what extend does an understanding of this crucial relationship between humanity and the R2P allow us to better explain the process of change brought about by the R2P so far, as well as the continuation of constraints regarding how the R2P can mobilize responses to atrocity crimes? Glanville (2016a) argues that decisions by states to adopt or not block a resolution connected to an R2P situation can be understood through the "power of the idea that the international community should do what it can to protect populations from mass atrocities" (193–4). The motivation behind this apparent international collective will is ultimately left untheorized by Glanville, and thus one is left to wonder whether it is possible to fully understand how the R2P is effecting state behaviour without also conceptualizing the role of the underlying normative ideals that are supposedly driving such change in the first place. In this regard, for Glanville, the power of the R2P comes from a universal feeling of collective responsibility that he believes states share. But to what extent can we view the international community as sharing such beliefs? And more importantly, how do moral ideals influence how we should conceptualize the R2P's key added value? Furthermore, while Welsh (2014b) is correct to highlight that the R2P must work alongside a range of competing considerations that are both normative and non-normative, the challenge of better understanding this complex web of competing obligations is left significantly underdeveloped, with no further engagement with the concept of humanity and the extent to which it may compete with or override other moral imperatives for action.

Furthermore, as William Burke-White highlights (2011), the strength of any norm or rule of international law can be measured by its ability to "alter the cost-benefit calculations, preference sets, or value choices of actors in the international system" (35); thus part of the challenge for R2P advocates has been to locate the core function of the norm and then address how the R2P can work to best influence state decision-making. Disagreements over the R2P's core function, whether understood as a policy agenda, a rallying cry, or a combination of the two, have at times clouded discussions concerning the depth of the R2P's influence on international policy-making and the potential effectiveness of the norm itself. Perhaps most significantly, R2P scholarship has tended to overlook questions concerning the overall global harm such crimes generate and thus the extent to which the R2P, as a distinct moral imperative, can influence how states, and the international community, approach discussions and practices of intervention. In this sense, there is a clear disconnect between debates around how the R2P changes international practice and why the R2P should pressure states to change their foreign policy calculus in mass atrocity crime situations.

THE R2P AS A NEGATIVE ACCOUNTABILITY CLAIM

In response to the limitations of the current debates so far highlighted, I want to introduce the idea of negative accountability claims. This normative concept can be used to better conceptualize the important added value of the R2P and further locate its potential to influence specific forms of state behaviour in response to mass atrocity crimes. By reconceptualizing the R2P in relation to the moral concept of humanity, it will be possible to reinforce the importance of ethical terms to the ways in which states communicate their actions and intentions to others (Frost 2009, 19). In this regard, rather than simply accepting that a shared universal feeling of collective responsibility is held by all states, one must examine how states are making use of universal moral language, for what purpose, and to what ends. Through this analysis we will be able to refine our understanding of the R2P's key added value in terms of its role as a negative accountability claim. This approach builds on the claims put forward by Welsh and Glanville, recognizing the importance of the R2P as a concept that can place political pressure on states to, at a minimum, discuss the outbreak of specific mass atrocity crimes; at the same time, it locates the R2P within the limitations of moral and normative arguments, rejecting claims that the R2P has so far made consistent progress in fundamentally changing the impetus for states to act in order to prevent mass atrocity crimes.

Furthermore, while Bellamy (2014, 72) has recognized the role the R2P has played in setting community standards and holding out the threat of criticism or exclusion, this approach also focuses on the central normative force that underpins the power of such criticism, namely the concept of humanity. It is this concept that actors claim states are accountable to, and thus there is a need to articulate how it interacts with the R2P principle. As this chapter will later explain, this theoretical reconceptualization will allow a more balanced assessment of the R2P's value to current debates, emphasizing its strengths as a framework for generating routine discussion and consideration of protection practices, as well as its limitations as a driving force for implementating such policies. This analysis will thus build on calls for greater expectation management (Gallagher 2015) regarding assessments of the R2P's impact on state behaviour and its future salience in a rapidly changing global order.

First of all, it is vital to substantiate what we can define as a negative accountability claim. The term can be understood in relation to the idea of "accountability for failure," in this sense: when a negative result occurs, who is to be held to account, and why? The politics of constructing a negative accountability claim against certain state actors have been dramatically reinforced by the creation of the R2P, with states most often appealing to its content in the breach (Doyle 2015, 11). In this sense, the R2P as a negative accountability claim must be conceptualized in regard to the idea of account-giving, whereby actors must increasingly explain themselves or their actions to other actors in response to failure, that is, inaction (Busses 2014, 39–40). Conceptualizing the R2P as a negative accountability claim thus makes it possible to more accurately pinpoint the impact the concept is having on international debates surrounding protection and prevention. This can be done by examining how states use normative appeals to humanity as part of ethical debates, in order to challenge and frame their responses to mass atrocity crimes, most often following the UN's failure to respond. As Andrew Linklater argues (2016), "demands for accountability can be issued directly, often more or less immediately, and those who are adversely affected by the actions of others may be able to mobilize public opinion by appealing to shared understandings of what is irresponsible or reprehensible conduct" (419). Accordingly, what the R2P can be seen to provide is a moral framework within which states can more easily trigger debates concerning the question of why we are not protecting.

As this book has so far emphasized, the concept of failure remains integral to the underlying normative power of the R2P. Critics like Lucas (2014) have therefore sought to conceptualize the R2P as "essentially a narrative of guilt on the part of dissident former UN diplomats," which is utilized to help "operationalize moral determinism more effectively" (37). This failure to act, along with the supposed moral inadequacy and complicity of states, has been consistently questioned by UN leaders, such as former UN Secretary-General Ban Ki-moon, who continually challenged the international community to live up to its responsibilities and obligations as part of the R2P agreement. Understanding the R2P as a negative accountability claim begins then with the recognition that "there is an international conversation happening on R2P, one that engages academics and policy-makers alike and reminds us of our global interconnectedness" (Falk and Skinner 2016, 504). In this sense, the R2P is fundamentally a political attempt to challenge global cultures of impunity and the clear lack of genuine accountability in regard to mass atrocity crimes; thus it serves as a moral challenge to member-states and the international community (Durham and Massingham 2015, 277–78). Yet in recognizing the R2P as a negative accountability claim, one must also accept that the R2P has often been a far more useful moral frame *after* atrocities have occurred, as states question the failures of the international community.

For example, while UNSC resolutions referencing the R2P have almost always focused on Pillar I of the doctrine to highlight the primary responsibility of member-states to protect their populations from genocide, ethnic cleansing, crimes against humanity, and war crimes, such claims cannot be seen to represent a substantial added value in regard to the development of greater global accountability for mass atrocity crimes. As previously highlighted, it is the idea of a shared responsibility to respond that is so critical to the R2P. In contrast, the responsibilities attached to Pillar I of the R2P can be more easily traced back to already embedded international law. Consequently, the R2P has generated the most important discussion around the responsibilities states should share as defenders of both international peace and security and the protection of our common humanity.

The concept of humanity is thus integral to reinforcing this added moral claim that the international community has a responsibility to protect those threatened by mass atrocity crimes, and not just their own populations. As a central component of the R2P's function as a negative accountability claim, humanity can be seen to provide a yardstick, or behavioural foundation, by which the international community has often attempted to rhetorically hold states morally into account. So whether states accept the notion of humanity or contest it, they are forced to grapple with it (Weinert 2015, 2). This is evident in a number of UNSC meeting records on the situation in Syria, most significantly the double vetoes by Russia and China in 2012 and 2014.

In response to the vetoing of the February 2012 resolution (S/2012/77) calling for an immediate ceasefire in the Syria conflict, many states fiercely challenged the idea that the international community had nothing to do with the atrocities taking place in Syria, as well as the Russian and Chinese positions on the issue; the representative for Pakistan argued that humanity was unfortunately still suffering from this outdated viewpoint (UN 2012b). Furthermore, following the Russian and Chinese vetoes over the referral of atrocities in Syria to the ICC, the concept of humanity was referred to on numerous occasions in the aftermath of the vote, most notably by Lithuania, which sought to shame those who stood against the referral, declaring that "today's veto is a stand on the wrong side of justice and accountability – a stand on the wrong side of humanity" (UN 2014a). The initial response to atrocities was thus in no way timely or decisive, and the Security Council was forced to concentrate its efforts on humanitarian assistance rather than direct protection from atrocity crimes (Welsh 2019, 67). The subsequent debates in the Security Council thus reinforced the way in which R2P was being utilized more to frame the failure to gain agreement to act as the driving motivation to respond.

The more recent decision by China to abstain and not to stand with Russia in vetoing a draft resolution condemning chemical weapons use in Syria (UN 2017) demonstrates a change in Chinese strategy that is in part connected to the increasing rhetorical pressure on the UNSC to not block potential action in response to the Syria conflict. During discussions, France in particular was quick to attack the Syrian regime, claiming that such acts broke "the most basic standards and elementary principles of humanity"; in this way, it reinforced appeals to the initiative to limit the use of the veto in the case of mass atrocities (UN 2017). In this regard, the concept of humanity has continued to be integral to the ways in which states justify why the international community should recognize shared obligations and values, as well as the moral imperative for states to challenge the actions and decisions of others. This is certainly reflective of what Frost (2009) has termed as "ethical contestation," in which a "central component of international interaction is a struggle for the ethical upper hand" (92–3). The R2P and the moral imperative of humanity that underpins it have thus become critical in raising awareness of humanitarian crises around the globe and in compelling states to acknowledge the impact of inaction and the need to do more when it comes to implementing protection practices. As a result, the R2P functioning as a negative accountability claim can be seen to have had a significant impact on how states now discuss the failure of the international community to respond to mass atrocity crimes, albeit its influence has arguably been most visible in examples of violation. As Bellamy (2014) previously acknowledged, the R2P has made it more likely that the UNSC will engage in discussion following the outbreak of humanitarian crises than it was during the Cold War. This has placed new normative expectations and pressure on states and has also led to greater use of naming and shaming tactics against state actors that are seen to have violated the principles of the R2P.

However, the generating of further dialogue and discussion among member-states has not directly addressed the gap that remains between commitment and action, demonstrating the limitations of ethical contestation in support of the R2P concept. As Pattison (2015) emphasizes, due to the generality and unspecified nature of the international responsibility to protect that state actors share, it is extremely difficult for any actor to hold others to account, particularly if they claim they have done what they can in such circumstances. It is argued that without more specific requirements, the international responsibility to protect will "not exert sufficient compliance pull on states and other actors" (196). Thus, though the international responsibility element of the R2P is arguably the most radical and significant added value, appeals to that responsibility have featured the least in R2P resolutions, in part due to lack of clarity concerning the scope of expectations for state actors to respond and the challenge of generating consensus. The enforcement of the international responsibility to protect relies more on the moral imperative of humanity rather than on a fixed legal obligation. As this chapter argues, the tools and institutional framework for addressing mass atrocity crimes are available to states; the question remains how to boost the importance of the responsibilities states have to humanity in their political calculations for action.

Moving forward, one must therefore examine how the R2P interacts with other humanitarian norms and the extent to which such interactions help reinforce an understanding of the R2P as a negative accountability claim. Kurt Mills (2015) writes that the R2P interacts with two contrasting state responsibilities in mass atrocity crime situations: the responsibility to palliate (provide humanitarian aid and assistance), and the responsibility to prosecute (international criminal justice) (223). Having tabled these two categories, Mills argues that the R2P functions most effectively as a marker of global concern, "which may then activate other responsibilities" (224). Consequently, "the responsibility to palliate and prosecute may sometimes only be activated if the R2P is invoked" and may even then be used as a substitute for the R2P (224). Mills here is highlighting the strength of the R2P as a trigger for discussion even while recognizing that the R2P is not necessarily the prism through which action will be taken.

In the case of Syria, the failure to generate political will in support of a coercive R2P response to the atrocities taking place in that country, and the vetoing of attempts to refer the situation to the ICC, meant that humanitarian assistance proved to be the only enforceable strategy. More than three years after the conflict in Syria began, the UNSC was finally able to adopt Resolution 2165 (UN 2014b), securing access for humanitarian assistance without the consent of the Syrian authorities. Yet while the UNSC did view the deteriorating humanitarian situation as a threat to peace and security, it did not choose to invoke Chapter VII (Rodley 2016, 200). The Syrian example thus highlights how the R2P has spurred moral concern, even though attempts to diffuse the R2P concept so as to encompass coercive enforcement measures have faced stubborn headwinds, even in the face of atrocity crimes.

All of this leads to an important question posed by Labonte (2013): "Why are humanitarian assistance and humanitarian diplomacy so often used as substitutes for political will, especially in direct cases where stronger measures appear to be both legitimate, responsible and practical to halt mass atrocity crimes?" (3). In light of ongoing diplomatic responses to the crisis in Myanmar (Smith and Williams 2021), this question remains critically relevant to today's discussion of the R2P's motivational capacity. Moving forward, the future salience of the R2P as a force for political change will require greater reflection on the role of reform as a process for readdressing this gap between rhetorical commitment and action. Moreover, it will also be vital to further unpack the complex interactions between competing humanitarian pressures and their impact on the goal of protection and prevention of atrocity crimes.

CONTESTING THE REFORM AGENDA: THE FUTURE OF THE R2P

Reform has been a central point of discussion in the R2P literature for well over a decade now and has come to define the positions of various R2P advocates and critics. By exploring the range of recent initiatives and proposals around the issue of international reform, this section will question the scope of such approaches and thus reinforce the limitations of institution-based responses. Taking into account the challenges facing the R2P that have been outlined in this chapter so far, it will be critical to provide a deeper focus on the question of what is behind the lack of "political will" and what other competing pressures on decision-making shape how states respond. It will then be possible to provide a more nuanced conception of both the core political constraints of decision-making procedures and the undertheorized role of moral appeals connected to the need to develop a stronger cosmopolitan consciousness. Through this broader focus on the challenge of motivation and its impact on the reform agenda, one can begin to unpack the factors that have been most detrimental to consensus building in response to atrocity crimes.

R2P ADVOCATES: DOUBLING DOWN ON THE STATUS QUO OR A MOVE TOWARD INCREMENTAL CHANGE?

For R2P advocates such as Bellamy, the continuing focus on reform, whether in regard to changes to the UN Charter or to the move to introduce a UN-based rapid reaction force, represents idealistic thinking that is both unlikely to ever be achieved and, most importantly, that is not necessary to the continuing goal of reducing outbreaks of atrocity crimes around the globe. In this regard, Bellamy (2014) has been clear in claiming that "the world already has sufficient law and institutional coverage to make it less tolerant of atrocity crimes and more protective of its victims" (15). Underpinning his approach is a belief in the idea that "we must not let the perfect become the enemy of the good," and thus a key strength of the R2P remains the decision to not change "the basic international rules governing the use of force" (11–12). Instead, Bellamy views the R2P as providing a way to persuade states to "act on their existing responsibilities" (12). His skepticism of reform initiatives is apparently grounded in the assumption that the UNSC's current structural decision-making procedures do not have to be an overpowering impediment to protection and prevention, and that the gradual acceptance of R2P principles will begin to fundamentally redefine how states approach the threat of atrocity crimes and their responses to them.

However, as this chapter has so far examined in detail, persuading states to reorient their interests in light of the R2P's focus on prevention of and reaction to mass atrocity crimes has posed an extreme challenge, and a considerable gap remains between rhetoric and action. Appeals in support of the status quo can thus seem self-defeating, particularly in light of recent trends, which have seen a steep rise in civilian casualties caused by war (von Einsiedel 2017) as well as indifference to war crimes "becoming an entrenched normality as the UNSC remains paralyzed by rivalries between permanent member states" (Amnesty International 2017). Moreover, in relation to the ongoing case of Syria, there has been an assumption in certain circles of the R2P literature that any intervention in Syria would likely have done "more harm than good" (Glanville 2016a, 185). Such claims reinforce the current status quo as well as the view that the concept is still functioning effectively and that it is simply a case of waiting for factors to coalesce in support of effective action.

Consequently, debate over the UNSC's failures to fully respond to the crisis in Syria have at times conveniently been blamed on geopolitical realities on the ground. As a result, there has been far less discussion of the R2P's potentially more serious long-term problems, which relate to a declining moral motivation to address mass atrocity crimes across the region. As a consequence, many advocates and critics still find it hard to accept that the current status quo in terms of collective decision-making may be as good as we can get when it comes to preventing and responding to such crimes. A number of R2P advocates now place much greater focus on the importance of developing incremental changes to the UNSC's decision-making processes in order to challenge the current global status quo.

Many of the most recent R2P reform initiatives put forward by advocates are premised on the idea that small changes to the decision-making structure at the international level can have a large impact, based partly on the belief that humanitarian impulses are being constrained by the UN's current structures, and thus it is simply a case of refining those structures to allow humanitarian sentiment to flourish. Such claims stem from the idea that the R2P is a neutral and agency-free concept that remains in thrall to the UNSC's whims. This is the view taken by Simon Adams (2015), the Executive Director of the Global Centre for the Responsibility to Protect, who argues that "the Responsibility to Protect is an international norm, but it does not possess independent agency. The failure to end atrocities and protect civilians in Syria is not a failure of R2P, but of the imperfect actors and institutions charged with its implementation" (3). This argument focusing on the imperfect institutional structures of the UNSC can be seen to be the central imperative behind initiatives such as the

"Responsibility Not to Veto (RN2V)," which asks states to not veto draft resolutions that have the explicit goal of halting potential mass atrocity crimes, while recognizing that the P5 may still use the veto in situations where critical national interests are at stake.

Perhaps most significantly, this agreement would not require an amendment to the UN Charter; rather, it would be a voluntary commitment of the P5. As discussed in chapter 1, such initiatives have been heavily promoted by Mexico and France as well as the Accountability, Coherence and Transparency group (ACT). Despite the general support for veto restraint, the assumption that the veto remains the biggest problem to both preventing and responding to mass atrocity crimes is arguably misplaced. As Justin Morris (2015) has argued, even if consensus was reached on "Responsibility Not to Veto" (RN2V), it would most likely have little impact, for it would exclude cases where vital state interests are at stake, and furthermore, the initiative would come into play only once the threshold of human suffering, outlined by the crimes of the R2P, has been reached or recognized by states (416). Moreover, the focus on the RN2V principle distracts attention from more inventive and possibly more effective solutions, such as supporting greater use of regional institutions, which are often seen as having more legitimacy as potential authorizers of a response to mass atrocities (Adediran 2018, 480). Energy would thus be better spent on considering how the R2P interacts with state behaviour and interests, rather than viewing the R2P as fundamentally separate from the agents and actors involved in its operationalization. So it appears unlikely that a voluntary agreement such as RN2V would sufficiently address the more fundamental problem of "moral under-reach" (Gallagher 2013, 166), whereby states are reluctant to adopt a genuine commitment to align their national interests with humanitarian causes. This, in spite of accountability claims increasingly being made against those states that have remained indifferent to the growing threat of atrocity crimes in many parts of the globe. The clear limitations of incremental change at the UN level force us to consider what further measures could be developed so that states took a much broader view of the R2P reform agenda.

THE R2P CRITICS: REIMAGINING GLOBAL INSTITUTIONS

In light of all this, many critics of the R2P have focused on the need to put forward more radical reforms to the governance of the international system, to help change how states respond to atrocity crimes.

For critics such as Hehir (2015b), part of the problem is that "the R2P industry champions moral advocacy rather than legal reform," with the focus being on "lobbying states to change their behaviour, rather than challenging the state-based international system per se" (676). Thus Hehir (2017) has remained skeptical of the exaggerated importance advocates have placed on the institutionalization of the R2P, arguing that "its frequent invocation is not a consequence of R2P having changed the behaviour of states" (343). What is required moving forward, then, is a more radical adaptation of the UN's current organizing structure to help compel greater change. The underlying sentiment of much of the critical reform literature on R2P is perhaps best encapsulated by a suggestion by Joshua Kassner (2013) that "if the system no longer serves humanity, then we ought not to hesitate to change it so that it does" (209). Central to such claims is therefore a questioning of the decision to leave intact much of the normative framework that resulted in the disasters of the 1990s (152), whereby the R2P was forced to function through the same decision-making processes. Similarly, for Pinar Gözen Ercan (2016) the inconsistency of implementation stems from "the nature of the institution tasked with implementing R2P" (107), that is, the UN and the Security Council. So as long as the R2P "remains dependent on the usual practices of the Security Council," the R2P will be unable to achieve its stated goals (124). Failure to advocate for greater change has left the R2P relying solely on interpretations of Articles 39 and 42 of the UN Charter, with the deliberation process most often left to the voluntary will of the five permanent members.

In response, a number of reform approaches have been put forward by R2P scholars like Ayoob (2010), Roff (2013), Hehir (2012), and Ercan (2016), all of whom have focused to some extent on the need to construct new independent decision-making organizations or to simply limit the UNSC's decision-making power by emboldening the UN General Assembly through changes to the UN Charter. While there is insufficient scope here to address each reform approach individually, it is vital to acknowledge at this point the wealth of scholarship that has developed around the issue of large-scale UNSC reform. Central to much of the R2P literature on this type of reform is the problem of inconsistency, which in light of the UNSC deadlock over Myanmar, Yemen, and Syria has led to the assumption that current decision-making structures are not fit for purpose. In this regard, introducing some form of independent body to oversee decision-making, and creating a rapid reaction force to implement protection, is often presented as the most effective approach to overcoming the UNSC's current selection bias. However, as this chapter acknowledged earlier, attempts to simply sign up permanent member-states to a voluntary agreement on veto use have proven extremely taxing, demonstrating the strong reservations of key UNSC powers to any form of change in their decision-making authority. Reforms such as the ones suggested here represent a significant and highly controversial reworking of the current global order, bringing into question the viability of such initiatives in the current global climate. As Gallagher (2015) has argued, such reforms raise the question of whether those skeptical of the R2P in its current institutional form "create overly high expectations of what is achievable" (271) so that a focus on extensive reform is at times counterproductive. This thread is picked up by Jason Ralph (2018), whose pragmatic understanding of the R2P's role leads him to be dismissive of potential legal fixes, which are often detached from political reality and thus can do more harm by heightening skepticism as to the norm's ability to address atrocity crimes effectively.

So it is useful to reflect further on the limitations of the institutional focus that has run throughout much of the literature on R2P reform and that is often built upon the assumption that attempts to constrain and redefine decision-making power within the UNSC can serve as a silver bullet for the R2P's implementation problem. Such critiques of institutional arrangements have a clear knock-on effect, whereby current multilateral procedures are at times seen to bear heavy responsibility for morally problematic "humanitarian under-intervention" (Recchia 2016, 20). Unilateral action has continued to be seen as an option that must always be on the table in order to bypass the restraints of a UNSC that is argued to lack just procedures and thus cannot be relied upon to make decisions "in a morally responsible way" (Pattison 2010, 188). However, as Stefano Recchia (2016) has argued, a strict focus on the problem of generating multilateral responses arguably misdiagnoses the problem, in that the lack of intervention in a particular situation is most often "because no major power is making a determined push for intervention (and for multilateral approval) to begin with" (71). In this sense, any attempt to bring about extensive reform, or even to generate action in regard to carrying out prevention initiatives, ultimately requires a strong dose of political will, which is constrained by the current decision-making processes at the international level. Moreover, interventions and other coercive responses to mass atrocity crimes have the potential to weaken institutional processes that were created to help guard against other wrongs, such as great power overreach. In this sense, other normative concerns often underpin why a state or group of states may be skeptical about supporting a particular approach to averting mass atrocity crimes.

To explore and expand on such claims in more detail, it is vital to return briefly to an assessment of past failures surrounding the concept of humanitarian intervention. While the case of Rwanda has been touched on at points throughout this book as having sparked the development of the R2P, it will be used here to demonstrate the limitations of the R2P's focus on sovereignty and of the UNSC's decision-making procedures. Through such analysis, it will be possible to then reconsider the challenges facing the R2P's motivational capacity and the role of future reform initiatives.

LESSONS FROM THE CASE OF RWANDA FOR THE R2P REFORM AGENDA

As argued by the 1999 independent inquiry into the UN response to the Rwanda Genocide, and by scholars such as Chesterman (2001) and Wheeler (2005), the lack of sufficient political will was the driving factor behind the failure to protect. Yet despite this conclusion, the decision by the international community not to act has continued to be used as an example to suggest that the international community's failure was not one of morality *per se*; rather, it stemmed from the prevailing view that the "principles and institutions governing the practical deliberations of states precluded states from considering moral reasons for action, that would require interference in the internal affairs of another sovereign state" (Kassner 2013, 89). Yet when one draws on the actions of states in bypassing sovereignty laws when confronted by terrorism or broader security threats, states have never been shy about contradicting their own rhetoric in regard to sovereignty. This highlights the limitations of understanding the R2P, or humanitarian intervention more generally, as a binary playoff between humanitarian objectives and sovereign rights. There is, then, a need to broaden out these debates and reflect on the variety of constraints states place on their own responses to mass atrocity crimes.

As Muller and Wolff (2014) highlight, the creation of the ICISS document recognized an explicit goal of "no more Rwandas" and sought to redefine the principles of sovereignty and non-intervention so that it would be more possible to prevent genocide (285). But as the authors go on to argue, the claim that Rwanda demonstrated the problem of "outdated international law" that impeded a humanitarian intervention can be argued to "sit uneasily with the scholarly record" (285). The Rwandan genocide thus revealed an important shift in the post–Cold War era in regard to the normative terrain of intervention debates. The case highlighted how states were no longer claiming that intervention for humanitarian purposes would be "illegitimate or an illegal breach of sovereignty" (as had been the case regarding India's intervention in East Pakistan in 1971), but instead were working to suppress information from Rwanda regarding the extent of the genocide so as to allow them to sidestep their obligations (Finnemore 2003, 80). US President Bill Clinton did at times make rhetorical references to sovereignty, but this was arguably a means to invalidate the humanitarian argument and thereby uphold self-interest over normative restrictions (Bentley 2017). The tragedy of Rwanda is therefore best understood as a failure of political will rather than the product of an increasingly "outdated" belief in the importance of traditional sovereignty claims.

This is significant, for the Rwanda case did a great deal to shift the focus of reforms during the initial development of the R2P and has continually been used to suggest that progress in responding to atrocity crimes in the future will rely on changing the decision-making processes within the UN so as to limit the influence of traditional sovereignty claims. Thus, what we must take away first and foremost from the case of Rwanda is that regardless of what decision-making procedures were in place, they would have had little impact there, for at the time, moral motivation was at an all-time low (Barnett 2002). Furthermore, specifically in regard to the challenge of mobilization, the Rwanda case brings to our attention the limits of our exposure to extreme violence in helping to generate stronger pressure on states to respond. With Rwanda, it became clear that the emotional component of the arguments in favour of armed intervention to halt the atrocities was in fact "dulled rather than enhanced by the large numbers" and thus did little to improve the salience of such arguments (Labonte 2013, 57). As Hugo Slim (1998) acknowledges, "knowing what is wrong is indeed distinct from knowing how to put it right" (44), and thus moral responsibility is often diminished once the inherent wrong of the situation has been identified. In this sense, it can be argued that it is not the magnitude of suffering and death that changes the decision-making of potential interveners; instead, the initial shock and moral bite of the atrocities weakens very quickly once competing obligations and risks become evident (Menon 2016, 129). Thus, it quickly becomes apparent that what matters is "not how many people are being killed, but where they are being killed and by whom" (129). The lack of political will for humanitarian action in Rwanda thus demonstrated how even the weightiest of human rights norms such as genocide are ultimately not enough to drive specific policy action.

These considerations take us right to the heart of the R2P reform agenda and the challenges it currently faces. As has been argued so far, the concept of humanity remains an integral moral imperative in support of the R2P and requires states to subscribe to a universal responsibility to protect. But the strength and success of the concept can only be as strong as our ability to place the needs of humanity as a universal claim above or in connection to those of national self-interest. This was made abundantly clear in the original 2001 ICISS report, which argued that "for all the rhetoric about the universality of human rights some human lives end up mattering a great deal less to the international community than others" (1). In the twenty years since that report, states have continued to weigh competing pressures: that is, their political responsibilities toward their own populations, and their moral responsibilities to end mass atrocity crimes and protect humanity. A case can thus be made that a focus on attempts to simply rearrange the institutional makeup of decision-making processes has caused many scholars to overlook the moral dimensions of political will that have arguably remained so integral to any attempt to gain consensus for action. That will be the focus of the final section of this chapter.

RETHINKING POLITICAL WILL: THE ROLE OF HUMANITY

Some supporters of the R2P assumed early on that the principle had already begun to radically redefine the procedures of state decision-making around intervention practice and thus represented "a revolution in the notion of sovereignty" (Carvin 2010, 52). However, in direct relation to the challenge of motivating responses to address atrocity crimes, it is certainly unclear to what extent it has in fact removed major obstacles that have inhibited consensus in the past. As Labonte (2013, 171) has argued, "the standing impediments to crafting effective policy responses to mass atrocities are virtually identical to those that existed before the World Summit." Thus, it is not sovereignty and non-intervention that have been the key obstacles to saving strangers, but political will, which remains essential to converting the apparent moral necessity for intervention into effective compliance pull on political actors (142). At this stage one must ask what is meant by political will. This section will argue that the key to locating political will is to first understand what a *lack* of political will looks like. In reference to previous cases of UNSC inaction during humanitarian crises in Rwanda and Darfur, it is clear that a lack of information about atrocities taking place is not a central factor in generating political will. In both examples, state actors and UN agencies received clear information about the atrocities taking place but were ultimately unable to generate sufficient will for action. When there is a lack of political will, it is much more about the limitations of normative arguments to motivate state actors to take on sufficient sacrifices or to frame potential action as aligning with other national interests, alongside the competing concerns states may have about the material resources required and the risks involved in protection. The ability to generate political will in support of protection and prevention therefore requires a complex balancing act by which moral sacrifice can be justified in the context of specific strategic and material interests.

However, the narrowness of approaches to understanding political will in R2P cases has meant there has been limited analysis of the interaction between competing humanitarian norms and the moral imperatives that underpin them. In this regard, any attempt to better understand how political will is generated in atrocity crime situations must engage with and examine further the role that broader humanitarian norms play in this process, particularly in terms of why states may contest some claims to protection but not others. Ignorance of such factors will only mask the complexity of the motivational processes underpinning the R2P and thus allow a misdiagnosis of the concept's apparent limitations.

There is a need to first view the challenge of inaction in R2P cases of protection and prevention through the wider lens of moral motivation for broader humanitarian responses, rather than focusing solely on the problem of reforming the UNSC's decision-making processes to avert the dominance of the P5 and the veto. Central to this challenge is thinking about how to better integrate and consolidate the mandates for conflict resolution, peacekeeping, human rights, and criminal justice with the R2P. This challenge is exemplified by Kirsten Ainley (2015), who highlights the lack of political will of the P5 states with regard to contributing to the relief of human suffering in Syria through refugee protection. It can be argued, then, that the failure to "generate an R2P response to Syria does not lie solely with Russia and China, or with the structure of R2P decision-making at the international level" (42). Thus, one must conclude that a change in UNSC decision-making in the case of Syria would not have fundamentally altered or solved the humanitarian crisis (42). The gap between rhetoric and action during this refugee crisis can thus be seen to challenge assertions as to the existence of an international community that shares common moral values regarding humanitarian protection (Menon 2016, 154). Today, many Western states spend billions of dollars to resist providing shelter to those seeking asylum, many of whom are fleeing political violence and mass atrocities, choosing instead to shift the responsibility onto weaker developing states (Glanville 2020, 4). These actions speak to the challenge of calling out the hypocritical divergence between state action and rhetoric and further underscore the need to better understand why states continue to place narrow self-interest above their responsibilities to a common humanity.

Moreover, one must recall that the most frequent use of force for human protection is not in cases in which there is no consent of the state, such as in Libya or Syria, but rather when there is consent, as in the cases of Mali and the Central African Republic (CAR) (Tourinho, Stuenkel, and Brockmeier 2016, 146). In these cases, finding the necessary resources was the greatest challenge for protection, and in the example of the CAR specifically, it took five months until sufficient resources were in place to start operations (146). Political will cannot therefore be understood solely through the constraints of UNSC decision-making processes; it also requires a recognition that states must be prepared to make sacrifices to address atrocities and their potential outbreak.

These two examples draw attention to the intersection of the central moral claims that are argued to underpin the concept of R2P with the wide array of other pressing humanitarian concerns. The reality is that often these appear to be out of sync. Consequently, R2P advocates such as Bellamy (2016) have been compelled to accept a clear disjunction, whereby many of the states that have been some of the biggest champions of the R2P have been the least hospitable to refugees through the winding back of protection. This points to the limitations of viewing R2P reform within the bubble of the UNSC: the domestic politics of protection have often taken a back seat in reform-based discussions. The challenge of protection moving forward then is not one of simply resolving the tensions in R2P decision-making procedures; required instead is a much deeper assessment of how to renew the connection between domestic and international decision-making so as to develop a more ambitious conception of political will that can at the same time promote cosmopolitan goals and aspirations. This is critical during a period of significant change in the current global order, in which statist visions of protection have gained increasing traction. A more ambitious conception of political will must start with considering which responsibilities are owed to others and in which circumstances. This will expand the framing of the R2P debate beyond just discussing whether the Security Council should act in this or that particular case, to one about how the interests of a state in terms of foreign policy are intimately linked to addressing the larger impact of mass atrocity crimes on the global political order.

CONCLUSION

There has often been a tendency in the R2P literature to see the debates surrounding how states should respond to the outbreak of mass atrocity crimes as a straight contest between cold hard national self-interest and the strength of moral cosmopolitanism. However, this simplistic binary overshadows the complexity of decision-making. As Cathinka Vik (2015) highlights, state decision-makers are often forced to choose between "a moral duty to follow an international norm and a countervailing duty to realize another equally important moral value that conflicts with the international norm" (22). One must therefore recognize that state behaviour is not driven solely by pragmatism and self-interest; clashes between contrasting normative considerations are another factor (Welsh 2014b, 137). In other words, debates around state decision-making in R2P situations cannot be condensed down to a simple question of how far we can "expand the notion of moral responsibility in international relations" relative to the sway of self-interest and domestic obligations (Vik 2015, 128). It is vital to recognize the points of moral contradiction that are also inherent in today's state system and how these contradictions affect the ability of states to make decisions and take actions to alleviate the human suffering caused by mass atrocity crimes.

As this chapter has examined, there continues to be a strong emphasis on the importance of sovereignty and the structures of current UNSC decision-making practices when it comes to debates surrounding R2P reforms. It has been argued that this focus has led both advocates and critics to overlook the role played by moral and normative considerations and their impact on the R2P's ability to generate consensus in response to mass atrocity crimes and the fallout from them. This chapter has argued that the R2P debate is too narrow and that the R2P's ambition must be linked to other agendas and goals, be it in terms of refugee protection or peacekeeping resources and funding. So we need to better understand how competing humanitarian norms interact with one another and to demonstrate how the goal of human protection requires states and civil society to rethink their approaches to generating political will. Also, by reconceptualizing the R2P's key added value as a negative accountability claim, this chapter has provided a more balanced assessment of the concept's key strengths and limitations. It has argued that the R2P has generated significant change in the way states now consider the impact of atrocity crimes. Clearly, however, accountability claims made against states that violate the norm have been ineffective in terms of both holding violators to account and closing the gap between rhetoric and action.

This chapter has drawn significant attention to how moral claims for protection or prevention can be significantly compromised, not just by international sovereignty claims but also by how states conceptualize the relationship between competing humanitarian norms and their own priorities and responsibilities. States may recognize mass atrocity crimes as a threat to humanity, but all too often they allow competing demands to override their responses to them. Changing this outlook therefore requires that more inventive and creative ways be developed to build collective and individual state interest for stopping mass atrocity crimes. To kick-start this, we must reject the binary nature of recent reform initiatives that focus too much attention on the role of international institutions. Greater recognition must be given to the critical role that nation-states themselves play in supporting cosmopolitan aspirations that can work to protect humanity. The next chapter discusses how rethinking the role of the state and the R2P is critical to developing new, practical drivers for meeting cosmopolitan responsibilities of human protection in a changing global order.

CONCLUSION

Motivation beyond Humanity in a Changing Global Order

This book has aimed first and foremost to challenge taken-for-granted assumptions concerning the connection between humanity and R2P in locating global harm and influencing state decision-making. In breaking down the complex role humanity plays in this relationship, it has outlined the distinct dual function of humanity both as a moral demand for ethical reflection, understood as its emotional pull factor, and as a moral imperative to motivate action and response in the name of humanity, understood as its motivational push factor. By applying this new theoretical understanding of humanity to key debates in the R2P literature – in particular, the ongoing contestation surrounding the R2P implementation gap – it thus challenged dominant assumptions concerning humanity's motivational influence on the R2P and its ability to significantly redefine state behaviour in response to mass atrocity crimes. It has been argued that while humanity continues to underpin the moral foundations of the four core R2P crimes as well as appeals related to their global impact, humanity's role as a motivational concept remains much more fundamentally contested, particularly in relation to other demands and pressures that shape state interests. By acknowledging humanity's diminished impact once the R2P is diffused into action, this book has brought to light clear limits to humanity's motivational influence that go beyond competing claims of sovereign rights. Moving forward, R2P research on addressing the current implementation gap will need to consider how to develop new practical drivers for steering state interest toward the principle's original cosmopolitan ambitions. Practical drivers would be conscious of the way humanity interacts with competing moral, legal, and political pressures at the global level. This is increasingly imperative, given the changing nature of the current global order, in which the previously Western-dominated value system is feeling the strain exerted by both external and internal forces. In this conclusion I will theorize on the current complexities of state motivation and discuss a number of practical starting points for developing new motivational drivers for state behaviour, focusing on the important role nation-states can play in supporting cosmopolitan ambitions.

IMPLICATIONS FOR THE R2P IN A CHANGING GLOBAL ORDER

The key to making sense of the recent changes in the international order is to examine the role of the rising powers and their challenges to the principles and norms of the Western-dominated system, as well as the extent to which liberal Western states remain willing to strongly support and defend their core values, such as human rights protection and the prevention of mass atrocity crimes. The past decade has seen a marked increase in the forces of nationalism around the globe, leading to a much more fractured multilateralism, as well as a greater reluctance to accept or recognize criticisms of human rights abuses (Ferguson and Mansbach 2017). This is reflected in both domestic and international policy in terms of responses to refugees, increased targeting of civilians during conflicts, and a growing reluctance among the major powers to acknowledge human rights atrocities as threats to international peace and security. Part of the explanation for this growing pushback against human rights norms is connected to the importance assigned to sovereign independence and non-interference – principles that have been strongly championed by rising powers in recent years. However, as noted earlier, the assumption that sovereignty remains the strongest barrier to human protection initiatives has long been overplayed, particularly in terms of the relatively nuanced position taken by the rising powers when it comes to discussions about preventing atrocity crimes.

For example, central to China's position on the R2P is an attempt to carve out a space between the idea of sovereignty as an absolute principle and the R2P's more expansionist cosmopolitan tendencies. This space in between allows China to highlight that there is a threshold to violations that break sovereignty but that this level is much higher than what Western states propose. By doubling down on their own interpretation of threats to peace and security, China has been able to remain broadly supportive of the ideas that underpin the R2P, such as Pillars I and II. Consequently, as Mauro Barelli (2018) argues, China will tend to take into account "not only humanitarian considerations but also the broader and complex realities of international politics, on the one hand, and its own security and development interests, on the other" (198). This suggests that China's issues with the R2P must be understood in connection to its contrasting ideological approach to the management of the global order itself. So while China still upholds values that support a type of liberal international order, its stance is decidedly different from the liberal order that existed throughout the 1990s and early 2000s, which ultimately gave birth to the R2P concept (Jones 2018, 181–2). This new era thus demands new and creative approaches to motivating prevention and protection initiatives during an even more contested period of global politics.

The rise of China's voice and influence on the international stage can be contrasted with a sharp decline in liberal states' willingness to directly call out and push back against challenges to liberal norms (Lynch 2020). Part of this shift can be explained by the influence of the Trump administration in the United States, but it must also be viewed in light of changing national priorities and internal populist politics across the Western world, which have sought to hollow out the previous liberal international order (Adler-Nissen and Zarakol 2020). A significant consequence of this shift has been the promotion of a much more insular world view, one in which shared empathy for people around the globe is in steep decline. The challenge, then, for the R2P moving forward is how to address the decline in cosmopolitan values while still supporting the R2P and making it more effective. As this book has explored, the R2P principle has long been linked to the idea of a growing cosmopolitan "we-feeling," yet as Linklater (2016) rightly acknowledges, it is still the case that "narrower and wider conceptions of 'we' come into conflict" (470), generating contestation over how states should respond to human protection challenges. In a world now increasingly hostile to elements of humanitarianism and human rights discourse, it is vital to examine more closely what space and value there still is for moral appeals and how these may interact with competing political and legal pressures in attempts to motivate responses to mass atrocity crimes.

THE CHALLENGE OF FOSTERING A COSMOPOLITAN CONSCIOUSNESS

As we examine how states respond to a variety of humanitarian pressures, such as refugee flows, we can first of all highlight the conflicting nature of a state's own circle of empathy, in that support for the R2P principle does not instantly correlate with a willingness to accept responsibilities for protection in a national context. This points to an increasingly weak relationship between empathy and moral sacrifice. Addressing this weak relationship requires greater reflection on how empathy functions at the global level and the extent to which states are willing to expend resources and political capital to offer protection to those beyond their borders. As Frans de Waal (2008) has argued, "without the emotional engagement brought about by empathy, it is unclear what could motivate the extremely costly helping behaviour occasionally observed in social animals" (292). Furthermore, as Martha Finnemore (2003) recognizes, "without emotion and effect, we have only information about the world and no particular reason to care about one outcome versus another" (154). Thus, in regard to protection practices, one can argue that we need to identify with others, to imagine ourselves as them, if we are to fully recognize their plight, "especially when intervention is not obviously a matter of national interest" (Sherman 1998, 109). Yet while the motivation to protect those threatened by atrocity crimes can often begin with an appeal to empathy or emotion, it certainly does not end there. In this sense, as this book has outlined, states will also weigh competing political pressures that ultimately dictate how empathy is translated into the motivation to respond. This has played out to devastating effect in terms of the ongoing refugee crisis across Europe, in the course of which those fleeing from mass atrocity crimes in Iraq and Syria have faced varying degrees of hostility, with states contesting moral responsibility through the lens of security claims and nationalist sentiment (Bauböck 2018; Nail 2016).

In specific regard to the R2P, the development of a supposedly cosmopolitan consciousness will require the scaling up of responsibility to a global and universal level. For Marlier and Crawford (2013), the R2P's "prioritization of a concern for protecting civilians rather than states marks the expansion of the United Nations Security Council's circle of empathy" (398). However, as they go on to highlight, the R2P at this point is neither deeply institutionalized nor deeply encultured, especially on the national level, and thus "many of us still don't see a moral relationship to a distant other" (413). This is reinforced by Linklater (2016), who also suggests that ethical concerns about distant suffering "do not automatically translate into strong public support for global assistance programmes" (454). So while empathy and emotions remain central to influencing how certain humanitarian situations draw our concern, persuading state actors to respond has often required making a clear connection to their self-interest as well. This is perhaps best encapsulated by former US President Barack Obama, who, in his remarks to the UN General Assembly in 2015, declared that our concern must be "driven not just by conscience, but should also be driven by self-interest. For helping people who have been pushed to the margins of our world is not mere charity, it is a matter of collective security" (Obama 2015). Obama was making an important strategic connection between human protection and its potential impact on state security, calling on leaders to adopt self-interest as a key motivator for response.

Nevertheless, as Luke Glanville (2016b) has pointed out, this form of "enlightened self-interest" is at times not strong enough to promote specific action, particularly in cases "where the suffering of others is more distant and less strategically important" (337) and thus the longer-term security threats associated with atrocity crimes are not recognized as sufficiently threatening to wider state interests. Enlightened self-interest as encapsulated in Obama's comments is clearly an imperfect solution to the challenge of mobilization; even so, his words point to the need for states to continue widening the scope of security concerns in order to draw closer attention to the impact that atrocity crimes clearly have on global security. As a 2015 UNA-UK report reaffirmed, atrocity crimes have serious consequences for global security and prosperity, for they destabilize regions and generate further violence and refugee flows across borders. Moving forward, then, it is vital to reconsider how the goals of protection and prevention, originally founded on a belief in the universal category of humanity, can be reconciled with a world that has become increasingly hostile to key elements of human protection, such as refugee protection and atrocity prevention. In this sense, one must recognize that a global climate of increasing isolationism and the strengthening of border security is one in which the moral traction of appeals to a universal humanity as a purely motivating tool may prove increasingly limited. As this book has argued throughout, the R2P has often relied too heavily on the power of humanity and empathy to drive change and reform at an institutional level.

In response to the challenges involved in addressing the R2P's motivational capacity and the reform agenda at large, there is a mounting need to consider what new tactics and initiatives are required and may be effective in responding to the current political climate. This will ultimately demand claims to the moral righteousness of protection; but in addition, states will need to care more about human suffering and make a more concerted effort to link the protection and empowerment of people to a human security agenda, grounded and reinforced by international law. Humanity as a motivating principle must be seen to represent more than "a disposition of empathy"; it must be grounded more strongly in the challenge of motivating political will (Wilson 2010, 28). Ultimately, this must also mean expanding our thinking beyond a traditional R2P-focused lens when it comes to the challenges of protection and prevention; and this will require greater recognition of how a broad array of humanitarian norms interact, if we are to shape the situations in which states view actions to be in their national interest.

For example, there are major inconsistencies in how states approach competing responsibilities to mass atrocity crime prevention, peacekeeping, and refugee protection – responses that are often severely out of sync with one another. The contrast in support between the R2P and refugee protection in particular brings to light the complexity of state motivation and the need to further map out how different regimes of protection and prevention can generate moral, legal, and political dilemmas for decision-makers. When we talk about motivation and political will in terms of the R2P and atrocity crimes, we cannot separate these out from broader discussions concerning how states approach the protection of human beings in a variety of contexts. The current political climate of human rights pushback must therefore be seen as greatly detrimental to further consensus on R2P mobilization and as directly challenging us to start rethinking our strategy for R2P reforms.

THE PATH FORWARD: RECONFIGURING THE MORALITY, LAW, AND POLITICS OF THE R2P

As the previous chapter examined in detail, R2P scholarship has often been extremely narrowly focused and has predominantly emphasized the problems of institutional arrangements at the international level. The challenge to the international community has largely been framed around the need to change decision-making structures and redefine core principles such as sovereignty. Yet as this book has argued, the limited scope of such discussions has often clouded judgments regarding the broader obstacles to R2P mobilization, most notably the challenge of generating stronger political will for preventing and responding to mass atrocity crimes. In his article "Reinvigorating Human Rights for the Twenty-First Century," Hurst Hannum (2016) argues that "social progress can only be achieved by appealing to law, politics and morality" (446), not by simply appealing to human rights as a remedy for all wrongs. In direct relation to the current R2P discourse, this argument is highly relevant. The enthusiasm of R2P advocates for their supposedly game-changing principle has at times overshadowed the intricacies of diplomatic decision-making around prevention of and intervention in mass atrocity crimes. The moral appeal of humanity has continued to be held up by both diplomats and academics as the concept that can best connect a shared empathy over human suffering to effective international decision-making, through the power of the R2P principle (Thakur 2015). This book has argued, however, that the motivational qualities of humanity have been largely overstated and thus the moral complexities of state practice, in regard to mass atrocity crime prevention and protection, have been somewhat oversimplified.

Central to this analysis is the recognition that the R2P on its own is no panacea for mass atrocity crimes. While the R2P is clearly a critical step, in that it has drawn a new global benchmark for state agreement on the inherent wrong of mass atrocity crimes, it must not be understood as a final piece of the puzzle, for that would blind us to the need for greater critical analysis of and reflection on the current impediments to changing state priorities when it comes to mass atrocity crimes. The R2P is best conceptualized as a stepping stone, one that has done much to generate negative accountability claims but that has not laid the foundations for a more stable and consistent approach to atrocity crime prevention and protection.

In this regard, the R2P, as Aidan Hehir (2013a) rightly points out, should be understood not as part of a liberal teleological process of change, underpinned by a belief in the progress of humanity, but rather as a reversible process that must not be taken for granted. This is reflected in comments made by the former UN Secretary-General Ban Ki-moon, who in his 2016 R2P report suggested that the UNSC's limited response to mass atrocity crimes over the preceding few years threatened to reverse years of progress. He also pointed out quite sharply that the frequency and scale of atrocity crimes had been increasing and would likely continue to do so "unless the international community takes more determined and consistent action to fulfil its responsibility to protect" (Ki-moon 2016a, 3). The current challenges the UN faces in attempting to address mass atrocity crimes remain complex and demand new thinking that moves beyond the often repetitive R2P debates over the past two decades.

MORALITY AND POLITICS

First, it is crucial to re-emphasize the complex interactions between moral claims and the political contexts in which they are referred to and acted upon. That has been a central focus of this book throughout, in which I have argued that assumptions made about the motivational impact of appeals to humanity have clouded discussion regarding how political actors translate moral claims to humanity into responses. Much of the R2P literature continues to take for granted that the rhetorical consensus upheld by states is a sign of the R2P's influence in shifting the debate beyond the previous moral dilemmas created by the humanitarian intervention concept. R2P advocates still assume that the principle is now in a stage of consolidation and that it is not worth expending energy on questions that have already been decided, particularly as they concern why states may have a responsibility to protect in the first place (Diggelmann 2014). Indeed, these advocates are promoting the R2P as the *future* and contend that we must now "concentrate on doctrinal questions and implementation" (408). As Rajan Menon (2016) points out, much of the literature surrounding R2P debates continues to be "suffused with moral certainty" (14) and fails to fully account for the complex interactions between specific moral claims and the political contexts in which they are applied.

In contrast, this book has provided a new theoretical understanding of how moral appeals to humanity function in international decision-making and the limitations of their application. Here, one can highlight how the emphasis placed on the motivational power of a shared concept of humanity in helping generate arguments in favour of moral sacrifice is often tested, perhaps most notably when states are asked to deploy ground troops to save foreigners from massacre (174). The responses by intervening powers to mass atrocity crimes from Kosovo to Libya suggest that moral sacrifice has always encountered clear political limits, particularly when it comes to the value of national lives when those being protected are not nationals. For example, the exclusive use of air power instead of ground troops, potentially weakening the effectiveness of the intervention, can be viewed as a tactic to reduce the casualties of the intervener. Acknowledging the clear human wrongs created by mass atrocity crimes has therefore not prevented state actors from setting clear parameters regarding what sacrifices and expenses are valid for the sake of protecting other populations. It can thus be argued that the "willingness to put resources on the line is often a more pressing concern than respect for state sovereignty" (Massingham 2009, 826). This is significant, for it brings into question the R2P's strong focus on and attention to the need to redefine the role of sovereignty first and foremost. This suggests that states carefully consider how much they are willing to sacrifice politically in order to address outbreaks or continuations of mass atrocity crimes and their humanitarian impact. These sorts of calculations bring into further question claims made by advocates, who suggest that R2P debates should now focus solely on assessing the practical constraints of implementation rather than the specific motivations that underpin the central obligation in the first place. In this sense, by generally ignoring the influence of moral dilemmas and pressures in the later stages of decision-making, advocates have sought to downplay the complexity of the interaction between morality and politics and have at times also sought to reinforce their own assumptions regarding the ease with which moral claims should translate into sufficient political responses to mass atrocities.

Yet another question continues to be posed: whether the UNSC "can act as the guarantor of the protection and security of humanity while at the same time remaining aloof from the machinations of politics" (Orford 2016, 31). However, when the R2P debate takes the shape of simply a dichotomy between the influence of politics and the protection of humanity – as it does at present – this masks the critical interaction between the two normative pressures and thus reinforces the idea of political decision-making as an apparent restriction on the goals of humanity. It is vital to reject this arbitrary separation and examine in more detail the politics of humanity itself in order to fully question the overall limits of humanity as a motivating force.

MORALITY AND LAW

Second, one must also rethink the interaction between morality and law at the international level. International law over the past seventy years has seen a significant shift in how states perceive their responsibilities to both the global community and individual human beings around the globe. Yet despite claims by some that it is "humanity's law" (Teitel 2011), the R2P is not a legally binding concept, so it is crucial to recognize that the principle was constructed to "fortify existing legal commitments, as opposed to an attempt to transform international law or create new legal obligations" (Tacheva and Brown 2016, 442). It is thus argued that the R2P must be understood as a moral imperative that functions within "existing customary and codified international legal channels" (443). This is significant, for it means that the R2P remains heavily tied to the interaction between the motivational power of moral appeals and the imposition of international law on state practice. As this book has examined, international law remains subject to competing interpretations by states, be it in terms of recognizing genocide or in terms of how states decide which crimes represent a threat to international peace and security and thus justify a collective response. The existing legal framework requires states to work collectively in more consistently calling out those who seek to divide and contest its structures and application. But states must do so from a position of strength. As Gallagher (2021, 11) argues, Western actors in particular need to gain the support of the Global South, which means they must reflect on their own practices and moral standing in the world. When Western states violate international law, it significantly undermines their efforts to build a vision of human protection that can challenge the growth of anti-cosmopolitan sentiment in the current global order. Morality and law must remain connected to avoid the imposition of an apparent dichotomy between the two that could undermine the fragile consensus on the R2P principle.

To summarize, the discussions concerning the R2P's creation and its recent implementation have reaffirmed the significant role moral arguments play in internationalist debates (Orford 2013, 84). Moral appeals play a powerful role in the fight against mass atrocity crimes. Yet appeals to morality cannot on their own provide the motivational force to drive significant change in how states respond to mass atrocity crimes. Instead, as this section has underscored, there needs to be a greater understanding of the complex interactions among law, morality, and politics when framing state decision-making around mass atrocity crime prevention and protection. As Cater and Malone (2016) have argued, "admirable principles of international law and diplomacy do not always mutually reinforce each other" and "often overlap uncomfortably or clash outright" (292). In this regard, any approach to conceptualizing how to address the current R2P implementation gap must be careful not to rely too heavily on political, legal or moral arguments; they must also at the same time recognize how each works to generate constraints and opportunities in the process of addressing mass atrocity crimes. Moving forward, it will be crucial for academics and practitioners working on the R2P to reject some of the more simplistic explanations put forward to justify the current R2P implementation gap, explanations that often rely heavily on perceived dichotomies between concepts (such as humanity and sovereignty) at the expense of offering a more complex theorization of how better to generate state motivation in atrocity crime situations.

HARNESSING STATE-BASED SELF-INTEREST FOR THE WIDER RECOGNITION OF COMMON HUMAN CONDITIONS

Recognition of the considerable limitations of common humanity as a motivating force ultimately demands more creative ideas and tactics to better conceptualize how the R2P implementation gap can be closed. An element of inconsistency is built into the R2P's framework (Paris 2014), yet space remains for new strategies and ideas to further the cause of mass atrocity prevention and protection. One such move would be to strengthen the link between cosmopolitan ambitions and the role of state-based self-interest in indirectly supporting such goals. Although state-based self-interest is often viewed as incompatible with cosmopolitan motivations to protect humanity, it is increasingly clear that the state is set to remain the dominant actor in world politics; thus, to exclude or play down the importance of state interests would only make it much harder to address the challenges the R2P faces. States, instead, must be seen as having the potential to play an increasingly critical role in promoting a more cosmopolitan condition even when this may not be couched in the language of humanity or a shared cosmopolitan consciousness (Beardsworth et al. 2019). This will require a stronger focus on identifying self-motivated drivers that could be used to further raise awareness of common human conditions (Brown and Jarvis 2019, 215). For the R2P, this will mean making stronger connections between security and global stability and the prevention of mass atrocity crimes.

Many of the debates in the early years of the R2P's development focused predominantly on the importance of Pillar III support and the need to pursue changes through reforms to the UNSC. At the same time, the growing emphasis on prevention initiatives under Pillars I and II at the diplomatic level have created new opportunities to reframe the norm's role and impact on global politics. Beyond the issue of political will, the R2P's third pillar highlights the unequal enforcement capacities of UN member-states, given that most states are unable to contribute significantly to military operations (Mabera and Spies 2016, 216). This shift in focus away from the third pillar thus opens up space to prioritize more reciprocal tools of foreign policy; it also creates the potential for middle powers to play a greater role in prevention activities, thereby bridging the power divisions between the great powers and the rest. Yet the record on atrocity prevention has so far been relatively poor, with many of the overly ambitious claims about prevention's potential effectiveness tending to start from the assumption that difficult political and ethical decisions can be avoided. One must recognize that the viability of prevention initiatives will always rely on support from a range of actors and that one cannot avoid the need to construct complex motivational pressures to help shape state behaviour. Now more than ever, creative atrocity prevention strategies are required, working beyond normative appeals to humanity alone so as to better connect ideas to states' self-interests. States have begun to find more creative ways to pursue mass atrocity prevention, including the greater use of initiatives such as Arria Formula Meetings, where new information and insights can be shared when UNSC discussion is blocked. Another strong possibility is the ongoing strengthening of regional organizations as mass atrocity prevention actors.

Outside the formal parameters of the UNSC, Arria Formula Meetings in particular have become an important aid to discussion and debate about peace and security issues that have not found their way onto the council's formal agenda. These meetings have become an important space for council members to engage and interact with Human Rights Council–mandated commissions of inquiry, with NGO representatives and civil society actors among the briefers. The R2P's renewed emphasis on prevention means that such discussions are crucial to raising the alarm about human rights atrocities even when the council has blocked discussion. Diversifying the range of actors and voices at Arria meetings is critical to driving greater state recognition of the direct threats posed to those on the ground; it also serves as an important step in building a collective consensus on responding outside the parameters of a divided UNSC. These meetings do not lead to definitive or legal outcomes; even so, the increased use of Arria meetings in recent years demonstrates their importance in giving members new information from independent sources regarding key country situations. Looking forward, Arria meetings could be used more often to help build early collective support for addressing the potential outbreaks of mass atrocity crimes, besides providing a forum where debates and concerns can be discussed "on the record" (i.e., publicly). These more informal settings also allow for stronger communication between competing interest groups and non-state actors.

For effective prevention and human protection outside the UN system, regional organizations will most likely have to carry the burden. Various individual actors have interpreted elements of the R2P in contrasting ways; that said, there has been evidence of regional organizations and states working to support early warnings by incorporating mass atrocity prevention into legislation and formal institutions, most prominently in the case of the African Union (Aning and Okyere 2016). As Bolarinwa Adediran (2017, 486) has noted, regional organizations often have unique insights into looming threats to peace and stability and are also likely to be further motivated by the need to avoid the devastating economic consequences of mass atrocity crimes resulting from regional destabilization. These factors, and the increased legitimacy that local actors are often seen to have (i.e., relative to Western powers) reinforce the potential advantages of greater cooperation between regional organizations and the UNSC. Again, this example highlights the need to build stronger motivations for states to act through and in connection with existing institutions rather than focus their energy on proposing brand-new institutional structures, which would often require radical changes to the UN Charter.

The rise of these new actors as sources of new approaches to atrocity prevention speaks to a growing recognition of the broader security and economic impacts of mass atrocity crimes. This development has the potential to incentivize contributions by a range of state actors. While currently imperfect, these forms of motivation offer a more universal driver for change that would weaken the dominance of Western states. In the long term, states must continue working beyond the "deescalation of risk within already present cycles of violence" and aim to build toward addressing the more structural determinants of violence. This will require long-term motivation beyond the immediate moral threat generated by mass atrocity crimes (Bohm and Brown 2020, 60). As this book has consistently argued, institutions and legal structures already exist that would allow mass atrocity prevention and protection to be more effectively delivered and supported. The challenges remain how to motivate various actors through the more creative use of these structures and how to better connect motivation to a more expansive understanding of state interests.

As Barelli (2018) has argued, the challenge posed by the rising powers to the effective functioning of the R2P should not be understood as requiring these states to simply be more willing to engage in forcible intervention. Rather, that challenge should be framed in terms of how we can get these states to make "more credible contributions to peacefully preventing and halting the commission of atrocity crimes" (173). When examining China's recent record on the R2P, one can point to its support of nearly all R2P-related UN peacekeeping and humanitarian protection missions, such as Côte d'Ivoire, Democratic Republic of the Congo, Mali, Somalia, South Sudan, and Yemen (Chen and Yin 2020, 781). The initial narrative regarding the negative response by Russia and China to the 2011 Libya intervention was to suggest that it marked a turning point in support; it was widely assumed that both states would now contest the R2P at every step; but the reality is in fact much more nuanced than this: China and Russia have both continued to support the R2P, albeit while contesting parts of the norm and its implementation in various contexts. Furthermore, while the language of sovereignty is still a large part of R2P discussions even when it comes to prevention, the record so far on support for human protection and prevention missions by the rising powers suggests, again, that sovereignty is never the sole deciding factor when support is given.

Another important strategy moving forward will be to continue forging stronger links to the security and economic stability implications of failing to prevent atrocity crimes, thereby more directly connecting the moral goals outlined by the concept of humanity to specific national security interests. The prevention of the four crimes concerns all states, but the motivation to address them may need to be more directly linked to discrete national security objectives alongside moral and ethical claims. This may at first seem counterproductive to the promotion of cosmopolitan ambitions. Finding shared ground among states for implementing atrocity prevention initiatives will eventually require an appeal to state-based security interests. So we must evaluate whether such initiatives will help produce, in part or in whole, outcomes that reflect and support common humanity, instead of simply assessing whether humanity is the sole purpose and motivator for action. Connected to this motivational focus is the need for greater awareness of how a state's image and status in global politics can be improved or damaged by its response (or non-response) to atrocity crimes. So we must appeal to states' pride and prestige, not just their shared idea of humanity. As Gallagher (2021) has argued, status in international relations can be impacted by strong negative criticism of state practices, which means that the use of collective international pressure can be an important lever for getting a state to change its policy or approach. Moreover, the future prosperity and security of the rising powers will depend increasingly on support for peaceful development and stability around the globe (Barelli 2018, 199). Likewise, the focus must be on emphasizing the practical implications of the global harms generated by mass atrocity crimes; far too often, states speak to the need to protect a common humanity without outlining exactly what is at stake if we fail to do so and what is to be gained if we succeed. What it means to be a responsible power in twenty-first century international relations will thus remain deeply connected to the shared moral agenda of maintaining international peace and security and preventing mass atrocity crimes.

Critical to the path forward for the R2P principle is a recognition that there can be no easy fixes and that the continuation of mass atrocity crimes accruing globally is a reflection of the complexity of state decision-making when it comes to setting national priorities and the moral limits of political life. While many rising powers, such as China and Russia, are likely to continue playing a vital role in decision-making on the R2P, as "permission givers" for international actions and shapers of the norm, there remain grounds for cooperation as well as potential for agreement on more effective preventive initiatives (Chen and Yin 2020, 804). However, overreliance on moral righteousness alone will not bring about greater motivational drive. Instead, reflecting on how state-based self-interest interacts with competing pressures must serve as the framework within which to develop new strategies for preventing and responding to mass atrocity crimes.

CONCLUDING REMARKS

As we look back over a significantly volatile decade in history, reflected in growing nationalist sentiment combined with a steady rise in outbreaks of mass atrocity crimes, it is clear that the R2P's promise has so far, sadly, fallen significantly short of many of the expectations first placed on it. It may be difficult today to find much hope for the future salience of the R2P principle, particularly in a world increasingly dominated by a return of nationalist priorities and fragmented multilateral cooperation. Also, there is growing evidence that support for humanitarian action is in steep decline,[1] reflecting growing isolationism and a lack of confidence in world leaders to address humanitarian issues. Yet the extent of the current challenges should not mean we lose sight of the long-term goal of reducing outbreaks of mass atrocity crimes wherever they occur. This book has argued that there can be no easy remedy for the horrific global harms generated by mass atrocity crimes, and thus we would be unwise to consider the R2P principle as representing a revolutionary shift in state priorities and behaviour. Instead, we must be prepared to view the potential for change in relation to a much longer-term approach, one that is conscious of the significant backward steps that may occur on this trajectory and (perhaps more controversially) the reality that the influence of R2P may at times be severely limited.

The former UN Special Advisor for the R2P, Jennifer Welsh (2017), has commented that there has in recent years been a significant "dampening of the cosmopolitan aspects of the R2P," with much less talk about individuals and human security. Thus, one can assume that it will be more and more of a challenge for the UN and individual states to construct and sustain the "cosmopolitan consciousness" that remains so integral to the core ethic of protection (Ralph and Gifkins 2017, 632). Humanity must therefore be understood less as a short-term motivator for rallying states in response to mass atrocity crimes and more as a concept whose strength lies in its ability to ground appeals that seek to regulate behaviour. It can therefore only be through a process whereby this regulative force is strengthened at the domestic *and* international levels that appeals to humanity can be more successfully reconciled with competing and interconnected state interests, in relation to mass atrocity prevention and response. Solutions will not be found in simply rearranging international decision-making structures, but must instead be located in changing how states weigh their responsibilities to those beyond their borders relative to competing political demands within their borders. This will be a slow, iterative, and incremental process; nevertheless, it is the most effective foundation on which to build toward the global challenge of bringing an end to mass atrocity crimes.

Notes

INTRODUCTION

1 The Global Centre for the Responsibility to Protect provides up-to-date information on Security Council resolutions that mention R2P, available at https://www.globalr2p.org/resources/un-security-council-resolutions-and-presidential-statements-referencing-r2p.

2 It is important to note here that this argument is different from that of deciding how such responsibilities such be distributed and assigned or what type of duty R2P should be understood as. For analysis of such debates, see Pattison 2010; and Roff 2013.

CHAPTER ONE

1 By March 2020, 103 member states and 2 UN observer missions had signed the declaration. See UN 70th General Assembly, "Political Statement on the Suspension of the Veto in Case of Mass Atrocities," https://onu.delegfrance.org/IMG/pdf/2015_08_07_veto_political_declaration_en.pdf.

CHAPTER THREE

1 Article 8 of the Rome Statute states: "The Court shall have jurisdiction in respect of war crimes in particular when committed as part of a plan or policy or as part of a large-scale commission of such crimes." International Criminal Court (ICC) 1998.

2 As Scheffer (2008, 320) has previously argued, the use of the term "mass atrocity crimes" serves as an important shorthand for grouping international crimes that require "the highest priority" in order to "react quickly and effectively to stop further commission of such crimes."

3 The concept of *erga omnes* obligations in international law relates back to the Barcelona Traction case at the International Court of Justice in 1970, where the court outlined four *erga omnes* obligations: the outlawing of acts of aggression; the outlawing of genocide; protection from slavery; and protection from racial discrimination. A distinction was thus made between obligations that the international community held and that all states had a legal interest in upholding and obligations of a state vis-à-vis another state. See Memeti and Nuhija 2013.

4 See ILC 1951 Draft Code.

5 See also the International Criminal Tribunal for Rwanda (ICTR) and International Criminal Court (ICC) as examples of this normative development.

6 For a further legal overview of these debates, see Jalloh 2013; and Robinson 1999.

CHAPTER FIVE

1 See also Scheid 2014.

2 See UN 2014b, S/PV.7180, Statement by Rwanda on Syrian Veto: "all of us must commit ourselves to putting action for humanity above inaction for interests." Also, Luxembourg stated its deep regret that "our shared humanity and values have not prevailed today."

CHAPTER SIX

1 The term "moral sacrifice" is used here to encapsulate the idea that global protection practices force states to make moral decisions about the value of both their own material capabilities and the value of soldiers' lives in relation to those they are protecting.

CONCLUSION

1 See Aurora Humanitarian Index (2017), https://auroraprize.com/en/aurora/article/humanitarian_index/10836/aurora-humanitarian-index-2017/2017.

References

Abass, Ademola. 2012. "The African Union and the Responsibility to Protect: Principles and Limitations." In *Responsibility to Protect: From Principle to Practice*, edited by Julia Hoffmann and André Nollkaemper, 213–36. Amsterdam: Amsterdam University Press.

– 2015. "Failure to Protect: Syria and the UN Security Council." https://reliefweb.int/sites/reliefweb.int/files/resources/syriapaper_final.pdf.

Adediran, Bolarinwa. 2017. "Implementing R2P: Towards a Regional Solution?" *Global Responsibility to Protect* 9(4): 459–87.

– 2018. "Reforming the Security Council through a Code of Conduct: A Sisyphean Task?" *Ethics and International Affairs* 32(4): 463–82.

Adler-Nissen, Rebecca, and Vincent Pouliot. 2014. "Power in Practice: Negotiating the International Intervention in Libya." *European Journal of International Relations* 20(4): 889–911.

Adler-Nissen, Rebecca, and Ayse Zarakol. 2020. "Struggles for Recognition: The Liberal International Order and the Merger of Its Discontents." *International Organization* 75 (Spring): 611–34.

Adorno, Theodor. 2000. *Problems of Moral Philosophy*. Cambridge: Polity Press.

Ainley, Kirsten. 2015. "The Responsibility to Protect and the International Criminal Court: Counteracting the Crisis." *International Affairs* 91(1): 37–54.

Akbarzadeh, Shahram, and Arif Saba. 2019. "UN Paralysis over Syria: The Responsibility to Protect or Regime Change?" *International Politics* 56: 536–50.

Altman, Andrew. 2006. "The Persistent Fiction of Harm to Humanity." *Ethics and International Affairs* 20(3): 367–72.

– 2012. "Genocide and Crimes against Humanity: Dispelling the Conceptual Fog." *Social Philosophy and Policy* 29(1): 280–308.

Amnesty International. 2017. "'Politics of Demonization' Breeding Division and Fear." https://www.amnesty.org/en/latest/news/2017/02/amnesty-international-annual-report-201617.

Anderson-Gold, Sharon. 2009. "Kant, Radical Evil, and Crimes against Humanity." In *Kant's Anatomy of Evil*, edited by Sharon Anderson-Gold and Pablo Muchnik,195–214. Cambridge: Cambridge University Press.

Aning, Kwesi, and Frank Okyere. 2016. "The African Union.". In *The Oxford Handbook of the Responsibility to Protect*, 355–72, edited by Alex Bellamy and Tim Dunne. Oxford: Oxford University Press.

Anghie, Antony. 2006. "The Evolution of International Law: Colonial and Postcolonial Realities." *Third World Quarterly* 27(5): 739–53.

Anghie, Antony, and B.S. Chimni. 2003. "Third World Approaches to International Law and Individual Responsibility in Internal Conflicts." *Chinese Journal of International Law* 2(1): 77–103.

Annan, Kofi. 1999a. "Secretary-General presents his annual report to General Assembly". Press Release, SG/SM/7136, GA/9596. shttps://www.un.org/press/en/1999/19990920.sgsm7136.html.

– 1999b. "Report of the Secretary-General to the Security Council on the Protection of Civilians in Armed Conflict." S/1999/957. https://unispal.un.org/DPA/DPR/unispal.nsf/0/62038AA80887F23A85256C85007230A4.

– 2000. "We the People in the 21st Century." http://www.un.org/en/events/pastevents/pdfs/We_The_Peoples.pdf.

– 2001. "Human Rights and Humanitarian Intervention in the Twenty-First Century." In *Realizing Human Rights: Moving from Inspiration to Impact*, edited by Samantha Power and Graham Allison, 310–19. New York: St. Martin's Press.

Arendt, Hannah. 1963. *Eichmann in Jerusalem*. New York: Viking Press.

Averre, Derek, and Lance Davies. 2015. "Russia, Humanitarian Intervention, and the Responsibility to Protect: The Case of Syria." *International Affairs* 91(4): 813–34.

Ayoob, Mohammed. 2010. "Making Sense of Global Tensions: Dominant and Subaltern Conceptions of Order and Justice in the International System." *International Studies* 47(2–4): 129–41.

Badar, Mohamed Elewa. 2004. "From the Nuremberg Charter to the Rome Statute: Defining the Elements of Crimes against Humanity." *San Diego International Law Journal* 73(5): 122–40.

Bain, William. 2007. "One Order, Two Laws: Recovering the 'Normative' in English School Theory." *Review of International Studies* 33(4): 557–75.

– 2010. "Responsibility and Obligation in the 'Responsibility to Protect.'" *Review of International Studies* 36(1): 25–6.

Baldry, H.C. 1965. *The Unity of Mankind in Greek thought*. Cambridge: Cambridge University Press.

Barelli, Mauro. 2018. "Preventing and Responding to Atrocity Crimes: China, Sovereignty, and the Responsibility to Protect." *Journal of Conflict and Security Law* 23(2): 173–201.

Barnett, Michael. 2002. *Eyewitness to a Genocide: The United Nations and Rwanda*. Ithaca: Cornell University Press.

Bartelson, Jens. 2009. *Visions of World Community*. Cambridge: Cambridge University Press.

Bassiouni, Mahmoud Cherif. 1999. *Crimes against Humanity in International Criminal Law*. The Hague: Martinus Nijhoff.

Bauböck, Rainer. 2018. "Europe's Commitments and Failures in the Refugee Crisis." *European Political Science* 17: 140–50.

Bauman, Zygmunt. 2001. *Community*. Cambridge: Polity.

Bauman, Zygmunt, and Keith Tester. 2001. *Conversations with Zygmunt Bauman*. Cambridge: Polity.

Beardsworth, Richard, Garrett Wallace Brown, and Richard Shapcott. 2019. *The State and Cosmopolitan Responsibilities*. Oxford: Oxford University Press.

Bellamy, Alex. 2002. "Pragmatic Solidarism and the Dilemmas of Humanitarian Intervention." *Millennium – Journal of International Studies* 31(3): 473–97.

– 2009. *Responsibility to Protect: The Global Effort to End Mass Atrocities*. Cambridge: Polity Press.

– 2010. "The Responsibility to Protect – Five Years On." *Ethics and International Affairs* 24(2): 143–69.

– 2011. "Libya and the Responsibility to Protect: The Exception and the Norm." *Ethics and International Affairs* 25(3): 263–9.

– 2013. "The Responsibility to Protect: Added Value or Hot Air?" *Cooperation and Conflict* 48(3): 333–57.

– 2014. *The Responsibility to Protect: A Defence*. Oxford: Oxford University Press.

– 2015a. "Still Hearing the Cries from the Graves: Srebrenica, R2P, and the Struggle for Human Protection," http://www.internationalaffairs.org.au/australian_outlook/still-hearing-the-cries-from-the-graves-srebrenica-r2p-and-the-struggle-for-human-protection.

– 2015b. "The Responsibility to Protect: A Wide or Narrow Concept." In *The Responsibility to Protect (R2P): A New Paradigm of International Law?*, edited by Peter Hilpold, 38–59. Leiden: Brill Nijhoff.

– 2015c. "The Responsibility to Protect Turns Ten." *Ethics and International Affairs* 29(2): 161–85.

– 2016. "R2P in a Time of Trump: Can Human Protection Weather the Storm?" Speech at the University of Oxford, 5 December 2016. https://www.politics.ox.ac.uk/departmental/r2p-in-a-time-of-trump-can-human-protection-weather-the-storm.html.

– 2020. "The Responsibility to Protect at 15: A Promise Unfulfilled." *Global Centre for the Responsibility to Protect*. https://www.globalr2p.org/publications/the-responsibility-to-protect-at-15-a-promise-unfulfilled.

Bentley, Michelle. 2017. "The Intervention Taboo(s): Strategy and Normative Invalidation." *Review of International Studies* 43(3): 557–80.

Beresford, Alex. 2015. "A Responsibility to Protect Africa from the West?" *International Politics* 52(3): 288–304.

Bilsky, Leora. 2010. "The Eichmann Trial and the Legacy of Jurisdiction." In *Politics in Dark Times: Encounters with Hannah Arendt*, edited by Seyla Benhabib, Roy Tsao, and Peter Verovšek, 198–218. Cambridge: Cambridge University Press.

Binder, Martin. 2009. "Humanitarian Crises and the International Politics of Selectivity." *Human Rights Review* 10 (3): 327–48.

Blitz, James. 2011. "Cameron Ardent in Support of Rebels in Libya." *Financial Times*, 10 March.

Bloomfield, Alan. 2015. "India and the Libyan Crisis: Flirting with the Responsibility to Protect, Retreating to the Sovereignty Norm." *Contemporary Security Policy* 36(1): 27–55.

Bohm, Alexandra, and Garrett W. Brown. 2020. "R2P and Prevention: The International Community and Its Role in the Determinants of Mass Atrocity." *Global Responsibility to Protect* 13(1): 60–95.

Boot, Machteld. 2002. *Genocide, Crimes against Humanity, War Crimes: Nullum Crimen Sine Lege and the Subject Matter Jurisdiction of the International Criminal Court*. Antwerp: Intersentia.

Booth, Ken, and Tim Dunne. 1999. "Learning beyond Frontiers." In *Human Rights in Global Politics*, edited by Tim Dunne and Nicholas Wheeler, 303–28. Cambridge: Cambridge University Press.

Botte, Auriane. 2015. "Redefining the Responsibility to Protect Concept as a Response to International Crimes." *International Journal of Human Rights* 19(8): 1029–43.

Boucher, David. 2011. *The Limits of Ethics in International Relations*. Oxford: Oxford University Press.

Brown, Chris. 2013. "The Antipolitical Theory of Responsibility to Protect." *Global Responsibility to Protect* 5(4): 423–42.

Brown, Garrett Wallace. 2009. *Grounding Cosmopolitanism*. Edinburgh: Edinburgh University Press.

Brown, Garrett Wallace, and Samuel Jarvis. 2019. "Motivating Cosmopolitanism and the Responsibility for the Health of Others." In *The State and Cosmopolitan Responsibilities*, edited by Richard Beardsworth, Garrett Wallace Brown, and Richard Shapcott, 203–23. Oxford: Oxford University Press.

Brunnee, Jutta, and Stephan Toope. 2006. "Norms, Institutions, and UN Reform: The Responsibility to Protect." *Journal of International Law and International Relations* 2: 121–37.

Buchan, Russell. 2013. *International Law and the Construction of the Liberal Peace*. Oxford: Hart.

Bulley, Dan. 2010. "The Politics of Ethical Foreign Policy: A Responsibility to Protect Whom?" *European Journal of International Relations* 16(3): 441–61.

Burke-White, William. 2011. "Adoption of the Responsibility to Protect." In *The Responsibility to Protect: The Promise of Stopping Mass Atrocities in Our Time*, edited by Jared Genser and Irwin Colter, 17–36. Oxford: Oxford University Press.

Busses, Mark. 2014. *Global Ethics and the Power Relations of Responsibility: The Politics of The Responsibility to Protect*. PhD diss., McMaster University. https://macsphere.mcmaster.ca/bitstream/11375/13794/1/fulltext.pdf.

Butler, Judith. 2009. *Frames of War: When Is Life Grievable?* London: Verso.

Byers, Michael. 2015. "International Law and the Responsibility to Protect." In *Theorising the Responsibility to Protect*, edited by Ramesh Thakur and William Maley, 101–24. Cambridge: Cambridge University Press.

Caney, Simon. 2005. *Justice beyond Borders*. Oxford: Oxford University Press.

Cannizzaro, Enzo. 2014. "Responsibility to Protect and the Competence of UN Organs." In *The Responsibility to Protect (R2P): A New Paradigm of International Law?*, edited by Peter Hilpold, 207–18. Leiden: Brill.

Carvin, Stephanie. 2010. "A Responsibility to Reality: a Reply to Louise Arbour." *Review of International Studies* 36(1): 47–54.

Cater, Charles, and David Malone. 2016. "The Origins and Evolution of Responsibility to Protect at the UN." *International Relations* 30(3): 278–97.

Chan, Phil. 2013. "A Keen Observer of the International Rule of Law? International Law in China's Voting Behaviour and Argumentation in the United Nations Security Council." *Leiden Journal of International Law* 26(4): 875–907.

Chandler, David. 2004. "The Responsibility To Protect? Imposing the 'Liberal Peace.'" *International Peacekeeping* 11(1): 59–81.

Chehtman, Alejandro. 2010. *The Philosophical Foundations of Extraterritorial Punishment*. Oxford: Oxford University Press.

Chen, Xunwu. 2013. "The Concept of Crimes against Humanity and the Spirit of Our Time." *Journal of East-West Thought* 2 (Summer): 3.

Chesterman, Simon. 2000. "An Altogether Different Order: Defining the Elements of Crimes against Humanity." *Duke Journal of Comparative and International Law* 10(2): 307–43.

– 2001. *Just War or Just Peace: Humanitarian Intervention and International Law*. Oxford: Oxford University Press.

– 2011. "Leading from Behind: The Responsibility to Protect, the Obama Doctrine, and Humanitarian Intervention after Libya." *Ethics and International Affairs* 25(3): 1–7.

Chimni, B.S. 2002. "Forum Replies: A New Humanitarian Council for Humanitarian Interventions?" *International Journal of Human Rights* 6(1): 103–12.

– 2018. "Customary International Law: A Third World Perspective." *American Journal of International Law* 112(1): 1–46.

Cicero, Marcus Tullius. 1998. *The Republic and the Laws*. Translated by N. Rudd. Oxford: Oxford University Press.

Clinton, William Jefferson. 1999a. Transcript of TV address to the Serbian people. 26 March. http://edition.cnn.com/WORLD/europe/9903/26/clinton.transcript/index.html.

– 1999b. Remarks at the Close of the North Atlantic Treaty Organization 50th Anniversary Summit. 25 April. https://www.govinfo.gov/content/pkg/PPP-1999-book1/html/PPP-1999-book1-doc-pg630.htm.

Coates, Anthony. 2006. "Humanitarian Intervention: A Conflict of Traditions." In *Humanitarian Intervention*, edited by Terry Nardin and Melissa S. Williams, 58–83. New York: NYU Press.

Coupland, Robert. 2001. "Humanity: What Is It and How Does It Influence International Law?" *International Review of the Red Cross* 83(844): 969–89.

Crossley, Noele. 2012. "The Responsibility to Protect in 2012: R2P fails in Syria, Brazil's 'RWP' Emerges." http://www.globalpolicyjournal.com/blog/28/12/2012/responsibility-protect-2012-r2p-fails-syria-brazil%E2%80%99s-%E2%80%98rwp%E2%80%99-emerges.

– 2016. *Evaluating the Responsibility to Protect: Mass Atrocity Prevention as a Consolidating Norm in International Society*. Oxford: Routledge.

Cunliffe, Phillip. 2010. "Dangerous Duties: Power, Paternalism, and the 'Responsibility to Protect.'" *Review of International Studies* 36(1): 79–96.

de Waal, Frans. 2008. "Putting the Altruism Back into Altruism: The Evolution of Empathy." *Annual Review of Psychology* 59: 279–300.

Del Sarto, R. Raffaella. 2006. "Security and Democracy: A Reprise." *European Security* 15(4): 507–18.

Deng, Francis, Sadikiel Kimaro, Terrence Lyons, Donald Rothchild, and William Zartman. 1996. *Sovereignty as Responsibility: Conflict Management in Africa*. Washington, D.C.: Brookings Institution.

Diggelmann, Oliver. 2014. "Ethical Dilemmas Connected with the 'Responsibility to Protect.'" In *The Responsibility to Protect (R2P): A New Paradigm of International Law?*, edited by Peter Hilpold, 405–16. Leiden: Brill Nijhoff.

Doyle, Michael. 2014. "Law, Ethics, and the Responsibility to Protect." In *The Ethics of Armed Humanitarian Intervention*, edited by Don E. Scheid, 187–208. Cambridge: Cambridge University Press.

– 2015. *The Question of Intervention: John Stuart Mill and the Responsibility to Protect*. New Haven: Yale University Press.

Dubler, Robert. 2008. "What's in a Name? A Theory of Crimes against Humanity." *Australian International Law Journal* 85: 85–107.

Duff, Antony. 2009. "Can We Punish the Perpetrators of Atrocities?" In *The Religious in Responses to Mass Atrocity: Interdisciplinary Perspectives*, edited by Thomas Brudholm and Thomas Cushman, 79–104. Cambridge: Cambridge University Press.

Dunford, Robin, and Michael Neu. 2019. *Just War and the Responsibility to Protect: A Critique*. London: Zed Books.

Dunne, Tim, and Eglantine Staunton. 2016. "The Genocide Convention and Cold War Humanitarian Intervention." In *The Oxford Handbook of the Responsibility to Protect*, edited by Alex Bellamy and Tim Dunne. Oxford: Oxford University Press.

Durham, Helen, and Eve Massingham. 2015. "Moving from the Mechanics of Accountability to a Culture of Accountability: What More Can Be Done in Addition to Prosecuting War Crimes?" In *Accountability for Violations of International Humanitarian Law: Essays in Honour of Tim McCormack*, edited by Jadranka Petrovic, 267–81. Oxford: Routledge.

Ercan, Pinar Gözen. 2016. *Debating the Future of the Responsibility to Protect*. London: Palgrave Macmillan.

Etzioni, Amitai. 2009. "The Common Good and Rights. A Neo-Communitarian Approach." *Georgetown Journal of International Affairs* 10(1): 113–19.

Evans, Gareth. 2006. *Responsibility to Protect: Unfinished Business.* G8 Summit 2006: Issues and Instruments. https://www.gevans.org/opeds/oped73.html.

– 2008a. *The Responsibility to Protect: Ending Mass Atrocity Crimes Once and for All*. Washington, D.C.: Brookings Institution Press.

– 2008b. "When Nations Kill their Own." *Christian Science Monitor*, 10 October 2008. https://www.csmonitor.com/Commentary/Opinion/2008/1010/p09s01-coop.html.

– 2009. "Implementing the Responsibility to Protect: The Need to Build on the 2005 Consensus." Speech at the UN General Assembly, New York City, 23 July. http://www.gevans.org/speeches/speech405.html.

– 2015. "The Evolution of the Responsibility to Protect: From Concept and Principle to Actionable Norm." In *Theorising the Responsibility to Protect*, edited by Ramesh Thakur and William Maley, 16–37. Cambridge: Cambridge University Press.

Falk, Barbara, and Sara Skinner. 2016. "The Responsibility to Protect: A Normative Shift from Words to Action?" *International Peacekeeping* 23(3): 493–505.

Falk, Richard. 1992. *Explorations at the Edge of Time*. Philadelphia: Temple University Press.

Fassbender, Bardo. 2002. "Uncertain Steps into a Post–Cold War World: The Role and Functioning of the UN Security Council after a Decade of Measures against Iraq." *European Journal of International Law* 13(1): 273–303.

– 2011. *Securing Human Rights? Achievements and Challenges of the UN Security Council*. Oxford: Oxford University Press.

Fast, Larissa. 2016. "Unpacking the Principle of Humanity: Tensions and Lessons." *International Review of the Red Cross* 897–8: 111–31.

Feldman, Ilana, and Miriam Ticktin. 2010. *In the Name of Humanity: The Government of Threat and Care*. Durham: Duke University Press.

Ferguson, Yale H., and Richard W. Mansbach. 2017. "The Decline of the Liberal Global Order and the Revival of Nationalism." In *The Global Community Yearbook of International Law and Jurisprudence 2017*, edited by Giuliana Ziccardi Capaldo, 31–70. Oxford: Oxford University Press.

Finnemore, Martha. 2003. *The Purpose of Intervention: Changing Beliefs about the Use of Force*. Ithaca: Cornell University Press.

– 2008. "Paradoxes in Humanitarian Intervention." In *Moral Limit and Possibility in World Politics*, edited by Richard Price, 197–224. Cambridge: Cambridge University Press.

Forst, Rainer. 2011. "The Ground of Critique: On the Concept of Human Dignity in Social Orders of Justification." *Philosophy and Social Criticism* 37(9): 965–76.

Fraser, Trudy. 2014. *Maintaining Peace and Security?: The United Nations in a Changing World*. London: Palgrave Macmillan.

Frost, Mervyn. 2009. *Global Ethics: Anarchy, Freedom, and International Relations*. London: Routledge.

Frulli, Micaela. 2001. "Are Crimes against Humanity More Serious Than War Crimes?" *European Journal of International Law* 12(2): 329–50.

Gaita, Raimond. 2000. *A Common Humanity: Thinking about Love and Truth and Justice*. Oxford: Routledge.

– 2005. "Refocusing Genocide: A Philosophical Responsibility." In *Genocide and Human Rights: A Philosophical Guide*, edited by John K. Roth, 153–66. London: Palgrave Macmillan.

Gallagher, Adrian. 2013. *Genocide and Its Threat to Contemporary International Order*. London: Palgrave Macmillan.

– 2015. "The Responsibility to Protect Ten Years on from the World Summit: A Call to Manage Expectations." *Global Responsibility to Protect* 7(3–4): 254–74.

– 2016. "Conceptualizing Humanity in the English School." *International Theory* 8(2): 341–64.

– 2021. "To Name and Shame or Not, and If So, How? A Pragmatic Analysis of Naming and Shaming the Chinese Government over Mass Atrocity Crimes against the Uyghurs and Other Muslim Minorities in Xinjiang." *Journal of Global Security Studies* [online first].

Gallagher, Adrian, and Garrett Wallace Brown. 2016. "The Responsibility to Protect 10 Years on from the World Summit: A Victory for Common Humanity?" *International Politics* 53(1): 8–13.

Gallagher, Adrian, and Jason Ralph. 2013. "Syria: Can Legitimacy for Intervention Be Found in a Uniting for Peace Resolution?" http://www.bss.leeds.ac.uk/2013/09/05/syria-can-legitimacy-for-intervention-be-found-in-a-uniting-for-peace-resolution.

Garwood-Gowers, Andrew. 2015. "R2P Ten Years after the World Summit: Explaining Ongoing Contestation over Pillar iii." *Global Responsibility to Protect* 7(3–4): 300–24.

Gehring, Thomas, and Thomas Dörfler. 2019. "Constitutive Mechanisms of UN Security Council Practices: Precedent Pressure, Ratchet Effect, and Council Action Regarding Intrastate Conflicts." *Review of International Studies* 45(1): 120–40.

Geras, Norman. 1995. *Solidarity in the Conversation of Humankind: The Ungroundable Liberalism of Richard Rorty*. London: Verso.

– 2005. "Genocide and Crimes against Humanity." In *Genocide and Human Rights*, edited by John K Roth, 167–81. New York: Palgrave Macmillan.

– 2011. *Crimes against Humanity*. Manchester: Manchester University Press.

Gifkins, Jess. 2016. "R2P in the UN Security Council: Darfur, Libya, and Beyond." *Cooperation and Conflict* 51(2): 148–65.

– 2021. "Beyond the Veto: Roles in UN Security Council Decision-Making." *Global Governance: A Review of Multilateralism and International Organizations* 27(1): 1–24.

Gifkins, Jess, Samuel Jarvis, and Jason Ralph. 2019. "Brexit and the UN Security Council: Declining Briitish Influence?" International Affairs 95(6): 1349–68.

– 2019. "Global Britain in the United Nations." United Nations Association of the UK.

Glanville, Luke. 2012. "The Responsibility to Protect beyond Borders." *Human Rights Law Review* 12(1): 1–32.

– 2013. *Sovereignty and the Responsibility to Protect: A New History*. Chicago: University of Chicago Press.

– 2016a. "Does R2P Matter? Interpreting the Impact of a Norm." *Cooperation and Conflict* 51(2): 184–99.

– 2016b. "Self-Interest and the Distant Vulnerable." *Ethics and International Affairs* 30(3): 335–53.

– 2020. "Hypocritical Inhospitality: The Global Refugee Crisis in the Light of History." *Ethics and International Affairs* 34(1): 3–12.

Graubart, Jonathan. 2015. "War Is Not the Answer: The Responsibility to Protect and Military Intervention." In *Theorising the Responsibility to Protect*, edited by Ramesh Thakur and William Maley, 200–20. Cambridge: Cambridge University Press.

Guterres, António. 2017. "Implementing the Responsibility to Protect: Accountability for Prevention Report of the Secretary-General." A/71/1016–S/2017/556. https://reliefweb.int/sites/reliefweb.int/files/resources/N1725138.pdf.

– 2019. "Responsibility to Protect: Lessons Learned for Prevention, Report of the Secretary-General." A/73/898-S/2019/463. https://www.globalr2p.org/resources/responsibility-to-protect-lessons-learned-for-prevention-2019.

Gyekye, Kwame. 2004. *Beyond Cultures: Perceiving a Common Humanity*. Washington, D.C.: Council for Research in Values and Philosophy.

Habermas, Jürgen. 1990. "Justice and Solidarity: On the Discussion Concerning Stage 6." In *The Moral Domain: Essays in the Ongoing Discussion between Philosophy and the Social Sciences*, edited by Gertrud Nunner-Winkler, Wolfgang Edelstein, and Thomas E. Wren, 224–54. Cambridge, MA: MIT Press.

– 2008. *Between Naturalism and Religion*. Cambridge: Polity Press.

Hannum, Hurst. 2016. "Reinvigorating Human Rights for the Twenty-First Century." *Human Rights Law Review* 16(3): 409–51.

Harrison, Graham. 2016. "Assessing the Responsibility to Protect: Moving from Theory to Practice." http://blogs.lse.ac.uk/politicsandpolicy/the-responsibility-to-protect-realism-and-the-second-political-question.

Haslam, Nick. 2006. "Dehumanization: An Integrative Review." *Personality and Social Psychology Review* 10(3): 252–64.

Hayden, Patrick. 2005. *Cosmopolitan Global Politics*. Aldershot: Ashgate.

Hehir, Aidan. 2011. "The Illusion of Progress: Libya and the Future of R2P." http://www.e-ir.info/2011/09/11/the-illusion-of-progress-libya-and-the-future-of-r2p.

– 2012. *The Responsibility to Protect: Rhetoric, Reality, and the Future of Humanitarian Intervention*. Basingstoke: Palgrave Macmillan.

– 2013a. "The Responsibility to Protect as the Apotheosis of Liberal Teleology." In *Libya, the Responsibility to Protect, and the Future of Humanitarian Intervention*, edited by Aidan Hehir and Robert Murray, 34–57. London: Palgrave Macmillan.

– 2013b. "The Permanence of Inconsistency: Libya, the Security Council, and the Responsibility to Protect." *International Security* 38(1): 137–59.

– 2015a. "The Viability of the 'Responsibility to Prevent.'" *Politics and Governance Journal* 3(3): 85–97.

– 2015b. "From Human Security to the Responsibility to Protect: The Co-Option of Dissent?" *Michigan State International Law Review* 23: 675–99.

– 2016. "Assessing the Influence of the Responsibility to Protect on the UN Security Council during the Arab Spring." *Cooperation and Conflict* 51(2): 166–83.

– 2017. "Utopian in the Right Sense: The Responsibility to Protect and the Logical Necessity of Reform." *Ethics and International Affairs* 31(3): 335–55.

Hill, Thomas. 1980. "Humanity as an End in Itself." *Ethics* 91(1): 84–99.

Hilpold, Peter. 2012. "Intervening in the Name of Humanity: RtoP and the Power of Ideas." *Journal of Conflict Security and Law* 17(1): 49–79.

Hobson, Christopher. 2016. "Responding to Failure: The Responsibility to Protect after Libya." *Millennium Journal of International Studies* 44(3): 433–54.

Honneth, Axel. 1995. *The Struggle for Recognition: The Moral Grammar of Social Conflicts*. Cambridge: Polity Press.

Hopgood, Stephen. 2014. "The Last Rites for Humanitarian Intervention: Darfur, Sri Lanka, and R2P." *Global Responsibility to Protect* 6(2): 181–205.

Hubert, Don, and Ariela Blätter. 2012. "The Responsibility to Protect as International Crimes Prevention." *Global Responsibility to Protect* 4: 33–66.

Hurd, Ian. 2012a. "The Selectively Expansive UN Security Council: Domestic Threats to International Peace and Security" (American Society of International Law Proceedings). http://papers.ssrn.com/sol3/papers.cfm?abstract_id=2488581.

– 2012b. "Libya and Responsibility to Protect: Great-Power Permission or International Obligation?" https://www.ethicsandinternationalaffairs.org/2012/libya-and-responsibility-to-protect-great-power-permission-or-international-obligation.

Hurrell, Andrew. 2007. *On Global Order*. Oxford: Oxford University Press.

– 2012. "Review of The Problem of Harm in World Politics: Theoretical Investigations." *Ethics and International Affairs* 26(3): 390–2.

Hwang, Phyllis. 1998. "Defining Crimes against Humanity in the Rome Statute of the International Criminal Court." *Fordham International Law Journal* 22(2): 457–504.

ICISS. 2001. *The Responsibility to Protect: Report of the International Commission on Intervention and State Sovereignty*. Ottawa: International Development Research Centre.

ICTY. 1999. *Prosecutor v. Jelisic*, Case no. IT-95-10-T, Judgment 68 (14 December).

Ignatieff, Michael. 2001. "Lemkin's Word." *The New Republic*, 26 February 2001. http://www.newrepublic.com/article/politics/lemkins-word.

Ikenberry, John. 2018. "The End of Liberal International Order?" *International Affairs* 94(1): 7–23.

ILC (International Law Commission). 1951. Report of the International Law Commission to the General Assembly, U.N. Doc. A/1858. https://legal.un.org/ilc/publications/yearbooks/english/ilc_1951_v2.pdf.

– 1996. Draft Code of Crimes against the Peace and Security of Mankind, U.N. Doc A/51/10. https://legal.un.org/ilc/texts/instruments/english/draft_articles/7_4_1996.pdf.

Jacob, Cecilia. 2018. "From Norm Contestation to Norm Implementation: Recursivity and the Responsibility to Protect." *Global Governance* 24(3): 391-409.

Jalloh, Charles Chernor. 2013. "What Makes a Crime against Humanity a Crime against Humanity." *AMU International Law Review* 28: 382–441.

Jones, Catherine. 2018. *China's Challenge to Liberal Norms: The Durability of International Order*. London: Palgrave Macmillan.

Kant, Immanuel. 1998. *Critique of Pure Reason*, edited and translated by Paul Guyer and Allen Wood. Cambridge: Cambridge University Press.

– 2002. *Groundwork for the Metaphysics Of Morals*, edited and translated by Thomas E. Hill and Arnulf Zweig. Oxford: Oxford University Press.

Kassner, Joshua James. 2013. *Rwanda and the Moral Obligation of Humanitarian Intervention*. Edinburgh: Edinburgh University Press.

Kateb, George. 2011. *Human Dignity*. Cambridge, MA: Harvard University Press.

Kerstein, Samuel. 2006. "Deriving the Formula of Humanity." In *Groundwork for the Metaphysics of Morals*, edited by Christoph Horn and Dieter Schönecker, 200–21. Berlin: Walter de Gruyter.

Ki-moon, Ban. 2008. "Responsible Sovereignty: International Cooperation for a Changed World." http://www.un.org/press/en/2008/sgsm11701.doc.htm.

– 2009. "Implementing the Responsibility to Protect. Report of the Secretary-General", A/63/677. https://www.un.org/ruleoflaw/blog/document/report-of-the-secretary-general-implementing-the-responsibility-to-protect.

– 2015. "A Vital and Enduring Commitment: Implementing the Responsibility to Protect: Report of the Secretary-General." A/69/981–S/2015/500. http://www.un.org/en/preventgenocide/adviser/pdf/N1521764%202015%20SG%20Report%20R2P%20English.pdf.

– 2016. "Mobilizing Collective Action: The Next Decade of the Responsibility to Protect: Report of the Secretary-General." A/70/999–S/2016/620. http://www.responsibilitytoprotect.org/SG%20Report%202016%20Mobilizing%20collective%20action%20the%20next%20decade%20of%20the%20responsibility%20to%20protect.pdf.

Korsgaard, Christine. 1996. *Creating the Kingdom of Ends*. Cambridge: Cambridge University Press.

Krasner, Stephen D. 1999. *Sovereignty: Organized Hypocrisy*. Princeton: Princeton University Press.

Krieg, Andreas. 2013. *Motivations for Humanitarian Intervention: Theoretical and Empirical Considerations*. Dordrecht: Springer.

Kymlicka, Will. 2001. *Politics in the Vernacular*. Oxford: Oxford University Press.

Labonte, Melissa. 2013. *Human Rights and Humanitarian Norms, Strategic Framing, and Intervention*. Oxford: Routledge.

– 2016. "R2P's Status as a Norm." In *The Oxford Handbook of the Responsibility to Protect*, edited by Alex Bellamy and Tim Dunne, 133–50. Oxford: Oxford University Press.

Lang, Berel. 2005. "The Evil in Genocide." In *Genocide and Human Rights*, edited by John K. Roth, 5–17. New York: Palgrave Macmillan.

Lanz, David. 2011. "Why Darfur? The Responsibility to Protect as a Rallying Cry for Transnational Advocacy Groups." *Global Responsibility to Protect* 3(2): 223–47.

Lee, K. Pak, and Lai-Ha Chan. 2016. "China's and India's Perspectives on Military Intervention: Why Africa but not Syria?" *Australian Journal of International Affairs* 70(2): 179–214.

Levinas, Emmanuel. 2005. *Humanism of the Other*. Champaign: University of Illinois Press.

Linklater, Andrew. 2009. "Human Interconnectedness." *International Relations* 23(3): 481–97.

– 2011. *The Problem of Harm in World Politics*. Cambridge: Cambridge University Press.

– 2016. *Violence and Civilization in the Western States-Systems*. Cambridge: Cambridge University Press.

Lu, Catherine. 2000. "The One and Many Faces of Cosmopolitanism." *Journal of Political Philosophy* 8(2): 244–67.

– 2006. "Whose Principles? Whose Institutions? Legitimacy Challenges for 'Humanitarian Intervention.'" In *Humanitarian Intervention*, edited by Terry Nardin and Melissa S. Williams, 188–216. New York: NYU Press.

– 2007. "Humanitarian Intervention: Moral Ambition and Political Constraints." *International Journal* 62(4): 942–51.

Luban, David. 2002. "Intervention and Civilization: Some Unhappy Lessons of the Kosovo War." In *Global Justice and Transnational Politics*, edited by Pablo De Greiff and Ciaran P. Cronin, 79–116. Cambridge, MA: MIT Press.

– 2004. "A Theory of Crimes Against Humanity." *Yale Journal of International Law* 29: 85–167.

Lucas, George R. 2014. "Revisiting Armed Humanitarian Intervention: A 25-year Retrospective." In *The Ethics of Armed Humanitarian Intervention*, edited by Don E. Scheid, 26–45. Cambridge: Cambridge University Press.

Luck, Edward C. 2010. "The Responsibility to Protect: Growing Pains or Early Promise?" *Ethics and International Affairs* 24(4): 349–65.

Lynch, Colum. 2020. "U.N. Chief Faces Internal Criticism over Human Rights." *Foreign Policy*, 4 February. https://foreignpolicy.com/2020/02/04/un-chief-antonio-guterres-internal-criticism-human-rights.

Mabera, Faith, and Yolanda Spies. 2016. "How Well Does R2P Travel beyond the West?" In *The Oxford Handbook on the Responsibility to Protect*, edited by Alex Bellamy and Tim Dunne, 208–26. Oxford: Oxford University Press.

MacIntrye, Alasdair. 1995. "Is Patriotism a Virtue?" In *Theorizing Citizenship*, edited by Ronald Beiner, 209–28. New York: SUNY Press.

Macleod, Christopher. 2010. "Towards a Philosophical Account of Crimes against Humanity." *European Journal of International Law* 21(2): 281–302.

– 2012. "An Alternative Approach to the Harm of Genocide." *Politics* 32(3): 197–206.

Manusama, Kenneth. 2006. *The United Nations Security Council in the Post-Cold War Era*. Leiden: M. Nijhoff.

Margalit, Avishai. 2007. "Human Dignity between Kitsch and Deification." *Hedgehog Review* (Fall): 7–19.

Marlier, Grant, and Neta C. Crawford. 2013. "Incomplete and Imperfect Institutionalisation of Empathy and Altruism in the 'Responsibility to Protect' Doctrine." *Global Responsibility to Protect* 5(4): 397–422.

Martin, Stevie. 2011. "Sovereignty and the Responsibility to Protect." *Griffith Law Review* 20(1): 153–87.

Massingham, Eve. 2009. "Military Intervention for Humanitarian Purposes: Does the Responsibility to Protect Doctrine Advance the Legality of the Use of Force for Humanitarian Ends?" *International Review of the Red Cross* 91(876): 803–31.

May, Larry. 2005. *Crimes against Humanity*. Cambridge: Cambridge University Press.

Mazlish, Bruce. 2009. *The Idea of Humanity in a Global Era*. New York: Palgrave Macmillan.

Medzihorsky, Juraj, Milos Popovic, and Erin K. Jenne. 2017. "Rhetoric of Civil Conflict Management: United Nations Security Council Debates over the Syrian Civil War." *Research and Politics* 4(2): 1–10.

Memeti, Ardit, and Bekim Nuhija. 2013. "The Concept of Erga Omnes Obligations in International Law." *New Balkan Politics* 14: 31–47.

Menon, Rajan. 2016. *The Conceit of Humanitarian Intervention*. Oxford: Oxford University Press.

Merry, Michael S., and Doret J. Ruyter. 2011. "The Relevance of Cosmopolitanism for Moral Education." *Journal of Moral Education* 40(1): 1–18.

Mills, Kurt. 2015. "What Responsibilities Does the International Community Have in Complex Humanitarian Crises and Mass Atrocity Situations?" In *Human Rights Protection in Global Politics: Responsibilities of States and Non-State Actors*, edited by Kurt Mills and David Karp, 223–44. London: Palgrave.

Mitchell, Audra. 2014. *International Intervention in a Secular Age: Re-enchanting Humanity?* Oxford: Routledge.

Morris, Justin. 2013. "Libya and Syria: R2P and the Spectre of the Swinging Pendulum." *International Affairs* 89(5): 1265–83.

– 2015. "The Responsibility to Protect and the Great Powers: The Tensions of Dual Responsibility." *Global Responsibility to Protect* 7 (3–4): 398–421.

Moses, Jeremy. 2013. "Sovereignty as Irresponsibility? A Realist Critique of the Responsibility to Protect." *Review of International Studies* 39: 113–35.

Müller, Harald, and Jonas Wolff. 2014. "The Dual Use of an Historical Event: 'Rwanda 1994,' the Justification and Critique of Liberal Interventionism." *Journal of Intervention and Statebuilding* 8(4): 280–90.

Murray, Robert. 2013. "Humanitarianism, Responsibility, or Rationality? Evaluating Intervention as State Strategy." In *Libya, the Responsibility to*

Protect, and the Future of Humanitarian Intervention, edited by Aidan Hehir and Robert Murray, 15–33. London: Palgrave Macmillan.

Nail, Thomas. 2016. "A Tale of Two Crises: Migration and Terrorism after the Paris Attacks." *Studies in Ethnicity and Nationalism* 16(1): 158–67.

Nasu, Hitoshi. 2011. "The UN Security Council's Responsibility and the Responsibility to Protect." *Max Planck Yearbook of United Nations Law* 15: 37.

Nersessian, David. 2007. "Comparative Approaches to Punishing Hate: The Intersection of Genocide and Crimes against Humanity." *Stanford Journal of International Law* 43(2): 251–76.

Newman, Edward. 2016. "What Prospects for Common Humanity in a Divided World? The Scope for RtoP in a Transitional International Order." *International Politics* 53(1): 32–48.

– 2021. "Exploring the UK's Doctrine of Humanitarian Intervention, International Peacekeeping." *International Peacekeeping* [online first].

Ntoubandi, Faustin. 2007. *Amnesty for Crimes against Humanity under International Law*. Leiden: Martinus Nijhoff.

Obama, Barack. 2011. "Address to the Nation on Libya." The White House, 28 March. http://www.whitehouse.gov/the-press-office/2011/03/28/remarks-president-address-nation-libya.

– 2015. "Remarks to the United Nations General Assembly, United Nations Headquarters." 28 September. https://www.whitehouse.gov/the-press-office/2015/09/28/remarks-president-obama-united-nations-general-assembly.

Oellers-Frahm, Karin. 2014. "Responsibility to Protect: Any New Obligations for the Security Coucnil and Its Members." In *The Responsibility to Protect (R2P): A New Paradigm of International Law?*, edited by Peter Hilpold, 184–206. Leiden: Brill.

Orford, Anne. 2013. "Moral Internationalism and the Responsibility to Protect." *European Journal of International Law* 24(1): 83–108.

– 2016. "The Responsibility to Protect and the Limits of International Authority." In *Reassessing the Responsibility to Protect: Conceptual and Operational Challenges*, edited by Brett R. O'Bannon. Oxford: Routledge.

Ossewaarde, Marinus. 2007. "Cosmopolitanism and the Society of Strangers." *Current Sociology* 55(3): 367–88.

Papamichail, Andreas, and Hannah Partis-Jennings. 2016. "Why Common Humanity? Framing the Responsibility to Protect as a Common Response." *International Politics* 53(1): 83–100.

Parekh, Bhikhu. 1999. "Non-Ethnocentric Universalism." In *Human Rights in Global Politics*, edited by Tim Dunne and Nicholas Wheeler, 128–59. Cambridge: Cambridge University Press.

Paris, Roland. 2014. "The Responsibility to Protect and the Structural Problems of Preventive Humanitarian Intervention." *International Peacekeeping* 21(5): 569–603.

Pattison, James. 2010. *Humanitarian Intervention and the Responsibility to Protect*. Oxford: Oxford University Press.

– 2015. "Mapping the Responsibilities to Protect: A Typology of International Duties." *Global Responsibility to Protect* 7(2): 190–210.

– 2018. "The 'Responsibility to Protect' and International Political Theory." In *The Oxford Handbook of International Political Theory*, edited by Chris Brown and Robyn Eckersley, 330–42. Oxford: Oxford University Press.

Peters, Anne. 2009a. "Humanity as the A and Ω of Sovereignty." *European Journal of International Law* 20(3): 513–18.

– 2009b. "Membership in the Global Constitutional Community." In *The Constitutionalization of International Law*, edited by Jan Klabbers, Anne Peters, and Geir Ulfstein, 153–262. Oxford: Oxford University Press.

– 2011. "The Security Council's Responsibility to Protect." *International Organisations Law Review* 8: 1–40.

Phillips, Anne. 2015. *The Politics of the Human*. Cambridge: Cambridge University Press.

Pogge, Thomas. 1998. "The Categorical Imperative." In *Kant's Groundwork of the Metaphysics of Morals: Critical Essays*, edited by Paul Guyer, 189–214. Lanham: Rowman and Littlefield.

Ralph, Jason. 2017. "The Responsibility to Protect and the Rise of China: Lessons from Australia's Role as a 'Pragmatic' Norm Entrepreneur." *International Relations of the Asian Pacific* 17(1): 35–65.

– 2018. "What Should Be Done? Pragmatic Constructivist Ethics and the Responsibility Protect." *International Organization* 72(1): 173–203.

Ralph, Jason, and Jess Gifkins. 2017. "The Purpose of United Nations Security Council Practice: Contesting Competence Claims in the Normative Context Created by the Responsibility to Protect." *European Journal of International Relations* 23(3): 630–53.

Ralph, Jason, Jess Gifkins, and Samuel Jarvis. 2020. "The United Kingdom's Special Responsibilities at the United Nations: Diplomatic Practice in Normative Context." *British Journal of Politics and International Relations* 22(2): 164–81.

Recchia, Stefano. 2016. "Authorising Humanitarian Intervention: A Five-point Defence of Existing Multilateral Procedures." *Review of International Studies* 43(1): 50–72.

Renzo, Massimo. 2012. "Crimes against Humanity and the Limits of International Criminal Law." *Law and Philosophy* 31: 443–76.

Reus-Smit, Christian. 2001. *The Moral Purpose of the State: Culture, Social Identity, and Institutional Rationality in International Relations*. Princeton: Princeton University Press.

Rhoads, Emily, and Welsh, Jennifer. "Close Cousins in Protection: The Evolution of Two Norms." *International Affairs* 95(3): 597–617.

Roach, Steven C. 2016. "Affective Values in International Relations: Theorizing Emotional Actions and the Value of Resilience." *Politics* 36(4): 400–12.

Robertson, Geoffrey. 1999. *Crimes against Humanity*. New York: New Press.

Robinson, Darryl. 1999. "Defining Crimes against Humanity at the Rome Conference." *American Journal of International Law* 93(1) 43–57.

Rodley, Nigel S. 2016. "R2P and International Law: A Paradigm Shift?" In *The Oxford Handbook of the Responsibility to Protect*, edited by Alex Bellamy and Tim Dunne, 186–207. Oxford: Oxford University Press.

Roff, Heather M. 2013. *Global Justice, Kant, and the Responsibility to Protect: A Provisional Duty*. London: Routledge.

Rorty, Richard. 1989. *Contingency, Irony, and Solidarity*. Cambridge: Cambridge University Press.

Roth, John K. 2016. "Crying Out for Action: Do the Dead Say Anything about the Responsibility to Protect?" In *Reassessing the Responsibility to Protect: Conceptual and Operational Challenges*, edited by Brett R, O'Bannon, 151–63. Oxford: Routledge.

Ruiter, Adrienne de. 2021. "To Be or Not to Be Human: Resolving the Paradox of Dehumanisation." *European Journal of Political Theory*. [Online first].

Sampford, Charles, and Ramesh Thakur. 2015. "From the Right to Persecute to the Responsibility to Protect: Feuerbachain Inversions of Rights and Responsibilities in State–Citizen Relations." In *Theorising the Responsibility to Protect*, edited by Ramesh Thakur and William Maley, 38–58. Cambridge: Cambridge University Press.

Schabas, William. 2009. *Genocide in International Law*. Cambridge: Cambridge University Press.

Scheffer, David. 2008. "Atrocity Crimes Framing the Responsibility to Protect." *Case Western Reserve Journal of International Law* 40(1): 319–24.

Scheid, Don E., ed. 2014. *The Ethics of Armed Humanitarian Intervention*. Cambridge: Cambridge University Press.

Schindlmayr, Thomas. 2001. "Obstructing the Security Council: The Use of the Veto in the Twentieth Century." *Journal of the History of International Law* 3(2): 218–34.

Schmidt, Carl. 2007. *The Concept of the Political: Expanded Edition*. Chicago: University of Chicago Press.

Schmidt, Megan, and Amelia Wolf. 2012. "The Responsibility to Protect: A New Norm to Make 'Never Again' a Reality." https://icrtopblog.org/2012/12/05/the-responsibility-to-protect-a-new-norm-to-make-never-again-a-reality.

Sensen, Oliver. 2009. "Kant's Conception of Human Dignity." *Kant-Studien* 100(3): 309–31.

Shapcott, Richard. 2008. "Anti-Cosmopolitanism, Pluralism, and the Cosmopolitan Harm Principle." *Review of International Studies* 34(2): 185–205.

– 2010. *International Ethics*. Cambridge: Polity.

Sherman, Nancy. 1998. "Empathy, Respect, and Humanitarian Intervention." *Ethics and International Affairs* 12(1): 103–19.

Sirkin, Micol. 2010. "Expanding the Crime of Genocide to Include Ethnic Cleansing: A Return to Established Principles in Light of Contemporary Interpretations." *Seattle University Law Review* 33(2): 489–526.

Sleat, Matt. 2016a. "Politics or Ethics? Assessing the Responsibility to Protect." http://blogs.lse.ac.uk/politicsandpolicy/the-responsibility-to-protect-the-politics-of-evil-and-good.

– 2016b. "The Politics and Morality of the Responsibility to Protect: Beyond the Realist/Liberal Impasse." *International Politics* 53(1): 67–82.

Slim, Hugo. 1998. "Sharing a Universal Ethic: The Principle of Humanity in War." *International Journal of Human Rights* 2(4): 28–48.

Smith, Claire Q., and Susannah G. Williams. 2021. "Why Indonesia Adopted 'Quiet Diplomacy' over R2P in the Rohingya Crisis: The Roles of Islamic Humanitarianism, Civil–Military Relations, and ASEAN." *Global Responsibility to Protect* 13(2–3): 158–85.

Smith, Karen. 2020. "A Reflection on the Responsibility to Protect in 2020." https://reliefweb.int/report/world/reflection-responsibility-protect-2020.

Stark, Alex. 2011. "Introduction." In *The Responsibility to Protect: Challenges and Opportunities in Light of the Libyan Intervention*, 4–6. http://www.e-ir.info/wp-content/uploads/R2P.pdf.

Stefan, Cristina. 2017. "On Non-Western Norm Shapers: Brazil and the Responsibility While Protecting." *European Journal of International Security* 2(1): 88–110.

Tacheva, Blagovesta, and Garrett Wallace Brown. 2015. "Global Constitutionalism and the Responsibility to Protect." *Global Constitutionalism* 4(3): 428–67.

Tan, Kok-Chor. 2006. "The Duty to Protect." In *Humanitarian Intervention*, edited by Terry Nardin and Melissa S. Williams, 84–116. New York: NYU Press.

Taylor, Charles. 1985. *Philosophy and the Human Sciences: Philosophical Papers 2*. Cambridge: Cambridge University Press.

– 1993. *Reconciling the Solitudes*. Montreal and Kingston: McGill–Queen's University Press.

Teitel, Ruti. 2011. *Humanity's Law*. Oxford: Oxford University Press.

Thakur, Ramesh. 2011a. "Rebalancing Interests in the Shifting Global Order: R2P was the Game-Changer in the Decision to Impose a No-Fly Zone." *Canberra Times*, 22 March.

– 2011b. *The Responsibility to Protect: Norms, Laws, and the Use of Force in International Politics*. London: Routledge.

– 2015. "R2P's 'Structural' Problems: A Response to Roland Paris." *International Peacekeeping* 22(1): 11–25.

Tourinho, Marcos, Oliver Stuenkel, and Sarah Brockmeier. 2016. "Responsibility While Protecting": Reforming R2P Implementation." *Global Society* 30(1): 134–50.

UN (United Nations). 1945. Charter of the United Nations.

– 1948. Convention on the Prevention and Punishment of the Crime of Genocide. A/RES/3/260.

– 1950. Resolution adopted by the General Assembly. A/RES/377 (V).

– 1966. Security Council Resolution S/RES/221.

– 1991. Security Council Resolution. S/RES/688.

– 1992a. Security Council Summit: The Responsibility of the Security Council in the Maintenance of International Peace and Security. 3046th meeting. S/23500.

– 1992b. Security Council Resolution. S/RES/794.

– 1993. Report of the Secretary-General Pursuant to Paragraph 2 of Security Council Resolution 808. S/25704. http://www.icty.org/x/file/Legal%20Library/Statute/statute_re808_1993_en.pdf.

– 1994. Security Council Resolution. S/RES/929.

– 1999a. Independent Inquiry into the Actions of the United Nations during the 1994 Genocide in Rwanda. S/1999/1257.

– 1999b. 3989 Meeting of the Security Council. S/PV.3989.

– 2005. Resolution adopted by the General Assembly. A/RES/60/1.

– 2008. 5933rd meeting of the Security Council. S/PV.5933.

– 2009. "Delegates Weigh Legal Merits of Responsibility to Protect Concept as General Assembly Concludes Debate, 100th and 101st Meetings, 28 July." http://www.un.org/press/en/2009/ga10850.doc.htm.

– 2011a. 6650th meeting of the Security Council. S/PV.6650.

– 2011b. Security Council Resolution. S/RES/1973.

– 2011c. Statement by the President of the Security Council. S/PRST/2011/16.

– 2012a. 6710th meeting of the Security Council. S/PV.6710.
– 2012b. 6711th meeting of the Security Council. S/PV.671.
– 2012c. Resolution adopted by the General Assembly.. A/RES/66/253.
– 2014a. Report of the Independent International Commission of Inquiry on the Syrian Arab Republic. A/HRC/27/60.
– 2014b. 7180th meeting of the Security Council. S/PV.7180.
– 2014c. Resolution adopted by the General Assembly. A/RES/68/182.
– 2014d. 7216th meeting of the Security Council. S/RES/2165.
– 2015. General Assembly, Seventieth Session, Agenda item 122, Strengthening of the United Nations system. A/70/621–S/2015/978.
– 2017. 7922nd Meeting of the Security Council. S/PV.7922.
– 2018a. Meeting of the Security Council. S/RES 8334.
– 2018b. General Assembly, 37th Plenary meeting. A/73/PV.37.
– 2019. General Assembly, 93rd Plenary meeting. A/73/PV.93.

UNA-UK. 2015. "Never Again? A Guide to the Responsibility to Protect and the Prevention of Atrocity Crimes." https://www.una.org.uk/news/never-again-una-uk-publishes-guide-r2p.

Vernon, Richard. 2002. "What Is Crime against Humanity?" *Journal of Political Philosophy* 10(3): 231–49.

Vik, Cathinka. 2015. *Moral Responsibility, Statecraft, and Humanitarian Intervention: The US Response to Rwanda, Darfur, and Libya*. London: Routledge.

von Einsiedel, S. 2017. "Civil War Trends and the Changing Nature of Armed Conflict." United Nations University Centre for Policy Research. Occasional Paper 10. https://collections.unu.edu/eserv/UNU:6156/Civil_war_trends_UPDATED.pdf.

Wald, Patricia M. 2007. "Genocide and Crimes against Humanity." *Washington University Global Studies Law Review* 6(3): 621–33.

Waldorf, Lars. 2016. "Inhumanity's Law: Crimes against Humanity, RtoP, and South Sudan." *International Politics* 53(1) 49–66.

Walzer, Michael. 1977. *Just and Unjust Wars: A Philosophical Argument with Historical Illustrations*. New York: Basic Books.
– 1994. *Thick and Thin: Moral Argument at Home and Abroad.* Notre Dame: University of Notre Dame Press.

Weinert, Matthew S. 2015. *Making Human: World Order and the Global Governance of Human.* Ann Arbor: University of Michigan Press.

Weiss, Thomas. 2011. "RtoP Alive and Well after Libya." *Ethics and International Affairs* 25(3): 287–92.

Welsh, Jennifer. 2008. "The Security Council and Humanitarian Intervention." In *The United Nations Security Council and War*, edited by Vaughan

Lowe, Adam Roberts, Jennifer Welsh, and Dominik Zaum, 535–62. Oxford: Oxford University Press.

– 2012. "Who Should Act? Collective Responsibility and the Responsibility to Protect." In *The Routledge Handbook of the Responsibility to Protect*, edited by W. Andy Knight and Frazer Egerton, 103–14. Oxford: Routledge.

– 2013a. "Norm Contestation and the Responsibility to Protect." *Global Responsibility to Protect* 5(4): 365–96.

– 2013b. "The Responsibility to Protect Principle Is Not the Problem: Interview with Jennifer Welsh." https://theglobalobservatory.org/2013/12/the-responsibility-to-protect-principle-is-not-the-problem-interview-with-jennifer-walsh.

– 2014a. "Responsibility to Protect and the Language of Crimes: Collective Action and Individual Culpability." In *The Ethics of Armed Humanitarian Intervention,* edited by Don E Scheid, 209–23. Cambridge: Cambridge University Press.

– 2014b. "Implementing the 'Responsibility to Protect': Catalyzing Debate and Building Capacity." In *Implementation and World Politics: How International Norms Change Practice*, edited by Alexander Betts and Phillip Orchard, 124–43. Oxford: Oxford University Press.

– 2016a. "R2P's Next Ten Years: Deepening and Extending the Consensus." In *The Oxford Handbook of the Responsibility to Protect,* edited by Alex Bellamy and Tim Dunne, 984–1000. Oxford: Oxford University Press.

– 2016b. "The Responsibility to Prevent: Assessing the Gap between Rhetoric and Reality." *Cooperation and Conflict* 51(2): 216–32.

– 2017. "Roundtable on the Global State of R2P, Peace, and Security Research: Women's Perspectives." International Conference on the Responsibility to Protect, Peace, And Security, 12 December, University of Leeds.

– 2019. "Norm Robustness and the Responsibility to Protect." *Journal of Global Security Studies* 4(1): 53–72.

Welsh, Jennifer, and Maria Banda. 2010. "International Law and the Responsibility to Protect: Clarifying or Expanding States Responsibilities?" *Global Responsibility to Protect* 2(3): 213–31.

Wheeler, Nicholas. 1997. "Agency, Humanitarianism, and Intervention." *International Political Science Review* 18(1) 9–25.

– 2002. "Decision-Making Rules and Procedures for Humanitarian Intervention." *International Journal of Human Rights* 6(1): 127–38.

– 2005. "A Victory for Common Humanity? The Responsibility to Protect after the 2005 World Summit." Paper presented to The UN at Sixty: Celebration or Wake? Conference, 6–7 October, University of Toronto.

Wilson, Richard A. 2010. "When Humanity Sits in Judgment: Crimes against Humanity and the Conundrum of Race and Ethnicity at the International Criminal Tribunal for Rwanda." In *In the Name of Humanity: The Government of Threat and Care*, edited by Ilana Feldman and Miriam Ticktin, 27–57. Durham: Duke University Press.

Wood, Allen. 1998. "Humanity as End in Itself." In *Kant's Groundwork of the Metaphysics of Morals*, edited by Paul Guyer, 165–188. Lanham: Rowman and Littlefield.

Wu, Feng-Wei. 2007. "Between Ethics and Politics: Reading Levinas through Kant." Taiwan Philosophical Association Annual Conference, Tunghai University, 21 October. http://tpa.hss.nthu.edu.tw/committee/tpaseminar/2007/5D.pdf.

Yamashita, Hikaru. 2007. "Reading Threats to International Peace and Security 1946–2005." *Diplomacy and Statecraft* 18(3): 551–72.

Zagor, Matthew. 2011. "Elementary Considerations of Humanity." In *The ICJ and The Evolution of International Law: The Enduring Impact of The Corfu Channel Case*, edited by Karine Bannelier, Théodore Christakis, and Sarah Heathcote, 264–292. Oxford: Routledge.

Zehfuss, Maja. 2012. "Contemporary Western War and the Idea of Humanity." *Environment and Planning D: Society and Space* 30(5): 861–76.

Zhang, Yongjin. 2016. "China and Liberal Hierarchies in Global International Society: Power and Negotiation for Normative Change." *International Affairs* 92: 795–816.

Zolo, Danilo. 2002. *Invoking Humanity: War, Law, and Global Order*. London: Continuum.

Index

www.ingramcontent.com/pod-product-compliance
Lightning Source LLC
LaVergne TN
LVHW040603130826
845408LV00028B/315

* 9 7 8 0 2 2 8 0 1 0 7 8 4 *